THE
GREAT SHOOTS

BY THE SAME AUTHOR
Tales of the Old Gamekeepers
More Tales of the Old Gamekeepers
Tales of the Old Countrymen
Tales of Time and Tide — Stories of Life on Britain's Coasts
Birds of Prey of the British Isles
Wildfowl of the British Isles and North-West Europe
Sporting Birds of Britain and Ireland
The Glorious Grouse
World Birds (Guinness)
British Gameshooting Roughshooting and Wildfowling
Game Cook/The Art of Game Cookery (with Rosemary Wadey)

Brian P. Martin

THE
GREAT SHOOTS

Britain's Premier Sporting Estates

· THE ·
SPORTSMAN'S
PRESS
LONDON

To Graham Marshall and the late John Povall,
my earliest shooting companions and lifelong friends

All colour photographs by the author unless otherwise stated

A Catalogue record
for this book is available
from the British Library
ISBN 0–948253 76 2

First published 1987 by David & Charles
Second impression 1987
Third impression 1988
Fourth impression 1991
Fifth impression 1995 published by
The Sportsman's Press

Typeset by ABM Typographics Limited, Hull
and printed in Great Britain
by Butler & Tanner Ltd, Frome and London

CONTENTS

INTRODUCTION

If the Duke of Westminster enthuses more about shooting wild quarry than about any other leisure activity, surely the sport has something very special, for he, as Britain's richest citizen, has virtually unlimited choice. Yet few disinterested people realise that shooting today is truly egalitarian with more people participating than ever before. It is indeed still the sport of kings, but it is also the preoccupation of many thousands of other folk at all social levels.

Researching this book was a tremendously enjoyable exercise, but in some ways the deeper the investigation the more confusing it became, in that so many shoots were recommended by informants. In the end I had to be ruthless in my choice and look only at a sample of the many fine shoots in each region of Britain both today and in the past. Of those discussed in detail, many are on great estates well known to the general public, but others are mostly known only to fieldsportsmen. I apologise if your favourite is not mentioned, but it was quite impossible to visit more in the time allotted. Before making my selection I did however consult many leading figures and organisations in the shooting world.

Even when my 'first eleven' was selected all was not easy, for some owners felt they could not co-operate, being genuinely worried about their image in today's social climate, extreme action by 'antis' or even increased poaching. There were also a few owners who were anxious about divulging their estate's management and finances; privacy is their prerogative and of course I must honour it. On the other hand, some owners seemed over-anxious to publicise their shoots in order to make commercial gain and in the main these, too, have been omitted. But by far the majority of owners were happy and even 'honoured' to participate, for they were well aware of the need for open-mindedness today, and welcomed the opportunity to show the public just what this shooting business is all about. And among all these shoot proprietors were a few exceptional men whose tremendous enthusiasm for shooting was out of all proportion to their wealth. There was that small-boy twinkle of excitement in their eyes, and with it the vital spark which can fire-up everyone connected with an estate and make the shooting there truly great.

It is very difficult to determine what makes a great shoot, and each person will have his or her own idea. After endless discussions with hundreds of shooting people across the land, I would say that it is one which provides consistently good sport in an environment where both game and wildlife flourish, where the landscape is aesthetically pleasing, where visiting Guns appreciate a sense of history, where everyone is thrilled to be

Her Majesty The Queen and The Queen Mother at a Scottish gundog trial. The Royal Family has always been closely associated with shooting

Date. *Dec 17th*	Number.	OBSERVATIONS. " *Allons! Justine!! *"
Red Deer		
Grouse		
Partridges		
Pheasants	168	
Snipe		
Wild Duck		
Wild Geese		
Woodcocks	1	
Quail		
Sea Fowl		
Wood Pigeon	2	
Hares	2	
Rabbits	70	
Various	2	
Total	245	
Webster & Co., 60, Piccadilly, W.		

Unusual quarry bird in Lord Ripon's gamebook

there and where there is sensible provision for the sport in future generations. Even the richest men in the world cannot create instant coverts. Long-term creation of suitable habitat by, for instance, tree planting, is essential. Some people would not consider all these ingredients necessary; others would insist on them all. For example, in discussing a fellow nobleman's famous shoot, one duke remarked that he never really liked going there because 'although the birds are always high, wide and handsome, there is no sense of history and it could never be classed as great'.

Of course, when an observer such as myself visits a shoot to record it for posterity, there is the chance that the organisers have put on a special display and that normally the scene is very different. To overcome this I consulted widely with visiting Guns and staff and in many cases had much of an estate's shooting history laid before me in complete sets of gamebooks. And 'make-up' is usually easy to spot; after much homework, when the big day arrives and the whistle signals the first drive, one can soon sense whether it is a slick, comfortable and effortless operation run by caring experts or a hopeless, frantic muddle in the hands of incompetents whose anxiety spoils everyone's fun. After all, in the end fun is what it is all about, for without it gamebirds might as well be reared for the table in the same way as poultry. The most important thing is that each guest enjoys the total experience of the day and wants to come again. And, of course, if he goes away happy he is more likely to reciprocate the invitation!

It is unfortunate that many people still associate organised gamebird shooting with very large bags, for the very inappropriately labelled 'Golden Era' of the late nineteenth and early twentieth centuries has gone for ever. Fortunately it is the long-established custom of shoots to maintain gamebooks and these show quite clearly how fashion has helped dictate the size of bags. Today Guns go for quality, not quantity, and anyone who deliberately tries to play the 'numbers game' will soon be alienated by true sportsmen, and risks bringing the whole sport into disrepute. Yet at the same time there must obviously be reasonable bags in order to maintain the Guns' interest and, where there is some commercialism, make the operation economically viable.

It could be argued that in some cases keeping bag records is merely a reflection of vanity, but as well as providing us with a marvellous insight into man's social behaviour they tell of the fluctuating fortunes of our quarry populations. In addition there are often innumerable notes on wildlife, weather patterns and legal cases. And it is only natural that most Guns want to know both the total bag and their personal bag at the end of the day and season. Some even record their kills-to-cartridges ratio, but this latter is best kept private for if the spirit of the chase is not the prime motivation, a Gun would do better to take up target practice for clay pigeon shooting.

A few shoots condemn any general discussion of the bag as ungentlemanly. But even here, when the guests have departed, you can bet your boots that the boss will have words with his keeper. After all, without some record of numbers how can trends be assessed and efficiency and habitat improved where necessary? Also a gamekeeper is entitled to job satisfaction and does not want to see his efforts wasted by a hopeless team of Guns. It may well be necessary to include one or two crack Shots as 'back Guns' to nurse the wets along, get the bag up to at least a respectable level and send all on their way with the feeling that they have not let the side down. This is especially important with complete novices who might otherwise abandon the sport through utter embarrassment. Where birds are reared there will also be investigation into percentage bag returns, not through greed but from a natural desire to realise the land's potential through increased efficiency. Outstanding day returns do not necessarily confer greatness on an estate; consistency has always been more important.

And where are the best shoots? Firstly, this book is generally concerned only with the major quarry gamebirds — pheasant, partridge and grouse — although other species are mentioned where traditionally they have been part of a shoot's typical day. To deal with wildfowl or waders comprehensively would require further volumes, and to treat them sketchily would not do them justice. Thus the majority of best shoots, but not all, are in areas where pheasant, partridge and grouse have been able to thrive with the provision of suitable habitat. However, climate and altitude are important too. Very briefly, the grouse are in those areas of the north and west where heather thrives, and the best grouse shoots are those where heather is well-managed, especially burnt on a strict rotational basis to provide both tender shoots for food and long growth for nesting cover. The pheasant seems to thrive in most areas with strong support from man, but undoubtedly it survives best, and often in a totally wild state, on the drier, lighter soils of eastern England. Partridges too are widely distributed, but they have suffered more through habitat destruction brought on by changes in agriculture, so today great partridge shoots are few.

The end of the day at Euston, Suffolk

I have had the good fortune to participate in many hundreds of shoots throughout the country over the last twenty-five years. These have ranged from one-man walk-abouts to 24-Gun DIY efforts, from big-business booze-ups to genteel forays with the local lord. In every category I have witnessed great *days*, but in no way could most of these shoots be called 'great'. To safeguard and improve our heritage of sport we need fire in our bellies and I decided that the best way to put it there was to write about those estates whose names alone are magic to many thousands of shooting men across the world, either for past or present greatness.

For me, and for most sportsmen, the countryside and its diversity of wildlife are as important as the bag. Bird shooting today, as practised by most people, virtually never prejudices the welfare of our fauna and flora. On the contrary, gameshooters are among the greatest defenders of fast-disappearing habitats and it is largely through the private ownership of land that so much has been preserved at all. Estate inheritance within traditionally caring and astute families has helped preserve great reservoirs of natural wealth which, increasingly, are available for the sporting and general public to enjoy.

Wherever I have been, shooting has been central in binding the country community together. My earnest hope is that this book will enable all those people whose world is dominated by urban thinking, and who can only dream of wild places, to understand what makes the average gameshooter tick. Whatever we do with our green acres in the future, we start now with a much better legacy because of the tradition of the sporting landowner.

BRIAN P. MARTIN
Brook, Surrey

CHAPTER 1

SOCIETY'S VIEW

Among fieldsports today gameshooting is unique in that it is the common pursuit of men from *all* walks of life. Foxhunting does, it is true, attract many enthusiasts from relatively poor as well as rich families, but the former are mostly foot-followers whereas the latter are those who get to enjoy the thrill of the chase in pole position — on horseback. Beagling — hunting the hare on foot — is somewhat more egalitarian as it does not involve the expense of keeping horses. In game fishing, only angling for trout can truthfully be said to be the occupation of 'all ranks', for the mighty salmon has been priced beyond the reach of most men. Coarse fishing, by its name alone, implies social stigma — I have yet to see a nobleman ledgering for bream or trotting for roach, though no doubt there are rare exceptions.

But shooting stands magnificently above all fieldsports as the lifetime love of representatives of every social stratum, because whatever the depth of your pocket there is a form of shooting to match it. Even in gameshooting, which is generally the most expensive form of 'live' shooting in Britain, there is room for the man of very modest means. Professional gamekeepers are not essential and today there are more and more DIY shoots, in which the Guns double-up as keepers in their spare time. And

The Duke and Duchess of Grafton with guests at Euston Hall, October 1928

King Edward VII was the hub of shooting society

if you are not an owner, land can often be rented quite cheaply — even had free in return for offering the owner a few days' free sport — and the costs of rearing shared among the Guns. On shoot days wives, children and friends are brought in as beaters or the Guns themselves shoot or beat on alternate drives. And as we shall see, more and more townsfolk now participate.

It is not unusual to find that a man who beats regularly for a great landowner is himself a Gun in another shoot. Because of the genuine widespread love of the sport in this country all ranks mix well in the field and this engenders tremendous loyalty. But this was not always the case. In the early nineteenth century, hunting was considered the proper exercise for men of rank and shooting a proper amusement for inferior persons; only a handful of gentlemen walked-up birds on their country estates and they were regarded by polite society as adventurous or even eccentric. Yet big changes were soon to take place.

When the breech-loading shotgun was introduced in the mid-nineteenth century, it became much easier to take large bags and the demand for artificial rearing and release of pheasants and partridges quickly developed. And in an age when no one even dreamed of voicing an objection, a great variety of game featured regularly on the menu. Larks, and plovers' eggs, for example, were entered alongside partridge, swan and duck in the game books as ordinary items. And by studying the way the early game ledgers meticulously recorded where all the game went, as well as when and where it was shot, one can appreciate how it was valued as a harvest.

Driven shooting became something of a novelty in the social scene and when the Prince of Wales (later Edward VII) led the way — in 1861 buying Sandringham expressly to cultivate his interest in the sport — the pattern was really set. All the big shoots vied to have him as a guest and naturally made sure that a big bag was at least available when he took their stands. He had neither the right body nor the right temperament for the hunt, but the well-drilled shoot was ideal. His likes and dislikes were noted with care so that his became the fashion to follow and grand shooting parties became an essential part of the smart set's winter entertainment.

King George V continued the royal interest in shooting and was a fair Shot

King George VI shooting at Sandringham. He was a fine and elegant Shot

At the same time communications took great strides forward, and with the rapid expansion of the railways, and later the road system, it became easy for Guns to commute between London and country estate. Remote areas were at last accessible and good game-holding land could receive the cash injection necessary to realise its full potential. In particular the flood-gates were opened on the glories of northern grouse. The magic of grouse shooting soon infiltrated society. In 1880 J. J. Manley wrote: 'Many a brain-worker from the Senate, the Bar, and other callings, many a harassed "City man", and many an idler for the greater part of the 12 months, adds years to his life by the wholesome work and unique excitement of grouse shooting.' The grouse was always the most keenly awaited as it was the first game bird to come into season, and grouse shooting drew those tired of London's summer commerce out in droves. Because of this, probably nineteen out of twenty gameshooters in the 1880s had had the edge taken off their appetites by the time partridge and pheasant came round, as they do to this day, on 1 September and 1 October respectively.

In the nineteenth century the partridge was still the premier game bird on many estates. It had a remarkable attraction for many statesmen including Peel, Palmerston, Lord Althorp and Lord Derby, and this helped to counter any early threats to gameshooting's social and moral acceptability. Pheasant shooting on a large scale was at that time chiefly confined to the wealthy as vast acreages had to be maintained and guarded at great expense, often to the detriment of agriculture. Eventually the scale of shoots was so vast that the necessary expense caused some surprising bankruptcies including those of Lord Walsingham at Merton, who even had to sell the Ritz Hotel, and Queen

R. H. Rimington-Wilson attracted high society to his Broomhead Moor in Yorkshire and (right) Archibald John Stuart-Wortley was an expert and popular Shot as well as a shooting author

Victoria's one-time favourite, HRH The Maharajah Dhuleep Singh at Elveden, so great was their obsession with the sport. Yet labour was very cheap and whole armies of keepers could be employed to bolster the bags. But fools were not tolerated and livelihoods were at risk if results were poor. Consequently many tricks were played, including bringing large numbers of pheasants in by train and releasing them in the coverts on the day of the shoot before the guests arrived. No one knew any different, the Guns went home happy, the host maintained his status and received reciprocal invitations and the keeper hung on in his tied cottage.

The growing demand for rented shootings made it daily more expensive. Bargain holdings were harder to get and prices became fixed. In 1893 A. Stuart-Wortley commented:

> Shooting is eagerly sought and handsomely paid for by all sorts and conditions of self-made and hard-worked men. It is no longer the exclusive privilege of aristocratic land-owners of ancient families and their friends and connections. The successful lawyer, doctor, stockbroker, or 'business-man', of whatever shade of politics, seeks nowadays the relaxation and distraction which his hard-worked brain requires in shooting. He comes into the market with his store of hard-won guineas, hires the land from the family of long descent and looks upon the whole thing as a luxury he has fairly earnt.

By 1907 Evan Mackenzie could declare that antagonism to shooting had almost disappeared from this country. No longer were 'the masses jealous of all privileges derived from the possession of land', but were 'quite aware that the property qualification for gameshooting had long been abolished' and that farmers were almost all 'gunners on their own holdings'. Shooting had at last 'obtained a broader and firmer hold on the regard of the people at large'. He noted how in 1881 there were 57,983 game licences issued in the UK, but for the season 1904–5 as many as 72,996 — 52,605 paid £3 to shoot all year, 6,011 paid £2 for the season, 8,113 paid for a fortnight and 6,267 were gamekeepers' licences. In 1883 the excise authorities had changed the commencement date of the full licence from 1 August to 5 April 'to suit public convenience' and despite duty reductions many Guns dodged the fee altogether.

Shooting was undoubtedly growing more popular because the increase in numbers of game and gun licences was out of all proportion to the increase in population. In 1881 the number of gun licences per thousand males in England and Wales was 9.7, in Scotland 7.78 and in Ireland 5.33, while in 1891 it had already risen to 11.37, 8.8 and 5.96 respectively. Part of the increase was no doubt due to improvement in firearms and the cheapening of certain grades of gun through new machine processes. Inanimate bird shooting (the forerunner of clay pigeon shooting) had also been introduced. Grouse shooting in particular had risen from obscurity to stardom and was, according to that industrious scribe Aymer-Maxwell in 1910, 'rooted in the attachment of large sections of society'.

> The romantic poesy and tales of Sir Walter Scott, and certain glowing descriptions of not much earlier writers, of the wonderful scenic beauty and grandeur of the Scottish Highlands — till then hardly known to more than a small number of adventurous persons — awakened a widely ranged desire to visit regions which in our own land were still strangely unfamiliar to the multitude.

Lord Ripon in his pony cart at Studley Royal, 1901

Many members of both Houses of Parliament became enthusiastic grouse shooters, as indeed many are today. To quote Aymer-Maxwell again:

> . . . nothing could be better fitted or more effectual to revive the jaded energies of the worn-out legislator . . . The letting of grouse moors is still much affected by the course of parliamentary business. A good letting season, or the reverse of this, to a considerable degree hangs on the point whether Parliament shall cease from its sessional labours in time for celebration of the day of St Grouse. Autumn sessions of Parliament are abhorred by Highland lairds and other owners of grouse moors.

But the sophisticated visitors to the wilds demanded many more creature comforts than the ancient Highland chiefs ever did:

> Your first-class sporting tenant — English or American; never Scottish or Irish, and seldom any of the continental peoples — gives liberally for his privileges, and exacts liberal advantages besides the bare right to shoot. The lodge must be commodious — furnished, and kept almost up to the standard of metropolitan modern life. Electric lighting, garage for motor-cars, facilities for yachting and salmon fishing where practicable, and many other luxuries, or, as some would say, superfluities, are now looked upon as indispensable.

And before leaving the age of Aymer-Maxwell I must quote one of the most intelligent and far-sighted pieces he ever penned:

> It is quite common to hear it said in the smoking room — 'Let's have a good shoot now; who knows whether there will be any shooting in 10 years time.' This deplorable attitude of *laisser-faire,* this philosophical pessimism, cannot be too strongly condemned. We game-preservers must realize that though the arguments of our detractors seem to us trivial and absurd, and scarcely worthy of contradiction, yet the masses do not share our special knowledge of the subject, and it is for us to enlighten their ignorance, dispel the fallacies before they take root, and lead them to a better understanding. It is neither right nor expedient to obscure the issue, and evade the question of game-preserving on public platforms.
>
> Rightly handled, our case is eminently a presentable one; lay it clearly before the people whenever the chance offers, and show how it rests on a firm base — the general welfare of the country. Do not talk overmuch about the rights of property; however strongly you may believe in them yourself, still you cannot expect them to appeal to those who only want a right to your property, nor indeed to the mass of the people, to whom property is but a name. You will not get them to admit the sanctity of human institutions, but on broader grounds they will listen to your pleading, and your voice will not have been raised in vain.

For surely we all share a belief in the reasonable nature of our fellow-countrymen; could they but understand some of the simplest facts about game-preserving, we may rest assured that they would listen with less patience to all the rant and cant, which, uncontradicted, is liable to work so much harm.

It has taken the fieldsports community over seventy years to wake up to these words of 1911, which the national shooting organisations today should print for every member. The problem now is to get the great bulk of the gameshooting public to become members of our shooting organisations — the percentages are abysmal!

But as country pursuits have grown sophisticated and more specialised, and wild places have become harder to find, there has been a curious rebellion among the rich against formal shooting, even in titled circles, where there is strong pressure to demonstrate affinity with 'ordinary' mortals. The covert shoot has always been a 'natural medium for social intercourse' and a 'place of pleasant meetings', but today much is spoiled by commercialism. The essence of shooting should be enjoyment, but those whose concentration is solely on social intercourse will rapidly tire of its attractions. The lifelong enthusiast is he who at least occasionally performs as the original hunter, bothers to become a naturalist and gets to know his quarry well. Sadly, our manicured land cannot possibly accommodate large numbers of Guns in the good old-fashioned way — mooching about the hedgerows for a rabbit and a bird or two — chaos would ensue. And commercialism means that fieldcraft is not necessary in order to find the game, because hired experts will bring it to you. A knowledge of nature is not essential to the average gameshooter, and he is all the poorer for it. In the end this promotes a curious craving to go off on one's own and this book contains some account of very rich men who privately prefer the less organised ways.

Much of the age-old system crumbled with World War I and many great estates began to break up. But a demand for big bags still continued. Writing in 1938, James Wentworth-Day thought this was due mainly to 'the growth of a fresh class of shooting man in the shape of persons whose rise to affluence was due to war conditions, but who, not having been used at all to country life and pursuits, were too old to take up riding, so that sports like hunting, polo and steeplechasing were beyond their scope, and they therefore took to shooting.' He also pointed to the growing demand for game, especially pheasants, for the table.

These new syndicate shooters may have saved large-scale shooting through their injections of cash but they also drove away much of the old gentlemanly code of conduct. All was cash and carry now — even the single brace of birds taken home might have been debited to a Gun's account. Books were as carefully kept and audited as the balance sheets of a joint stock bank — very different from the days when all the Guns were guests and no one would dream of hinting at financial compensation; the day was for sport alone and excess game was often given away to local hospitals or the poor. Few could afford to carry on in this way. Yet today there are still landowners who are rich enough and generous enough to have all guest-Gun days. On the other hand, some are strongly motivated by the reciprocal invitations they will receive and therefore choose their guests with care! Whatever the system and whatever the motive, cash flow continues to support game preservation on a large scale and there is no doubt that in the UK today there are more pheasants (some 12 million estimated) shot each year than ever before.

Another very important social aspect of gameshooting has been the sport's ability to draw local communities together. It has always been the custom for landowners and farmers to include neighbours among their guest Guns, and this has done much to promote rural harmony. Sometimes the invitations are made with favours in mind, or as a reward for services rendered, perhaps by the estate agent or local businessmen; but more often than not less wealthy neighbouring farmers are included simply through true benevolence. One thing is certain — invitations today are far less class-orientated than they were in Edward VII's time. Unfortunately, some shy away from holding big shoots simply because the organisation of the social side is too much of a headache. Quite apart from worry about producing enough birds of sufficient quality to make the guests happy, there are endless domestic arrangements to make. The timing of invitations is an art in itself, as is the acceptance, for it is only human nature to go for the best on offer. Add to this the complications of last-minute illness and other excuses for non-attendance, and in the end the assembled party may be very different from that planned, their mix of temperaments auguring certain failure.

But country life without shooting would be very dreary indeed; so much is it part of the rural scene, and always has been, that it is little wonder that the bulk of the non-shooting community regards it with reverence and fascination. But not all, as we saw from the quotation from Aymer-Maxwell, and no one would deny that gameshooting has had a bad Press in recent years. As in so many walks of life, the position has become worse as the age of instant communication has projected the voice of everyman onto the national platform; the overwhelming mass of impartial opinion goes unheard among the extremist view. Gameshooting is traditionally associated with wealth and privilege,

Partridge shooting at Sutton Manor between the wars

King George V shooting at Sandringham

and the Press, instead of reporting more straight news, prefers to mount campaigns righting centuries of what it calls 'injustice'. But its vision is clouded, for shooting today is entirely different from that portrayed in the recent film *The Shooting Party* set in the Edwardian era.

When gameshooting was predominantly a way to augment food supplies there was little outcry, and it was not until the 'driving' of birds and hand-rearing facilitated big bags in the second half of the nineteenth century that dissent grew louder. No less a person than the USA's President Theodore Roosevelt said 'laying stress upon the mere quantity of game killed, and the publication of the record of slaughter, are sure signs of unhealthy decadence in sportsmanship'. Yet the age of the battue was all part of man's education, brought on chiefly by technical development of guns, rearing techniques and transport, and it would be very wrong to assume that many of the birds shot were 'easy' or unsporting. Study of early diaries quickly reveals how the novelty of mere execution of game soon wears off. Schizophrenic man wants to hunt and kill but at the same time he wants to stack the odds in favour of the quarry. This is no problem for the wildfowler, who must pit all his wits and fieldcraft against truly wild, migratory duck and geese; but the pheasant shooter is always struggling to re-create a satisfactorily wild arena for his sport in a land where man has tamed the entire environment. And

Driven partridge was the mainstay of many big shoots up to about 1950, as here at West Barsham, Norfolk

whatever is seen as a relatively easy exercise will always inspire antagonism. Not bothering to do its research properly, the Press sometimes takes up the cudgels on behalf of the uninitiated.

Yet it is certainly not at all easy to shoot even a low pheasant with a shotgun, and beginners are always surprised just how precise and well-timed the placement of the shot pattern must be. Today most Guns want high birds but unfortunately 75 per cent of people can't shoot them and never will — it is a rare art. And because of this it would be silly for a shoot with Guns of moderate ability to concentrate on extreme-range birds; this could result in excessive 'pricking' (wounding), which would certainly be cause for complaint. Most Guns are happy with birds coming over just above the trees, regarding a 25yd bird as testing, although 40–50yd birds can be brought down consistently and cleanly by competent Guns. The experienced know when a bird is out of range and should have the sense to avoid letting the novice 'have a go' because he will prick more than a few and before you can say 'Jack rabbit' the story will be blown up out of all proportion in the local paper.

This alleged cruelty is a continual source of friction and a bad Press for shooting. But after many years of allowing its strong rural base to fend for itself, the fieldsports community has at last organised its public relations effort and there are already signs that the 'anti' movement is waning. Concerted work on local and national Press through letter writing, lobbying of MPs and local councillors has at last seen extremists rebuffed, and the question of fieldsports is no longer the potential vote-catcher that some misguided politicians saw it for only a few years ago. Yet no matter how well the sporting Press puts its own case for continuance, and no matter how keen the sporting organisations are in laying on splendid events, both are largely preaching to the converted. The concentration must be on ways of putting the truth before the general public who, through no fault of their own, are concentrated in towns where the only place they are likely to come across game is hanging up in the butcher's shop. Most would be happy to sample the meat and would be pleased not only because it is infinitely more tasty and less fat-saturated than farmed meat but also because the creature which provided it at least lived wild with the sun on its back rather than in the shadow of some cramped, alien fattening unit.

Finally we come to the sporting Gun as the well-worn butt of endless jokes and cartoons, presumably stemming from the great British tradition of lampooning all seen to be in a position of 'unfair' advantage. The noble lord was always a 'short, fat peer' in order to cut him down to his true worth, his gun would 'spew lead in every direction' and his progress across the moors in tune with nature was condemned as 'a wretched massacre'. Perhaps all would have been different if King Edward VII, whose enthusiasm for shooting was second to none, had not presented the cartoonists of his day with the archetypal contours of over-indulgence. He was even reported as using 'twelve-inch guns'!

Today most of the nobility have got their public relations acts together and are seen as expert estate managers, so the Press has latched onto the Sloane Ranger, whose green wellies have epitomised the unfairly privileged 'hooray Henry haves'. Since these are seen as pathetic, weak individuals, it is a mystery why they are so frequently associated with fieldsports because, irrespective of their position in society, they just would not be tolerated by enthusiasts who walk the moors and fields all day in all weathers.

Grouse shooting, understandably, is mocked more than other forms of shooting because its season opens first — on 12 August — at which time the popular Press is freer to resurrect a hardy perennial in the shape of the tweedy image of Colonel Blimp. Yet, apart from the fact that driven grouse shooting is indeed expensive today, nothing could be further from the truth. The grouse is a truly wild, exciting and testing quarry and to shoot it requires considerable calmness, keen vision, skill with the gun, great co-ordination and at least reasonable fitness in getting from one line of butts to the next over treacherous, boggy, uneven and hilly terrain.

Fine sport always deserves a cultured approach and if men are willing and able to spend their income in buying all the extras to make the day memorable and enjoyable, why shouldn't they? A Range Rover is not just pretty: it is simply one of the best vehicles for shoot transport.

Yes, shooting has had a bad Press of late, but it has taken the broadsides well, and with surprisingly little effort has survived to fight the real battle — the battle against relentless habitat destruction which threatens to wipe both game and wildlife from the face of the earth.

CHAPTER 2

MAINLY ECONOMIC

Long ago, at times when the law would allow, great gameshooting could be had for virtually nothing, when wild game was prolific and there was no rent to pay because vast tracts of land had not been claimed by agriculture. All a sportsman had to find was the price of powder and shot. Today, in very rare cases, the same can apply, but for most people the true cost is proportional to enthusiasm and efficiency.

The main costs are labour, land and rearing, but there are so many variables it is hard to generalise. It all depends on the scale and social involvement of the sport, but the greater the commercial importance the poorer the sport is likely to be in terms of satisfaction, though not necessarily in bags.

Today, whether the emphasis is on reared or wild game, allocation of land to game preservation is, on paper at least, expensive, because everything is measured in terms of possible economic returns. For example, the more an owner diverts his agricultural programme for shooting, the more he has to pay in diminution of efficiency through loss of benefits from economies of scale. On moorland the uncertainties of grouse 'production' have increasingly been abandoned for blanket afforestation programmes which favour tax relief, and in some cases where shoots have been near to urban sprawl, owners have sold off great chunks of their estates for building development. Others have turned their parks into playgrounds. Thus even if an owner shoots on his own land there is hidden cost in terms of lost potential, and it can be considerable. For example, a farmer's 'sacrifice' of agricultural land to woodland useful to game might well cost him several hundred pounds per acre per annum. On the other hand, retaining hedges primarily for game can benefit agriculture by providing shelter for stock, which can increase liveweight gain and milk yield; and windbreaks can prevent soil erosion, raise soil temperatures and reduce moisture loss through evaporation, all of which factors will hasten crop development and thereby increase turnover.

Where an owner is not prepared to divert his agricultural or other land use to game he must rely more heavily on periodic injections of artificially reared stock and this is a great direct expense, chiefly through provision of labour — perhaps 60 per cent of the whole cost. Little wonder then that the number of gamekeepers has plummetted dramatically this century down to about 3,500 full-time. Today each man is under great pressure to be efficient, but even so he must be provided with expensive accessories such as a vehicle, fuel, and rent-free accommodation on site. Beaters and pickers-up have also to be paid. The whole thing has become so expensive that the sale of game excess to the Guns' needs has to be strictly controlled to reduce overheads.

Yet a shoot can be good and not too expensive if the Guns are prepared to provide the labour themselves. A common arrangement is for one or two of the Guns to do all the keepering in return for free shooting. This practice has grown rapidly, but DIY shoots are rarely truly great because they do not generally have inspirational surroundings or any sense of history. And no matter how good the labour organisation, efficiency cannot be guaranteed and the newly formed DIY shoot will be at a disadvantage through lack of passed-on expertise, lack of local knowledge and the inability to create instant coverts. For these same reasons many large-scale shoots fail to be great.

Where birds are reared there is also the cost of feed and equipment — incubators and heating, rearing and release pens etc. And when all these factors are allowed for it is said that today it costs something like £14–15 to put a bird in the air and, as we shall see, most shoots charge on a cost-per-bird-shot basis.

Where estates have gone very commercial, into what is generally regarded as factory production, there is a fair profit to be made, but these places rarely have any attributes of greatness. On the other hand some famous estates sell their names merely to break even on the shooting and allow the owners a few days 'free' sport to which they can invite their friends. This often works well and such estate owners can retain sufficient enthusiasm to permit their shoots' overall continuing greatness. There are also shoots which sell themselves so well that, although they make little on the shooting, they make a good profit on the total package, through provision of accommodation and meals with the lord of the manor, and other activities such as fishing or clay pigeon shooting. These too can remain great, and indeed need to remain on their toes if they are to attract very wealthy, discriminating customers who would soon go elsewhere if dissatisfied.

As already indicated, there are owners who appear to continue in the old tradition of private shoots, charging guests nothing at all. Yet most of them pick their guests carefully, knowing that a certain number of reciprocal invitations are assured. Thus it might be argued that they have paid for 'x' number of days shooting on various estates through paying for the whole cost of their own shoots! Very, very few owners indeed are wealthy enough today to be sole supporters of their own great, large-scale shoots with no or little interest in shooting elsewhere.

Another growth area in recent years has been in the sale of shoot days to companies who wish to entertain their clients and associates in a novel way while at the same time benefiting from tax relief and providing a jolly day out for senior host executives. Generally these work well with a good atmosphere. But what certainly does not work is where a nouveau-riche Gun wheedles his way into what had been a happy private shoot and tries to talk business. Most businessmen treat their shoots as escapes from the drudgery of commerce but even in the field some seem unable to escape and are in constant contact with the distant office through the wizardry of electronics. Of course, there is something of the showman in this, just as there is in the man who receives so many 'vital' phone calls during almost every shoot lunch — one must suspect that he has arranged them!

A hundred years ago, in an average year on a well-stocked moor it cost the renter only around £2 per brace for all the grouse he killed. At that time vast areas of shooting land could be rented for very little in remote places because few people could, or were bothered, to reach them. The real pressure was on good shooting country in the home counties and eastern England, and prices reflected this, especially as most owners wanted the shooting for themselves. There has been a surprising lack of awareness that sporting rents can be a significant source of income where agricultural production is marginal, such as in hill country on poor soil. If one farms one's own land, or the shooting one rents is farmed by a landlord who looks on the shooting rent as part of the profits on the farms, game-preserving is very much easier: the amount of game killed can be almost doubled without any appreciable harm to the land.

Ownership of land gives incentive for long-term work on habitat improvement, and this is very important in relation to the most valuable hardwood coverts. But there is also growing awareness of these trees as a crop in themselves and, as long as there is a continuous programme of felling and replacement, there can therefore be two crops for the price of one. But renting, even on a long lease, is precarious, and relies heavily on the co-operation of the farmer: therefore tenant farmers and their foremen are often guest Guns. The shoot owner can, as long as he can afford it, insist on what he wants; but the lessee can only persuade or offer financial compensation to farmers for growing special game crops or leaving cover.

Some owners prefer to hand the management of their shoots over to others in return for retaining a gun in the shoot. Up to April 5 1995, in Scotland sporting rates were levied irrespective of whether or not the owner shot his own land, and in England and Wales VAT has been a considerable burden to commercial shoots. VAT has been the cause of considerable cutbacks in some cases where large back payments have become due after much wrangling.

One very shrewd move, which has been recognised for a long time in the battle to keep down labour costs, is doubling-up of employees' duties. Estate workers doubling as beaters is the obvious example; less obvious is keepers as unpaid policemen of great estates in remote areas. Farm workers too have long been induced with gifts of game to work as unofficial watchers of game and property. Without such 'bribes' many would have become some of the worst local poachers, being in an excellent position to help themselves.

Shooting can be let for a season to one man or a syndicate, or days can be sold off at flat rates, with a surcharge per bird above a certain bag or on a cost-per-bird basis for the entire bag. The actual shooting can be controlled so accurately that Guns can actually order a certain bag. This, though, rather demeans the whole exercise, as an essential of any form of hunting should be the unpredictability of the bag. There seems to be no way round this.

Sadly, when a day is purchased by an inexperienced group they will often be intent on getting their money's worth so that on the first few drives they will be less fussy about selecting quality birds. Thus they will often approach the planned bag well before the day is ended, requiring the skilful headkeeper to hold the birds back on remaining drives where there is no surcharge on extra birds killed. This will lead to disappointment among the Guns, who may well voice complaint. But they will never be allowed to shoot significantly more than was forecast, though a prudent operator will allow just a few more 'free', hoping the customers will come back. Where a day is

Lord Walsingham of Merton
had severe financial problems

charged entirely on a birds-killed basis there is the temptation for the organiser to send over streams of poor or mediocre birds, but such easy shooting has only novelty value and no self-respecting Gun would return to this type of outfit.

The syndicate shoot is still frowned upon by some but there is no doubt that it saved the day when shooting — through increased personal taxation, agricultural depression and the changes brought about by World War I — seemed doomed. However, full-syndicate and part-private shoots had already been in existence for many years. Opponents of the system have argued that syndicate shooters are greedy, tend to overshoot their ground and leave little stock to regenerate, their members lacking the instincts of true sportsmen. But this is not generally the case today, and with the increased opportunity for people from all walks of life to 'buy-in', there is bound to be greater support for gameshooting from the community in general. Today syndicate shoots are the backbone of the shooting world.

Unfortunately it is inevitable that in any syndicate there will be occasional turn-over of members, and the incomers may not fit in, but once a group settles down all is generally well. The problem of fitting in also applies on those commercial shoots where a day is sold to various Guns rather than to one man who takes his own group along. Obviously, being thrown together with a group of strangers for the day can be tedious, but the skill of the organiser can play a part and some Guns relish the challenge so much that they buy odd days on different shoots all over the country rather than face what they consider to be boredom with the same old faces.

Since the nineteenth century much shooting has been let through sporting agents, most of them very good with reputations to safeguard. Others are unscrupulous and may well take advantage of the generally less knowledgeable, once-in-a-lifetime overseas visitor 'doing the rounds'.

Agents can be particularly helpful in locating shooting for those with little idea of where to find it. This was specially important around the turn of the century when it was the fashion to change one's grouse shooting every year, largely because of feminine influence, in great contrast to the 1850s and 1860s when 'Old Snowie', in his Bond Street, London, office had no competitors in the letting of Scottish shootings. His recommendation was enough as sportsmen believed he would never mislead them. Yet then, as now, there must have been disappointment, for no one can predict grouse bags very accurately because of disease and other factors. But, because rentals were much lower then in real terms, sportsmen were prepared to take more risks.

Today most of the agents are enthusiastic, lifelong Shots themselves and they have established their reputation through painstaking examination of the ground, sampling sport for themselves and with meticulous attention to detail. It is quite common for the agent or his representative to be present on every let day to ensure that things run smoothly. Thus, though rents and agents' fees may have rocketed over the last hundred years, there is overall better value. There is more sport, closer protection, more good quality accommodation and more luxury for those who want it.

And on the economic front one must not forget the importance of shooting to the national economy. Quite apart from the direct income to shoot owners, there is the steady employment of gamekeepers and game farmers. Also significantly dependent on gameshooting revenue are gun and cartridge makers, gamefood suppliers, rearing equipment manufacturers, dog trainers, dogfood suppliers, country clothing manufacturers and many more. And particularly in remote parts of Scotland, hoteliers and ghillies, for instance, are greatly dependent upon the income derived from visiting sportsmen. Today we are dealing with a multi-million pound industry.

There is no doubt that if gameshooting in Britain ceased thousands of people would join the dole queue and the nation would lose an important and welcome food supply. The great resurgence of interest in game as food because of its flavour and low fat content is generating more jobs through marketing and selling. And while these economic factors should not be in the forefront of any defence of sport shooting, considerations such as conservation and freedom of choice of legitimate pursuit being of greater weight, this is still an age when matters are assessed according to material good.

PRINCE DHULEEP SINGH

LORD HUNTINGFIELD   LORD WALSINGHAM

MARQUESS OF RIPON

Probably the four most well-known big Guns of the late nineteenth century

CHAPTER 3

GAME LAWS AND GAMEKEEPERS

The main gameshooting seasons have changed surprisingly little since driven shooting came into vogue, but the variety of bird species which can legally be bagged has been narrowed considerably as conservationists have argued for protection. But there has never been any question of stopping shooting of the mainstay species — partridge, pheasant and grouse. Such has been their importance to the rural community that they, along with a number of other birds and mammals, have long been the subject of a special section of legislation known as the Game Laws. Today all our wildlife is subject to the Wildlife and Countryside Act 1981, but those species officially classified as game are also subject to the Game Laws.

At one time, hunting of game animals, chiefly deer, was regarded as a royal prerogative. As early as 1389, following the Peasants' Revolt, Richard II decreed the pursuit of game lawful only for those qualified by land ownership. So long before the gun became the hunter's main weapon the stage was set for the centuries-old battle between poacher and the 'establishment'. It continues today.

By 1603 it was already necessary to ban the sale of pheasants, partridges and hares to try to stem the increase in poaching. Park walls were often knocked down and poaching continued virtually unchecked during the Civil War and Commonwealth (1642–59) and many forest laws were repealed by the Long Parliament, which took over the royal forests. But when Charles II was restored, an Act of Parliament introduced a gentleman's 'game privilege' based on a high land qualification. This allowed only a tiny percentage of the population to hunt game, and lords of the manor 'not below the degree of Esquire' were empowered to appoint gamekeepers 'who shall have power within the manor to seize guns, nets and engines kept by unqualified persons to destroy game and, by a warrant of the Justice of the Peace, to search in the daytime the houses of unqualified persons upon the ground of suspicion'.

In 1723 an attempt was made to strike terror into the hearts of poachers with the notorious 'Black Act', introduced to combat poachers with blackened faces who had been raiding Waltham Chase. After regular renewal it was made permanent in 1758, providing capital punishment for over two hundred offences.

Another harsh line was taken in 1770 with the Night Poaching Act. Under this, for poaching armed or unarmed between an hour after sunset and an hour before sunrise, a single magistrate had the power to give a minimum of three months imprisonment for the first offence, and a public whipping plus a minimum of six months gaol for the second. A modification in 1773 permitted just a fine for the first offence. Yet, on looking into the history of various estates it is obvious that not every poacher

Early-nineteenth-century keeper persuading a rabbit to leave cover for his master

apprehended was prosecuted: there was a considerable amount of humanity among some of the great estate owners even then, and alternative systems of local justice were not unusual. This might include insisting that the offender paid a fine to a local charity.

Apart from the fact that these restrictive game laws were a bone of political contention, they were also a considerable hindrance to tenant farmers who were legally prohibited from killing the game on their land even though this meant letting rabbits and hares, and to a lesser extent gamebirds, ruin crops.

In the early nineteenth century further legislation was introduced, confirming poaching as a criminal offence with harsh penalties. The Night Poaching Act of 1816 brought transportation for seven years merely for being apprehended 'armed' with net or stick with intent to take game or rabbits. Further market restrictions were sought, too, in order to counter the increase in poaching partly due to the beginnings of a population explosion and inevitable unemployment and poverty caused by variation in demand for goods and services. Bankes's Act of 1818 made it illegal to *buy* game, the sale already being an offence, with a fine of £5 per head, half to the informer. Some owners were so jealous of their property and game they had their keepers conceal grim mantraps and spring-guns about their woods and fields, but Lord Suffield's Bill to make these outlawed finally won the day in 1827.

But changes were underway and a slow process of amelioration began. In 1828 the Night Poaching Act introduced transportation for up to fourteen years for poaching gangs of three or more, only one of whom need be armed; but individual poachers would get seven years transportation for the third offence and, to distinguish from game proper, rabbits must have been killed to establish guilt. At about the same time some enlightened owners employed rabbit catchers to kill game on their tenants' land and even reduced rents on farms adjacent to game preserves or granted concessions to tenants to allow them to kill ground game. For example, when the 2nd Earl of Yarborough succeeded to the Brockleby Estate in 1846 he allowed his tenants to shoot game as long as they did not disturb the fox coverts. Few were as keen as Elveden's owners who specially retained land in hand to avoid conflict with tenants.

A big change came in 1831 when the Game Reform Bill swept away qualification of any kind and for the first time gameshooting was open to any purchaser of a game certificate, and game trading could be carried on by any purchaser of a game dealer's licence. The fine for day poaching would be £5, but a Lords' amendment retained transportation for night poaching, and it was determined that game was the property of the owner, not of the occupier of the land.

In 1846 there was another concerted attack on the morality and economics of game shooting, but although a select committee on the game laws was set up, no action ensued. In 1862, however, the Poaching Prevention Act gave rural police the power to search carts and persons on the highway as well as persons suspected of coming from preserves.

The next major change came in 1880 when the Ground Game Act was passed, following Gladstone's landslide Liberal victory at the polls. At last tenant farmers had the 'inalienable and concurrent right' with the landowners to shoot rabbits and hares eating their crops. Opposition had been strong in the Lords but, once again, confrontation was often avoided by landlord–tenant agreements.

Today it is hard for us to imagine the extreme poverty of the nineteenth century, but few people looking into its history could fail to sympathise with the occasional poacher struggling for survival. The incentive was considerable; for example, a labourer's income was but 1s a day in the 1820s when a pheasant fetched 5s and a hare 2s 6d on the open market. Our man of the backwoods was a Robin Hood of the people, unlike the vicious poaching gangs of the 1980s who have no hesitation in threatening violence to succeed in their big business.

Poacher working an Essex hedgerow. In the old days he was merely a 'one for the pot' man

Yet there have always been owners whose skill and benevolence has avoided much of the conflict. In 1859 'Stonehenge', a prolific nineteenth-century writer, noted how labourers were often regarded as the best preservers of game:

> If they are with you all the poachers in the world may be defied, while if they are against you no keeper can be sure of showing you good sport. The best plan is to make all the labourers feel an interest in the preservation of the game. Let every man receive at Christmas a certain sum proportionate to the head of game killed during the season, and the outlay will be found to be well bestowed, since it will go much further than the same sum laid out in extra watchers. . . The poaching labourer is the worst of all poachers, because his attacks on the game are insidious and constant.

Early action was recommended to stop a labourer embarking on a career of 'destruction', and 'Stonehenge' noted how the 'certificated' poacher was a great nuisance, a fine of only £2 plus costs being possible, and that most had good fieldcraft, good dogs and the ability to escape time and time again:

> . . . the systematic poacher is of all ages and classes. Some are brought up in luxury, but refusing to work, they descend in the scale, and consider poaching the only gentlemanly way of earning money. Others have been as labourers . . . Poachers will never go, by choice, where they know they are sure to be recognised; while on the other hand, wherever there is a keeper who relies upon his brute strength, the poacher goes at once, preferring a good thrashing, or the chance of a shot, to the certainty of identification, which spoils all his other prospects. The moment he goes into court all the keepers in the neighbourhood put their mark upon him.

When conditions were right for poaching, watchers would be set to observe the cottages of suspects.

Writing in 1880, J. J. Manley thought owners were not tough enough when it came to poachers:

> Owners of preserves should take measures to back up their keepers more efficiently than is now often the case. Regular patrols should be provided and the keepers and assistants instructed to teach the marauders a stern lesson of repression at all hazards. [Some preservers had] become overawed by the nonsense talked by the anti-Game Law League fanatics. Many owners of covers will not now provide their keepers with guns or dangerous arms of any kind; and the poachers, well aware of this, enter preserves with slight fear of capture, and are rendered bolder every year by the circulation of pamphlets and speeches in which their calling is described as a kind of honourable guerilla warfare against those who are interfering with their *rights*.

And there is little doubt that the excessive leniency established then in many quarters continues to this day.

Unfortunately, shoots close to or accessible from towns and cities have always suffered at the hands of poachers. For example, London has always posed a threat to eastern England. Yet technology continues to thwart the poacher where the law cannot. In 1938 James Wentworth-Day noted that 'many modern inventions such as the telephone and the portable electric torch have operated to defeat the old-fashioned gangs of poaching ruffians'; and early warning has often enabled the police to secure convictions and prevent loss of game. In addition, in recent years the walkie-talkie, increasingly used on estates, has helped, as have the many electronic alarm systems now available.

On the other hand, the motor car has brought a new breed of totally mercenary and ruthless poacher who tours the land to meet his requirements. Even otherwise quite respectable people use their cars to pick.off odd birds and rabbits from quiet verges. And today the serious poacher has the best of both worlds — the speed and accuracy of a gun plus the cloak of the silencer.

What the law has failed to do is mete out punishment to fit the crime. In many cases the comparatively rich professional poacher has received the same paltry fine as a genuinely poor man. The game dealers have often been at fault, too; they know full well when game is illegally handled and should do more about it. Many poachers deal direct with hotels and restaurants and they too could have more regard for the law.

But little is likely to change and as long as gameshooting continues there will be poachers. As far as the law goes, the main threat to shooting remains the erosion of the quarry list, but that is of greater concern to the wildfowler and roughshooter. The main gamebirds remain very common, but whether or not society will continue to allow artificial rearing and release is another matter.

Another complication, apart from those connected with the game laws, has come about through the public's increasing mobility and interest demanding more access to the countryside. This is to be encouraged, and most of the great shoot owners I have spoken to agree that public access is acceptable as long as it is controlled and the visitors respect the private property which they cross or pass by. But sometimes friction erupts, as in 1932 when ramblers organised a mass trespass over the Kinder Scout grouse moors. They were met by a force of gamekeepers and police and five offenders were subsequently gaoled. Since then similar actions have become almost as much a ritual as the annual Press send-up of the opening of the grouse-shooting season.

Yet some owners have made very generous concessions to ramblers, naturalists, geologists and the like who wish to go on their land. In most cases a reasonable request is met with sympathy and verbal agreement or even an official pass given. Sadly there is a loutish minority who damage crops, release livestock, let their dogs worry sheep, leave litter, cause fires and generally disturb game and wildlife, having no sense of country code whatsoever. When faced with such adversity from a largely urban-based population who are surprisingly ignorant of country ways, it seems astonishing that landowners generally are so accommodating.

The law is always slow to change, but on the whole that is good as far as country matters are concerned and it is quite unfair for townspeople to try to force unworkable and unreasonable law through at space-age pace. Without the goodwill of the rural community it will never succeed.

In most respects the great shoots of the type discussed in this book have for their part always been very careful to stick to the letter of the law, their owners having so much to lose as pillars of the community. But until very recently there was one area in which many failed to uphold the standards, though through neglect rather than intent.

Gentlemen of the 1820s walked-up game and loaded, primed and fired their own flintlocks

Gamekeeping tends to be a job for life, and throughout an average span the law usually changes considerably; many keepers have clocked up forty years service, some even more than sixty. It is very difficult for some men to change the habits of decades, and when Parliament ordered that certain birds would henceforth be protected they found it difficult to follow suit. Why should they not continue to shoot owls and other birds of prey, they argued, especially when their livelihoods depended on it. Of course, they were wrong, for if ever there is any question of contravening the accepted conservation law of the day, the gun should be laid aside. But quite a few owners were more to blame because they did not bother to find out if their keepers obeyed the new legislation meticulously.

Today, after much campaigning, and with a generally better educated generation of keepers, blatant abuse of the law is rare. Sadly, indiscriminate poisoning of rare and protected species still occurs, chiefly where baits such as eggs are illegally left out for pests such as crows; such incidents tend to be in remote areas of north and west Britain and also involve hill farmers. It is up to estate owners to ensure that such behaviour ceases, for even very rare cases can bring the whole sport into disrepute.

The proud profession of gamekeeping goes back centuries, at least to the already mentioned Act of the Restoration whereby gamekeepers could be appointed with power to seize unlawful articles and to search houses of suspected persons. But many owners abused this privilege and used the law as an excuse to employ whole armies of bodyguards and oppressors of the people. By the beginning of the eighteenth century it was necessary to restrict each estate to one keeper, but for the first time he was allowed to kill game as well as protect it. But to enable his servant to kill game the master had to pay a further 3 guineas on top of the annual 1 guinea gamekeeper's licence, to the government.

In those early days there was less regard for the law in remote rural areas, and 'border wars' between rival estates were commonplace. It was always tempting to steal a neighbour's eggs. There was also very little science in keepering and more regard to old wives' tales such as the necessity to mix saffron in the feed to make pheasant head feathers glossy. This, incidentally, persisted into the 1970s.

Today's keeper is concerned more with the methods of intensive poultry rearing, except on those rare estates where wild birds are still significant. The age-old coop and broody system, which was very labour-intensive, has been almost entirely replaced by a system of catching-up hens for laying pens, and hatching in vermin-proof, electric incubators; rearing under bottle-gas, electric or paraffin brooders; and acclimatisation and exercise in covered, vermin-proof runs. The birds are put into release pens in late summer when they are too large for most predators, the 6-foot high wire-netting pens usually having a low strand of electrified wire to dissuade foxes. Many amateur keepers fail by siting these pens too near public footpaths and potential poachers, or in too wet and windy situations. Birds are fed in the pens and soon learn to fly out to forage, but they are too stupid to fly back so 'pop-holes' have to be provided. These are too narrow for them to get out again easily, so they pace about until roosting time and fly out again in the morning. Thus roosting sites must be provided in the pens.

Elveden range of fixed hatching pens, 1880

In 1936 pheasant feed had to be mixed the hard way, often with secret recipes. (right) Improved hygiene has greatly improved pheasant 'production'. Here eggs are washed and sterilised at Lambton Park prior to artificial incubation

Before wildlife legislation came in, and when reliance was on wild stock, the keeper was concerned with a very wide range of so-called vermin, most of which has since been discounted as unimportant. Today's conservationist would have been horrified to see eagles, kites, peregrine falcons, harriers, merlins, owls, ravens and the hobby on the common gibbet alongside fox, polecat, pine marten, magpie and crow. As early as 1859, 'Stonehenge' listed the domestic cat as enemy Number One: 'The moment a cat takes to a covert she is doomed, for war must be waged against her to extermination.' Trap, poison and gun were all used to this end. Today puss is still despised.

The question of fox control has always been difficult because of foxhunting interests, especially where landowners have followed both sports. Today, despite wide efforts to encourage co-operation, there is no doubt that most shoots will exterminate as many foxes as possible, yet still they proliferate. And shooting was the method used more than a hundred years ago when, again to quote 'Stonehenge', 'In the Highlands of Scotland and North Wales, and indeed in some of the hills of Ireland, inaccessible to hounds, the mountain fox is so destructive to game, and even to lambs, that in each district in the first country a "tod-hunter" is appointed to the office of finding and destroying the litters, as well as the full-grown foxes when he can reach them.' Economics came into this too as southern masters of hounds were always willing to pay for such 'bagged' hill foxes taken alive, as they were thought to provide better sport. Today the keeper is very occasionally interested in bagged foxes for favours in kind, but more significant is the value of the fox pelt on the open market. Hence trapping is preferred to shooting in order not to damage the skin unduly.

The age-old conflict between hunting and shooting interests now centres very much on the keeper. If he happens to be a foxhunting man, and many are, all is well for he will bend over backwards to accommodate an ancient, exhilarating sport. But the keeper directed by a commercial shoot is not so interested in his standing in the local community and, unless his masters direct him otherwise, will only be interested in pheasant production. Sadly, when money comes into sport etiquette usually goes out of the window.

The open way in which the keeper's trapping practices were discussed is an interesting reflection on Victorian society. Much of the detail was horrendous. 'Stonehenge' again: 'A good plan of trapping egg-destroyers is to set the trap in water, so that it will drown them when caught, and thus prevent them from alarming their own species and from escaping with the loss of a leg.' Yet even in the 1850s many keepers were sensitive to unnecessary wildlife destruction and, wherever possible, did their best to prevent indiscriminate poisoning or taking unwanted birds in gins. Nonetheless, strychnine was still commonly placed in flesh baits left in the open.

Apart from being skilled in trapping, and in more recent times rearing, the keeper must be thoroughly honest, and this concerned Victorians just as much as the modern employer. In fact, their obsession with this often led to an 'outsider' getting a job. On the rare occasion when the vacancy was not taken by a son, other relative or long-standing associate, a newcomer to the district was often preferred because a local man would be too concerned with doing his chums a favour.

Selling game and eggs on the quiet to other estates or keepers has been common in the past, but an interested employer should be able to keep this to a minimum. Major difficulties arise when the owner is non-resident or does not have a good resident agent, but such frauds usually occur through excessive meanness on the part of the boss. This temptation to sell eggs became significant when rearing got underway, and at one time was on such a scale that few prosecutions were brought because so many keepers had 'dirty' hands. In the 1890s there were advertisements offering for sale as many as 20,000 eggs at one time, Norfolk and Suffolk being the principal hunting grounds of the 'eggers'.

Criticism has also been levelled at keepers generally in their approach to bag levels. In the *Country Life Book of Shooting,* 1903, the editor went so far as to say 'Keepers, speaking generally, are a race of butchers', and that they positioned Guns so that large bags were inevitable and everyone would be pleased.

The keeper is also always under pressure from the farm manager who, understandably, wants to maximise his yields whether for his own profit or to please his master. Pheasants can do considerable damage to crops, pecking away at roots,

Keeper testing eggs in 1880

scratching up seed and, to a lesser extent, eating grain prior to harvest. But there are ways to make amends. Apart from the obvious one of inviting the farmer to shoot occasionally, the keeper can ensure that serious agricultural pests such as rabbits and pigeons are kept down, that birds are well fed and are not so inclined to wander around eating the farm's produce. Most important on the great shoots with a large head of game is to kill the stock right down each year to avoid plundering of crops.

Another essential on great estates with large rearing fields has always been scrupulous cleanliness — be it hens, food, quarters or utensils — because the threat of disease is ever present. Today there is excellent veterinary advice and medicaments for ailing birds, but a great deal of money and frustration can be saved through preventive action. In the old days it was said, 'show me the man's aviaries, sitting boxes, coops and cooking, and I will hazard a good guess as to his results'.

Partridge rearing is particularly exacting and 'a good man' always hard to find. He was the key to success on every great estate. Charles Alington commented in 1904:

> A man to look after partridges must be content to work hard, knowing that there may be little or nothing to show as the results of his labours. He must be observant and have more than his share of intelligence. If the services of such a man are obtained, it must be remembered that they are not likely to be retained for 16 shillings a week. As a rule, very young men are given this job as a stepping-stone to higher wages and pheasant rearing.

Smaller tips was another reason why partridge beats were avoided.

Tipping is one of the most talked-about aspects of shooting; Guns always want to do the right thing and keepers get to rely on this considerable perk. Today tipping is based on a head count with a generally accepted rate of at least £10 for the first 100 birds and £5 per 100 thereafter. Yet it makes sense for the keeper to look after his Guns for I have seen quite a few tips of £50 and even £100 change hands. A man shooting four days a week on first-class estates is probably spending at least £200 a week on tips to keepers and loaders alone! Thus the keeper on a modern syndicate is certainly not going to get much in the way of tips compared with one lucky enough to land a job on a rich man's estate with its constant stream of wealthy visitors.

There are Guns who try to turn the system to advantage. The rich newcomer may think that by flashing a fat bundle he will get pole position or secure some useful knowledge, but the prudent keeper will give only the impression of dispensing advantage, knowing full well that his employer is watching every move. On the whole, true sportsmen will respect the thorough professionalism of the keeper and tip according to the latter's total contribution to a successful day. A good keeper will always attend to the fine-positioning of every Gun irrespective of reward. Today the partridge man would certainly not be under-tipped. On the contrary, good partridge days have become such a privilege that guest Guns are likely to be exceptionally generous.

Tipping by results is really unfair and a discerning Gun should judge for himself whether or not a keeper has done well according to the means at his disposal. Personally I would like to see most keepers paid more for the very long hours put in and greater flexibility in tipping.

In Edwardian times a keeper earned about £70 a year but, although he was very much a servant, his tips would amount to a minimum of around £20 per annum. A generous tip was half a sovereign, a good one 5s, a moderate one 2/6, and anything below that close to meanness. In his *Memories of a Highland Gamekeeper,* Dugald Macintyre recalls how, at Tulchan, King Edward put £5 in the keepers' box and the German emperor £20. But the King did give the headkeeper an inscribed gold watch. Young keepers made fortunes by selling cartridge cases 'as fired by King Edward and his guest'. Real 'King Edwards' brought 6d each, but the Kaiser's just 3d!

The average headkeeper on a great shoot today is a fine general who conducts his troops admirably, conferring with his boss, the field marshal, who sometimes knows as much as he does. Obviously disputes can arise and usually the word of the master prevails, but often not without subsequent embarrassment. For example, it is reported that Lord Cardigan, of Balaclava fame, once ranted at his keeper for lack of birds. 'Go and beat the covert at once, sir,' he shouted, 'and if there are not more birds, instant dismissal.' 'But, my lord', began the keeper. 'Not a word; do as I bid you', said his master, and the poor man scuttled off to obey orders. When hardly any birds came, Cardigan's language was as sizzling as the famous charge itself. But when he had finished the keeper replied, 'But, my lord, the covert is not yours.'

Most great shoot owners are directly involved in the employment of all their keepers, but generally it is the headkeeper alone who is responsible for mustering the necessary team of beaters and pickers-up. But many changes have taken place in the world of beating. Grand shoots no longer work on the old hired-servant basis where estate workers were commonly commandeered to double-up as beaters. Today not

IMPORTANT TO GENTLEMEN .

GAME PRESERVERS AND POULTRY KEEPERS.

BAILEY'S

Patent Improved PHEASANT FEEDER

IS, without doubt, the best Feeder made, as it fully saves half the usual quantity of Corn used without it. It insures the Birds being regularly fed ; it is quite vermin proof, and cannot get out of order. It has a glass front, showing the corn, which is a great attraction for the birds, and is warranted to be most substantially made. It holds quite half a bushel of corn, which is a great saving of time, as once filled it does not require looking to so often as other feeders do.

For price and particulars, apply to

T. DAINTITH, Gunmaker, 82, Bridge-st., Warrington.

Victorian pheasant feeder
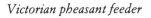

1935: gamekeepers help with research in picking out ants' pupae for analysis at the ICI Game Research Station (now the Game Conservancy)

only are there far fewer men on the land to call upon, but also their unions might have something to say about the matter.

But beaters are never difficult to get; so many people have been cut off from their roots in country pursuits that droves are queuing to join the beating line. Their pay is meagre — perhaps £5–£10 for a hard day's slog in all weathers, but there is often free lunch and beer, and sometimes a bird or two to take home. The chief reward is a day out in the fresh air, in a totally different environment where nature is close. To others it represents a way of making an extra useful 'bob or two'. Regular beaters are, however, still highly valued, for they can contribute much to the average day. They are traditionally rewarded with a gun on the keeper's day at the end of the season, though in Victorian times the idea of beaters shooting would have been unthinkable.

Today most beaters merge into the background in their green waxproofs and tweeds and it is not uncommon for them to look even smarter than the Guns. But in the old days visibility was regarded as more important than being in tune with a green environment. Also everyone needed to be reminded of his position and it was common practice to issue smocks for the beaters to wear. One estate at least is said to have put letters on the smocks but the men resented this convict-like approach and were not averse to arranging themselves to spell words of a dubious nature when the ladies joined the party after lunch!

To sum up, good game country, vast amounts of cash and a keen owner are not enough to make a shoot great. It still needs an outstanding headkeeper — a man who knows his patch intimately and commands both the loyalty of his team and the respect of his employer. He is a man who takes his vows for life, regards materialism as quite unimportant and has the strength of character to say 'No!' to rich, pompous Guns who would seek to dominate him. He is not just a game harvester but a lover of nature who is thoroughly in keeping with the whole environment.

Today there are dozens of people chasing every keeper vacancy, for the vogue has never been greater to enter occupations which get back to man's roots in the countryside. Technical advice, courses and even certificates in gamekeeping are widely available, but none takes the place of practical experience. The importance of having a successful keeper who knows how to apply all the theory to local requirements cannot be overstressed.

Elveden circa 1900. *Keepers in bowlers, beaters in smocks*

CHAPTER 4

THE QUARRY BIRDS

Before man increased greatly in numbers and when wild game was plentiful, if he wanted swan on the menu, so be it. But when increased demand brought the first shortages, ways to ration natural 'crops' were sought, although not before the rich and powerful had had a good go at keeping most of the bounty for themselves.

Even in the Middle Ages there was snobbery in the pursuit of game, for many of the birds and animals accorded 'game' status had no more meat on them and were no more tasty than 'lesser' creatures; wildfowl in particular have been ignored by 'gentlemen of leisure'. Thus, for somewhat arbitrary reasons, a comparatively small number of birds and mammals came to be regarded as 'game' and of these only three are of central interest to this book. Today Britain's 'bread-and-butter' gamebird is the pheasant, but only because the English or grey partridge has had a tough time this century, and I will deal with the latter first as most sportsmen prefer its challenge. The third bird is the red grouse, whose aura brings Guns from all over the world every year.

A shoot is restricted in its quarry list not only by law but also by climate and habitat. For example, it would be exceptional for a gamebird shoot to be good, let alone great, in a very wet, flat, featureless area where agriculture has turned the fields into prairies and a perpetual chemical storm rains down on insect life. In recent decades the widespread change to winter corn has meant that autumn stubbles, a traditional favourite for holding game, have become something of a rarity and they are always ploughed in quickly to make way for the next regime. Sometimes special crops are planted in small patches to provide food or cover for game, but the farmer will usually want compensation for devoting land to this. The great landowner who farms in-hand can usually please himself. Some shoots, such as those on the southern downlands, have planted cover to hold game in recent times, yet in some cases are now truly great because they have the advantage of ideal land contours. But where natural food is plentiful in areas of thick cover feeding is specially important to draw the birds out into position.

Overall, the South and East have the advantage when it comes to provision of cover and choice of food for pheasant and partridge, but the North and West have most of the hills to launch quality birds from. Grouse, of course, need the heather of the North.

In the South there is often time to grow a 'catch' crop such as mustard, stubble turnip and fodder radish, which are of value to game. Compensation to the farmer is then not necessary, but this is only really worthwhile where a winter crop will not be grown. The timing is so critical that sometimes mustard seed is scattered into winter corn several weeks before the harvest, to gain precious time.

PARTRIDGE

Many Guns would rather shoot one partridge than a dozen pheasants, but there is much nostalgia in their thinking. The English or grey partridge was Britain's premier gamebird before this century, and even up to about 1950 it was very significant in some areas. Today it is still common, but its numbers are much reduced because it has not been able to adapt to the new agricultural practices which have decimated its habitat and killed off much of its insect food. Probably some half a million partridges are shot each year in Britain, but that is nothing when compared with around 12 million pheasants. And many of these partridges are of the French, or red-legged variety, a species introduced here in the eighteenth century but largely confined to drier and warmer parts of the South-East. But before its decline the species had enjoyed a period of great increase at the hands of farming. After about 1830 many estates recorded a sudden, sharp increase in bags beyond that expected through growing popularity of shooting or climatic change. Undoubtedly it was due largely to much more land going under the plough (which provided that valuable stubble for long periods) and to the increase and consolidation of the vast hedgerow network.

The partridge has been highly regarded as a table bird for many centuries. Ben Jonson (1573–1637), in his 'Staple of News', wrote:

> Fetch me a pheasant, or a brace of partridges,
> From goodwife poulterer, for my lady's supper.

In 1880, J. J. Manley reflected the feeling of the day: 'There is no sporting anniversary so popular as the First of September, partly because partridge shooting is a pastime which has more followers than any other fieldsports, and partly because the sport itself is the most enjoyable of all connected with the gun.' Yet Manley also noted that it was 'but little more than a hundred years since netting, not shooting, was the ordinary way of securing partridges', when 'the lord of the manor, in his laced hat, tie wig, flapped waistcoat, capacious coat, and high-topped boots, rode over the stubble, directing his servants who drew the net, while the dog, crouching close to earth, patiently submitted to be enclosed therein along with the birds'.

In the 1890s the eastern counties were regarded as best for partridges, with Yorkshire and Nottinghamshire a short way behind. But reasonable bags were always expected in Cheshire, Shropshire and Staffordshire in the North West, Northamptonshire and Hertfordshire in central parts and Wiltshire, Hampshire and Dorset in the South, where there were thousands of acres of stubbles and fallow, turnips and clover. Yet many areas had not realised their potential. This was quite the reverse of the position in Hungary where Baron de Hirsch led the way with partridge shooting on a vast scale.

The lack of partridge shooting to meet demand at the end of the nineteenth century was blamed on lack of specialist keeping, excessive egg stealing and poaching, and over-shooting. With Norfolk, Suffolk and Cambridgeshire then regarded as the pick of English counties for game, everyone was astounded when, in 1887, Hampshire set new records. It was said that such a thing could not have happened without wholesale

1903 game cart for partridges

buying of eggs, artificial rearing of birds, sacrifice of agriculture, and use of nets, wires, kites 'and other illegitimate means' in a 'second-class game country'. In the event none was true and the remarkable performance of The Grange was entirely fair. The estate went on to provide the biggest weeks' partridge driving in England for some years through good keepering, good management and good understanding between owner, keepers, farmers and labourers.

Red-legged partridges featured more and more in bags everywhere at the turn of this century, having spread remarkably since their introduction in 1770 by two Suffolk landowners and neighbours, the Marquis of Hertford and Lord Rendlesham. In 1903 Charles Alington was astounded to find that on one shoot in Wiltshire a third of the bag were redlegs. But he could not agree that a sprinkling of redlegs was necessary for driving; he thought the French leader of a covey ridiculous and 'the invention of an incompetent keeper'. Driving was regarded as essential to kill the old birds off, and the general disturbance and splitting of families good in order to prevent excessive inbreeding. But introduction of Scottish as well as Hungarian birds was regarded as just as useful for these reasons. Fresh blood was thought particularly good even in counties such as Devon where driving was mostly difficult because of terrain, thick cover and fences. Estates were urged to help themselves by shifting eggs from one part of their ground to another. But purchase of eggs for hatching under fowls was always suspect, as eggs were often stolen from a neighbour or even from the buyer's own estate!

Overall then it had been realised that by artificial means the less favoured counties with heavier soils could easily compete with those which supported a good head of partridges naturally on light land. But walked-up days were increasingly a novelty and mere exercise, as driving became the method of serious men. Pheasant shooting was very well established at the beginning of this century, but to some extent it remained the pursuit of hill country where partridges were less numerous. Thus up to World War II the partridge was still generally considered the most sporting quarry the lowland shooter could find. Wildfowl and snipe could not be compared because their distribution was much more local.

Up to 1939, they were relatively good days for the partridge man. Agriculture had not yet blitzed the land, the human population level was tolerable, the weather was in an exceptionally kind phase and improved knowledge of keepering and rearing brought ways to augment and help the stock. By 1940 it was the custom to have a special partridge keeper on the best estates and each man would be expected to chart the progress of each nest on his patch. Eggs would be removed from nests in vulnerable situations and infertile ones left in their place. The hen partridge knew no difference and her eggs would be incubated under chickens until they reached the chipping stage, when they would be returned to the nest. This greatly improved the success rate. Alternatively, eggs could be moved to nests in safer positions and left there, as it is rare for a partridge to lay the maximum clutch of some twenty-five eggs. In recent times some keepers have also reduced the number of eggs in wild partridge nests to, say, ten or twelve, in the strong belief that with food scarcity on modern farms the remaining chicks will have a much higher survival rate. Those removed are looked after very well with the aid of very efficient modern incubating systems.

Others believe that management of the habitat to aid wild game is more productive than a rearing-and-release programme and that wild birds are generally better parents. An increasingly important consideration is that what's good for game is good for wildlife generally, and there is hardly a better indicator of the health of the countryside than the partridge. In some drier areas no partridges are released at all, but the red-legged partridge is better adapted to modern agriculture. Despite everything, however, it must be said that today there are very few shoots where there are sufficient wild partridges to make driving worthwhile. And as the partridges disappear so too do the skills required to drive them.

The grey partridge can provide marvellous sport even on level ground as long as there are tall hedges. Sadly, we all know what has happened to our hedgerows over the last thirty years — mile after mile have been ripped out year after year. Fortunately, some of the truly great shooting men, who had the funds to put their ideas into practice, planted up hedgerows specially for partridges in the 1930s and 1940s. But even where reasonable hedgerows remain they are not enough because the excessive tidiness of most farms now removes all the rough margins and untidy corners where weed seeds, berries and other partridge foods should abound. They can't eat barbed wire and conifers. Where a sterile environment exists winter feed bills are high, and this in turn means that the summer stock is artificially high and will not be successful on that ground.

Predator removal continues to be important but the battle can be hopeless if neighbours neglect this duty. On the other hand, better food supply on adjoining shoots will draw your birds away. The great partridge shoots are those where managers always make allowance for the weather and always leave enough wild stock. Too often today the small, inexperienced shoots get over-excited when partridges re-establish themselves and they shoot them too hard on the selfish last-chance principle.

PHEASANT

Much of what has been said about the partridge applies to pheasant as far as habitat management is concerned, but although an introduced Asian species the latter is much more able to cope with man's obsession with uniformity in the countryside.

It seems likely that pheasants were reared for the table in Romano-British households, but they were certainly not then bred for sport. The species does not seem to have been thoroughly naturalized in Europe until the thirteenth century, though they were commonly found in England during the reign of Henry I (1100–35), when a licence to kill them was necessary. The goshawk was used to take pheasants in woodland. By the reign of Edward I they were marketable commodities, making 4d each; but they must have been considerable luxuries because 4d was all a fat lamb could be expected to fetch 'except from Christmas to Shrovetide'. They were particularly relished as a table bird when killed by a hawk after a violent flight, which was supposed to make the flesh more 'short, tender and disposed to corruption'. It is even said that on the last night of his life, 29 December 1170, Thomas à Becket dined off a pheasant 'more heartily and cheerfully than usual'. Although King Richard II's cook seemed to have little regard for pheasants, boiling them with curlews for the royal banquets, they were usually treated better in great kitchens and were, no doubt, a welcome change from the swans, herons and lesser fowl of the commonplace menu. In fact, medieval household account books are full of references to pheasants and to the hawks used in their capture.

Henry VIII was interested in pheasants, but his proclamation of 1536 alludes to a very different London from that of today. Its purpose was to preserve the pheasants, herons and partridges from his palace at Westminster to St Giles in the Fields, and from thence to Islington, Hampstead, Highgate and Hornsey Park. The only pheasants there today are in butchers' shops.

Not surprisingly, there were laws to safeguard the pheasant. An Act of Queen Elizabeth I imposed a penalty of 20s or a month in gaol for every pheasant taken by night, and a statute of James I fixed a close season between 1 July and 31 August. Any person hawking at or destroying a pheasant during those months would be fined 40s for hawking and 20s for each pheasant taken. A Scottish Act of 1594 threatened with dire and divers penalties any enterprising individual pursuing pheasants 'either with gun, croce bow, hand bow, dogges halkes or girnes or be uther engine quhat-sum-ever in the king's haill wooddes, Forrestes and Parkes'.

It is not clear when pheasants were first reared and released for sport, but it was probably in the eighteenth century. The practice was clearly alluded to by Henry James Pye in his poem 'Amusement' (1790).

> The Wing'd tribe, by care domestic bred,
> Watched with attention, with attention fed,
> Where'er the sportsman treads in clouds arise.

1903 game cart for pheasants

This was a satire on the degeneracy of the age, particularly regarding fieldsports. There was also an Act passed in 1762 which made it illegal 'to take, kill, destroy, carry, sell, buy, or have in his, her or their possession . . . any Pheasant, between the First Day of February and the First Day of October, in any year . . . Provided always, That nothing in this Act shall extend to any Pheasant which shall be taken in Season and kept in any Mew or Breeding-place', indicating that pheasants were then habitually caught-up and kept in confinement for breeding, but it is not clear whether this was for sport.

Game records show that after modest beginnings at the end of the eighteenth century, pheasant rearing really got underway about 1825. Records from Hewell Grange in Worcestershire, and the Buccleuch estates, show that large numbers were then reared. In those early years there was more interest in October pheasant shooting because woods, generally speaking, were much larger and few 'rides' had been cut for hunting or shooting. Once the birds had retreated among the trees it was very difficult to get at them and you bagged what you could while they still lingered in the hedgerows and copses near their nests and rearing places. But by the 1880s hardly anyone thought of making a bag before the leaves were off the trees: birds could be got at in covers arranged for the purpose, where by the end of November both wild and tame birds would have assembled. This led to very large bags which included poor birds, but today much of the theory behind leaving birds until November is more concerned with late-developing birds being stronger on the wing by then.

By 1903 a clear pattern was established and Alfred Watson remarked: 'the science of rearing has now reached such a pitch of excellence that, given a competent keeper,

Pheasants driven out of kale at Gurston Down. Today they have replaced partridges as the major quarry on most estates

(page 49) Flintlock pheasant of yesteryear; a painting by Ben Marshall (photograph courtesy of Christie's)

(pages 50–1) Early partridge shooting, said to be at Six Mile Bottom in 1833, but not resembling the estate today; a painting by J. F. Herring (photograph courtesy of Christie's)

Ex-headkeeper ·the late Charles South remembers the many special days recorded in the Six Mile Bottom gamebooks

Light-hearted decoration in Lord Ripon's personal gamebooks. Once the owner of Studley Royal, he is said to have been the best Shot of all time – and not a bad artist either (photograph courtesy of Sotheby & Co)

Date. *Nov 24*	Number.	OBSERVATIONS. 5204
Red Deer		*Blankney Wood*
Grouse		
Partridges		
Pheasants	208	
Snipe		
Wild Duck		
Wild Geese		
Woodcocks		
Quail		
Sea Fowl		
Wood Pigeon		
Hares		
Rabbits	40	
Various *Jays*	3	
Total	257	*Let em rise !*

Webster & Co., 60, Piccadilly, W.

moderately favourable soil, and plenty of money, it becomes in these days merely a question of how many pheasants the woods on a property will hold'. And in that age of the big battue there was already a variety of plumages in the bag because the ring-necked or Chinese pheasant, having been introduced from southern China at the end of the eighteenth century, had freely interbred with the old English black-neck stock. Other varieties have since been introduced and mixed freely to provide many talking points when bags are examined. Some shoots prefer a strong element of melanistic (black) birds; others regard odd white ones as almost sacred and fine any Gun who bags one, for bad luck might result!

November pheasant shooting follows on well from October partridge driving for those who are in the fortunate position to follow both. However, it is not easy to confine pheasants to one area — perhaps the main park — and partridges to another — probably the arable areas around the park — on a great estate. The pheasant is a great wanderer, especially where large numbers are turned down, and it will move into partridge territory, doing mischief such as laying in partridge nests. On small estates in particular, which have sought unreasonably large bags, it became necessary literally to shepherd the pheasants. On one estate in the Black Country where 25,000 pheasants were turned down every year, 56 men and boys were employed to act as permanent 'stops' in this way. Most great estate keepers have agreed that the ideal partridge ground is one denuded of pheasants, for under pressure the partridge will migrate; most owners, of course, have always sought compromise.

Just as there were early attempts to mix partridge stock to improve the blood, so too have some of the great shoots very recently brought in pheasants from wilder counties to breed faster, lighter and more sporting birds. On the other hand, no less a person than Bill Fenwick, until recently the Queen's headkeeper at Windsor for many years, believes the small fen-type pheasants are no good for a driven day. 'They might be all right for one drive but they don't have the stamina of the heavy, reared birds.' In recent decades, in many parts of the country a kind of race developed to shoot the heaviest pheasant of the year, but the idea was self-defeating as a fat pheasant is a poor mark. The Game Conservancy estimates that a pheasant drains the energy reserves in its muscles in just eight seconds, then it glides. Excess fat will shorten that time, and this should be born in mind when positioning Guns, who should be where the birds reach maximum height and speed.

When it comes to rearing, the great estates have advantages of large-scale production over the small man, who would do better to buy poults from game farms rather than rear from the egg stage. The small shoot is better employed in improving the habitat to receive the birds. Also the large shoot is often in a position to sell excess eggs or birds and thus defray costs. And sometimes they take in eggs from other shoots to maximise incubator use.

There is a wealth of advice available today on rearing and keepering, species selection, habitat control etc, but few of the great shoots I have been to have ever made use of visiting experts such as those from the Game Conservancy. They have been in the fortunate position to be able to learn through their own mistakes and have built up great stores of local knowledge. The importance of this cannot be over-emphasised. On a predominantly wild-bird pheasant shoot it is obvious that sufficient stock must be left to suit the habitat, and this is where the excellent keepering and management of the great shoots comes into play. Here predator control is very important.

On both pheasant and partridge shoots tagging systems are commonly used, to ascertain bird movements and study efficiency. Many shoots take great pride in getting a high percentage of their tagged birds in the bag, but overall the average for reared pheasants on well-keepered ground is only 40 per cent. Very recently the experts have been doubting the wisdom of flooding a ground with birds and are much more preoccupied with the provision of ideal habitat. There is no doubt that Guns on commercial shoots tend to over-shoot more than Guns on private or syndicate shoots, and have less regard for quality. It is very encouraging indeed that on many of the most famous shoots visited the owners and managers have deliberately and systematically reduced the bags in recent years and sought to improve sport through continual experimentation with drives and introduction of fresh blood. Shoots which once thought nothing of a 1,000-bird day are now more interested in a maximum of around the 350 mark for the traditional team of about eight Guns.

Even great shoots have their problems as the British weather is so unpredictable, but this is no bad thing for if every breeding season were good not only would shooting men have nothing to talk about, but much of the mystery would disappear and we would be all the poorer for that.

RED GROUSE

The approach to red grouse shooting is entirely different from that to partridge and pheasant for, although this very wild bird of northern and western Britain can be reared, it is very difficult to get the birds to adapt to a natural diet when released onto the moor. Thus overwhelming concentration has been on habitat control since the introduction of driven shooting largely superseded walking-up in the nineteenth century.

This is another bird which was first valued for its flesh rather than sport and it was once sought with the falcon rather than the gun. But living in wild, remote regions it was not so easy to exploit as the lowland gamebirds, though its range was rather more extensive before gross habitat destruction got underway.

Grouse shooting is far less predictable than sport with partridge and pheasant because the species has always been perplexingly subject to cyclical population fluctuation. Many reasons have been put forward for this, including outbreaks of disease, loss of heather vitality, competition with sheep, reduction in vigour of the stock and, of course, the weather. Tentative studies have been going on throughout this century but it is only very recently that there have been major investigations.

Much of the new interest in grouse research and the funding of programmes has been generated by the fact that the bird is a major dollar earner, especially in Scotland. But it is heartening that there is considerable desire to sort out the grouse problems simply because this species above all is a symbol of the jealously guarded and seriously threatened upland habitat. Though primarily a man-made habitat, the grouse moors

1903 game cart for grouse

are important reservoirs of wildlife, much of it scarce or rare, and the strong move to preserve them is keenly supported by Britain's conservation organisations. In some instances the two 'sides' have joined forces to resist pressures from excessive public disturbance and the greater evil of blanket forestry which threatens to smother the purple hills with a sea of conifer green where botanist, zoologist and sportsman find little interest.

The major debate in the nineteenth and early twentieth century was whether grouse could co-exist with sheep, but inevitably the practice of the day reflected the greatest financial return. It is perfectly possible to crop both grouse and sheep on one moor and the income from sheep in lean grouse years is always welcome, but over-grazing by sheep is a disaster as the heather will rapidly decline and be replaced by rough grasses useless to grouse and virtually unpalatable to sheep. The situation is exacerbated by winter grazing when supplementary hay and feed blocks are necessary because the sheep must concentrate around the feeding points in harsh weather and may then graze remaining heather to extinction. Thereafter both sheep and grouse may be abandoned in favour of forestry with its tempting tax relief.

Highland lairds who once ranged the hills to crop the grouse, salmon and deer for their festivities had no idea that the southern craze for shooting would one day contribute to their income. Their eyes were first opened to the possibilities when Highland cattle had to give way to sheep in the first quarter of the nineteenth century. The first grouse shooters began to offer small rentals as better access meant that they could at last get there regularly and in relative safety. They would buy the shooting rights over extensive sheep farms; in the 1830s just £20 was paid for a year's shooting over 50,000 acres.

In the early years of let shooting there were still no railways so coach travel for days on end was necessary to reach the remote glens far removed from steamers. But competition soon set in for the small number of moors let and rents escalated, though they were still insignificant compared with those paid by the sheep farmers, then at the peak of their prosperity. Eventually the rents were comparable and the landlords had the best of both worlds. The bubble burst when sheep farming went to the wall as Australia's wool production got into full stride. Grouse rents continued to rise through the third quarter of the century and many men abandoned sheep, deriving higher incomes from grouse and deer than they ever did from wool and mutton. The economic importance of grouse was established and later enhanced further by overseas Guns coming as tourists.

Fortunately the early opening of grouse shooting on 12 August ties in well with the sportsman's social calendar. It was the common custom of the great landowners in the last quarter of the nineteenth century to remain on their grouse moors from that date well into September, when they would return to their lowland shoots to walk-up a few partridges before the big driven partridge days in late September and October, followed by the first of the big pheasant days in late November. Today there are very few people with the time and money to follow such a way of life. Yet they do exist, and there are men who are both wealthy enough and keen enough to shoot driven game for as many as five days a week for much of the season.

Unlike pheasant and partridge shooting, grouse shooting surroundings are almost always attractive and this is very much part of the fascination for both British and overseas sportsmen. But it is quite another thing to achieve the consistently good bags which can make a moor great and which very much determine the colossal rentals which have been paid in recent years as well as the outright purchase of moors for very large sums by foreigners, including Arabs. This often leads to disappointment because not everyone can inspire loyalty, get the best results and still have the long-term interests of the land at heart.

Most people are surprised to learn that the introduction of driven grouse shooting brought about a sharp increase in bags out of all proportion to that expected through increased firepower. The main reason for this is that the old birds tend to come over the Guns first and a larger proportion of them are killed than would be the case if the birds were walked up. This is good for the stock because the older birds are more territorial and combative and interfere considerably with the nesting of younger birds. Secondly, by driving, the danger of killing off whole broods is obviated, especially during the early part of the season when walking-up can easily wipe out an entire covey as the birds rise in twos or threes. Driving also moves the birds around more and refreshes the blood of local stock, and there is no doubt that driving has reduced the incidence of disease.

There is a reference to driven grouse on the Bishop of Durham's Horsley Moor in 1803 and it is certain that an informal type of driving was practised on Mr Spencer Stanhope's moors on the Penistone Range in Yorkshire in about 1805. When the owner became tired towards the end of a day he used to sit in an old sandpit, and if his sons were walking nearby on Snailsden Moor he soon discovered that he got more shots in that position. From then on things developed rapidly, there was experimentation with butts, and over the next few decades many people copied the system. Regular driving probably started in the mid-1830s.

It is most important that a grouse-moor owner and his keepers understand their business. If the moor is not shot hard enough disease will be a certainty among the thronging birds, many of which will die anyway through lack of territory and food. On the other hand, when there has been a bad breeding season, or a run of bad seasons, it is essential to shoot a moor only lightly. The man on the ground must know his patch well.

When lowground gameshooting was perfected towards the end of the last century, many landowners were happy to stay at home and this enabled the nouveau-riche without estates to buy into grouse shooting more easily. This still forced the rents up, but more and more of the newcomers were not traditional sportsmen. As Evan Mackenzie wrote in 1907:

> Some of them certainly are not sportsmen; they do not even desire to be regarded as fond of sport of any kind. They hire a moor as they would a steam yacht, or a villa at Scarborough, as an easy way of spending the holidays in a bracing and health-giving, even if expensive, atmosphere. In the absence of birds through disease or other cause, they instinctively perceive they are not receiving value for their cheques, and as businessmen they resent what they cannot help regarding as imposition.

True sportsmen will always accept the vagaries of grouse shooting because it is the only gameshooting available during a time of year when it is pure delight to be out in the country. All return refreshed to the grim, grey world of commerce and industry.

Many people would say that the best grouse moors in England, if not in the British Isles, are those of Yorkshire and Derbyshire. Before World War I, grouse were plentiful throughout the northern counties of England, in Northumberland, Durham, Westmorland, Cumberland and Lancashire, with good moors along the Pennines and in Cheshire, Shropshire and Staffordshire. Since then there has been considerable contraction, especially in the latter three counties, but the others still include many of the very best shoots. Before World War I grouse were also thriving in Wales, and increasing substantially in areas where management was good. Denbigh, Flint, Caernarvon, Montgomery and West Merioneth in particular were outstanding. Today it is a tale of woe, for so many fine moors have been lost to forestry there. The position in Ireland is even worse, for poaching has always been a particular problem, not to mention a puzzling loss of vigour in the stock, and lack of vermin control. Scotland, of course, has always been *the* land associated with grouse, and good moors are numerous. Yet the generally steeper terrain is more difficult to drive than the gently rolling hills of northern England and larger teams of beaters are needed. Also, in England on the great shoots, continuity of owner-interest and involvement has been much better than north of the Border where, traditionally, the desire to maximise incomes has often superseded love of the sport.

There is no doubt that the first big grouse bags were achieved on those moors where careful attention was paid to moor management through systematic burning, draining, fertilising, livestock control and so on. Yet none can guarantee the weather and that is why grouse shooting has always been much more liable to sudden cancellation or reduction in level than any other form of gameshooting. Nothing has changed today, though there has been a puzzling run of very bad seasons of late. Even so, there have been exceptions where management has been particularly skilful.

Predator control has also always been particularly important on the grouse moor, but in this activity the modern owner is more restricted as some of the traditional 'enemies' such as the harrier are now fully protected, and quite rightly so. Trapping must be done with great care and sensitivity and, of course, indiscriminate poisoning is outlawed.

Walking-up grouse is very popular and, if anything, has enjoyed something of a boom in recent years as sporting agents attract many Guns who could never even entertain the great expense of driven grouse. Such days generally bring very small bags but the pleasure of getting those hard-won birds through many hours tramping over the most invigorating moorland, where there is always so much for both sportsman and naturalist to enjoy, is almost unsurpassed. There is much fun too in watching pointers and setters work the ground in the age-old way, bringing peace to the generally overwrought mind. There are those who will always insist that the economic benefits of the grouse 'industry' are unimportant, being insignificant when compared with the land's potential for food production for the people. But if we always followed this dictum, there would be no nature conservation either and we would live in a boring state where everything was geared to efficiency.

Of course, one cannot have cake at every meal, or the perfection of down-wind drives every time. We cannot always hope for the great days of the past — off the hill at Broomhead, over the Shipka Pass at Wemmergill, 'the face of the rock' at Drumour, among the top Guns at the fourth drive on the home beat at Dungavel — but it is a very rare day indeed when a grouse shooter does not go to bed a happy man. If he is not satisfied, the answer almost always lies in his poor gun-handling.

MIXING IT UP

So far I have talked about only specialist gameshooting, but many Guns regard a mixed bag as essential to a great day and a great shoot. In the ordinary course of a pheasant or partridge day there may well be a smattering of woodcock, duck, hare, rabbit etc in the bag, but there are really outstanding shoots where the day is specially planned to take in the variety required. And even in grouse-shooting country, the moorland visitor will be hoping to account for a few black grouse or even ptarmigan. In addition, along the way every Gun will take pleasure in reducing the local predator population, knocking down the odd jay, crow, magpie, squirrel etc which, at the end of the day, will be entered in the game book under the quaint heading 'various'.

Rabbit In the nineteenth century rabbit shooting was very important indeed, for, apart from the great sport afforded, the rabbit was a major agricultural pest and its meat highly valued. In 1859 the authoritative 'Stonehenge' wrote:

> In my opinion rabbit shooting affords the very best sport in covert of all, excepting only wild pheasant and woodcock shooting. This, of course, has reference to the hunting them with dogs, and shooting them while going at their best pace, which is undoubtedly a racing one. Warren rabbits removed to a covert, and there allowed to breed, soon attain the same characters as the prior denizens of the same locality. The sport of shooting rabbits is never carried on in the warrens, because the warrener does not wish his property wasted, and prefers trapping them, for obvious reasons – one being, that the wounded rabbits often escape into the holes and die out of reach.
>
> Rabbits are now much encouraged in large pheasant preserves, partly for the sake of the keepers, whose perquisite they are, but chiefly because they afford food for the foxes preserved for fox hunting, which would otherwise prey upon the pheasants. The keeper feeds foxes when young regularly upon rabbits wounded and left near their earths; and, consequently, these rabbit-fed animals keep to the same fare, and are thus prevented from interfering with the pleasure of the battue.

The main rabbit shooting came in February and March when pheasant shooting was over and the foxes had been thinned, but before the rabbits could damage the young crops too much, 'several hundred couple being often killed in a single preserve'. Well-stocked coverts would be properly ferreted the night before, burrows blocked and the rabbits driven in droves towards five or six waiting Guns the next day.

Woodcock Today rabbit shooting is left to the keepers and is not the sport of gentlemen in the old-fashioned sense; woodcock, on the other hand, have always maintained their position as the most revered of all quarry. In 1846 'Craven' wrote of woodcock shooting: 'Here is, indeed, a stirring subject — the pursuit of at once the daintiest and most sporting of all our feathered quarry.' Also in the nineteenth century, the famous Colonel Hawker described it as 'the foxhunting of shooting', saying that 'a real good sportsman feels more gratified by killing a woodcock, or even a few snipes than bags full of game'. The same holds true today. The woodcock's pin (or pen) feather is still taken for the hat, and the sportsman still prefers to take a brace of 'cock home rather than six brace of pheasants.

Woodcock do breed in Britain but by far the largest number shot are winter visitors which congregate in western areas where there is less likelihood of frost to prevent them probing the soft ground for food. Indeed, some parts of Ireland, the western Scottish isles and Cornwall have traditionally received such an influx of wintering woodcock that special drives have been possible. In most other areas the Guns have to be content with a handful of 'cock which are put up in the ordinary course of a pheasant day.

Woodcock shooting is very unpredictable and the species very vulnerable to severe frost, when it must be shot sparingly. Through a quirk of legislation many are shot illegally every year because most are bagged on pheasant drives. Pheasant shooting ends on 1 February, but many Guns seem ignorant of the fact that woodcock shooting must cease on 31 January, though from a conservation point of view this means little.

Snipe Snipe shooting has always been held in high esteem, the birds offering a truly testing mark besides being superb on the table. But while woodcock have enjoyed some increase through afforestation in recent years, snipe have suffered considerably as farming has continued to drain every possible piece of land. Some of the great estates can still provide a little snipe shooting because they can afford to let rough corners remain. Apart from these one must generally go west to find snipe, to the frost-free bogs of Ireland, south-west England, Wales and Scotland. Driven snipe are rare in England because numbers are insufficient, so most Guns have to be content with walking-up. Yet any form of snipe shooting is testing.

Traditional hare shoot in Hampshire. Far fewer hares are shot now as the population has declined in most areas

Hare Hare shooting is a very controversial subject today because the brown hare has declined so much in the last twenty years. The reasons are not entirely clear because the decline has been patchy, but it is probably connected with poisons used in agriculture as well as habitat abuse. Very many shoots have stopped killing hares altogether, but in areas where they remain a significant agricultural pest special hare shoots are still held after the end of each gamebird shooting season.

There is no link between hares and great shoots today. When driven, the fleet-footed mammal offers good sport, but the Guns tend to be all and sundry locals who probably never shoot at any other time of year so it is a dangerous affair. Much greater fun is had when a few hares form part of a mixed day's walking-up, yet even then the hare is often spared because no one wants to be burdened with its great weight. In addition, the hare's flesh is nothing like as popular today as it was last century when it was regarded as a most valuable 'crop' on the great estates.

Few people realise that the large hare population we had all become used to was a relatively new phenomenon; in the last quarter of the nineteenth century there was fear for the mammal's extinction. Enlargement of fields, removal of woodland and ploughing-up of much land saved the day.

Long ago the hare was revered as a sporting quarry. According to the *Boke of St Albans,* 1486, it was second only to the red stag:

> Fowre maner bestys of venery there are:
> The first of them is the Hart, the seconde is the Hare,
> The Bore is oon of them, the Wolff, and not oon mo.

Very much later there was considerable interest in hare shooting on the great partridge estates as variety for the Guns. Great bags were made, such as those of Lord Chesterfield at Gedling in 1869 when 781 and 823 hares were killed on two separate days in one week, or of Lord Londesborough in 1878, when 1,217 were killed in three consecutive days. But such bags could not continue, as pressure from agricultural tenants increased.

Yet the presence of a large number of hares on the ground when gameshooting opened was always regarded as a feather in the keeper's hat, not only because the Guns welcomed the chance to try their skill on a hare when walking in line for partridges, but also because hares were always keenly poached and to see them in quantity meant the keeper had been vigilant.

Woodpigeon Woodpigeon shooting has never been significant on great game shoots. Most owners have been content to let their keepers organise the shooting of this great agricultural pest in the covert roosts as soon as 2 February came with, later, decoying on the stubbles. Just a few great landlords, whose tremendous enthusiasm for all forms of shooting drew them to more solitary sport, took large pigeon bags.

Woodpigeon shooting is tremendously popular today because the bird's population has continued to expand greatly and exert much pressure on agriculture. Thus its shooting is often to be had free and can be enjoyed by anyone, although game interests

Tree-top pigeon shooting in Banffshire. Only the more enthusiastic great shoot owners have regarded the woodpigeon as a special quarry

(right) Mallard flighting in Hampshire. Many shoots now rear duck to shoot at either end of a pheasant day

must always take priority and the coverts must not be disturbed until the keeper agrees.

Duck Of all the quarry in the mixed bag, the duck fits in best with the modern gameshoot because it is usually flighted at dawn and dusk and can be shot in an organised way either before or after the day's main sport takes place. It is a challenging and welcome diversion on great private shoots, but where commercialism takes over there is a tendency to use duck as a relatively easy means of bolstering poor pheasant bags. Here we are talking of inland duck shooting, which is entirely different from the wonderful wild sport of coastal wildfowling. Inland duck are generally concentrated

through a heavy rearing-and-release scheme, followed by a generous feeding programme. A few wild birds will also come into a fed water, but generally the reared duck
are very predictable and can be embarrassingly tame.

On the day of a shoot the birds are usually forced off the water and shot as they circle
to return home. They are often tame, and sporting shots are dependent upon a Gun's
self-control and selection; but on a commercial day the Guns will often be greedy and
take easy birds. Sometimes the organisers are more subtle and arrange for the duck to
be driven off unseen in the half-light and get the Guns ensconced in naturally set hides
as quietly as possible. When carried out tastefully and sportingly a satisfactory time can
be had.

Probably more rewarding is to shoot inland duck when they come to feed on the
stubbles in autumn, but that takes up precious daylight hours in preparation and could
interfere with a full day's pheasant shooting. However, this is unlikely on a great shoot
where the main pheasant days are from November whereas the duck days are mostly in
September, before pheasant shooting has commenced.

Just a few great shoots have had extensive natural waters or proximity to the sea to
enable them to 'major' in duck, but in most cases the bag has been augmented by
rearing, chiefly of mallard. At the turn of the century the most notable shoot was Sir
Richard Graham's Netherby in Cumberland, where as many as 10,000 duck were
reared in one season. The days when large estates had extensive swamps where fowl
could multiply at leisure and Guns take their fill whenever it took their fancy have now
gone.

Dislike of 'artificial' duck is nothing new. In 1913 Aymer-Maxwell commented: 'Some
of us may resent his presence on days of formal sport, finding something distasteful in
this tamer counterfeit of a true wild bird.' But duck-rearing seems here to stay and has
even been carried on by coastal wildfowling clubs. In the early days it was seen as a way
to boost bags but now, for fowling clubs, it is more of a public relations exercise and the
emphasis is on habitat management.

As we shall see, there have been remarkable mixed-bag days on great shoots, as indeed
there are today, but generally these are not planned and their incidence is a bonus.
Their great attraction will probably become more significant as emphasis switches from
rearing schemes to improved habitat management and predator control. After all,
variety is the spice of life.

CHAPTER 5

IT'S THE WAY THAT YOU DO IT

Once the law has decided what you *can* shoot and you have made up your mind what you *want* to shoot, what goes into the bag will be determined largely by your methods. These have been evolved over centuries partly according to fashion but chiefly in line with technical development.

Britain lagged behind Europe in entering the age of the big bag. While gentlemen pottered about our woods and fields after a handful of birds in the eighteenth century, it was already the fashion on the Continent to kill great numbers of game on single days. There it was the custom to round up hares, and even flying game, by means of nets and surrounded by the Guns. Up to a thousand peasants — men, women and children — were ordered to act as beaters and the game was steadily and carefully driven out from the enclosed area over the shooters, each of whom had up to six guns loaded for him by three attendants.

Shooting at flying birds was established in Italy in the first half of the seventeenth century and in 1688, in England, Richard Blome stated in his *Gentleman's Recreation* that 'It is now the Mode to shoot flying'. Previously the guns had not been up to the mark. But everyone soon caught on and by 1792 *The Sportsman's Directory* was able to report: 'The rage for shooting was never at a higher pitch than at present . . . the art of shooting flying has arrived at tolerable perfection'. Previously, apart from royal enthusiasm for staghunting, most interest in game had centred around the table with men more concerned with the certainty of killing. With extensive use of nets and sitting shots at birds, ideally in flocks, there was little notion of sport.

At first those large Continental bags were regarded as improper by our sporting gentry. The Reverend William Daniel even suggested at the beginning of the nineteenth century that 'the real sportsman feels a twinge whenever he sees a hen pheasant destroyed'. Killing more than one bird — except in the case of wildfowl — was considered worthy of punishment by fine. One shooting lodge in Sussex is said to have hung the following list of fines in the breakfast room:

	£	s	d
Killing a *hen* pheasant	1	1	0
Shooting at ditto	0	10	6
Shooting at a pheasant on the ground or in a tree	1	1	0
Shooting at ditto at more than 40 yards unless wounded	0	5	0
Shooting two or more partridges at one shot	0	10	6
Shooting at ditto on the ground	1	1	0
Shooting at ditto at more than 45 yards, if not before wounded	0	5	0
Shooting at a hare in her form	0	5	0

Half of the above fines go to the Poor of the Parish: the other half to the Keepers.

Highclere, 1957. Once highly regarded as a major quarry on big shoots, the rabbit is now gassed as a pest. Watching the demonstration are the late Lord Carnarvon (right) and Lord Porchester (centre), the current Lord Carnarvon

In general, similar principles apply today, but many Guns' range-judging leaves a lot to be desired and partridges do not get the extra five yards. And if anyone gets two partridges with one shot he is thought damn lucky rather than evil.

PARTRIDGE

The major change in shooting practice was from walking-up to driving, which at once facilitated both larger bags and the development of shooting as a fashionable social sport. But, where land was not specifically reserved for shooting, Guns always had to modify methods according to farming practice. For example, in 1859 'Stonehenge' noted:

> When wheat was reaped, and the stubble fields left unploughed till November, partridges might be shot in the stubbles as late as the end of October; but these fields are now shorn so close in 'bagging' them, or are so soon broken up, that the sport cannot be protracted beyond the middle of September. Some of the finest lands in England for partridge

shooting are those parts of our downs which are under the plough; for they are mostly planted with turnips sufficiently to hold birds, while at the same time the plants are not high enough to prevent a dog finding birds in them. In spite of this, however, it is now the fashion to dispense with the use of a pointer, and beaters are employed in partridge reserves as well as in covert, by those who take the lead in fashionable circles. Here the 'bag' is considered all important.

This was reiterated by J. J. Manley in 1880. General habitat destruction made it much harder to approach partridges, especially those surviving the close attention of the first week of September. Because of this there was renewed interest in driving and shooting under the kite, or artificial hawk. Flying a hawk-shaped kite over a field, the operator concealed behind a hedge, would cause the increasingly wild partridges to sit tight and allow the Guns a closer approach. On some estates, where they tried to cling to the old methods of walking-up, the partridge beats were over-shot because every area would be covered early in the season and driven later.

The ascendancy of driving in the late nineteenth century renewed interest in the partridge, which had waned with increased pheasant rearing and shooting. Guns also soon discovered how thrilling driven partridge were. They were particularly welcome on flat ground where pheasants proved difficult to launch. But there had to be a good stock of birds to make a shooting party of five or six Guns viable. Driving was also more likely to ensure continuance of good breeding stock, as the coveys would all be more or less equally thinned out. Walking-up frequently exterminated a whole covey and the remaining birds were thus more inclined to inbreed. Driving reduced the number of wounded birds but increased the number fit for the table. Obviously, as driving took over, the trend was away from questing and pointing dogs towards retrievers. Pace became important, too, in gathering up in the short time after each drive and picking up 'runners'.

But when it came to driving, partridges proved more difficult than grouse because they are much less predictable. On the moor, permanent butts could be established according to contours — many of today's have been in constant use since Victorian times; but on the partridge manor there had to be constant reappraisal of drives according to crops and factors known only to the birds. However, the manor man was, as now, less dependent on the wind than the moor manager, for whom an adverse wind on the long sweeping drive of the morning, intended to collect grouse for the shorter drives of the afternoon, can completely spoil the rest of the day.

One theory is that partridge driving started on some Suffolk manors in the 1850s when elderly Guns grew tired of toiling all day after the forever-running Frenchmen, and rested their limbs under a hedge while the keepers brought the birds to them. This soon spread through the redleg's great Suffolk stronghold, but Norfolk men pooh-poohed the idea and continued to walk in line for some time. Initially Guns stood under the hedge with their backs to the drive and only shot at the birds going away. It didn't take long to discover the advantages of taking birds in front and swinging round after others.

In 1911 Aymer-Maxwell considered the near extinction of walking in line after partridges a good thing. It was 'a clumsy business, and the endless repetition of the

Richard Cowen takes a red-legged partridge from his labrador at Sutton Scotney

same end-on shot compared but poorly with the almost infinite variety of pace, angle and curl that driven birds offer.' Given his 'dreary monotony of the interminable turnip-field in which you solemnly wheeled, marched, counter-marched, and wheeled again for half the livelong day', it is amazing that so many of the great shoot owners went out on so many consecutive days. As soon as one half of a field was cleared, fresh birds were driven onto the old ground and you had to retrace your footsteps 'till at length it was with a heart-felt sigh of relief that you stumbled over the last turnip by the gateway'.

Mr Aymer-Maxwell was, however, excessively hard on the old ways and today Guns still enjoy the rare opportunity to walk-up partridges because the birds provide reasonable marks when allowed to achieve a fair range; there is skill in getting near the coveys, and the solitude of the sport is a perfect antidote to an overcrowded world. It is also the best way for a young Shot to get to know his quarry well.

PHEASANT

In nineteenth-century England many large coverts were planted specially to protect pheasants, but the clever landowner also positioned the woods so that birds could be systematically driven to afford a full day's sport. It soon became the fashion to drive the coverts with beaters, aided by a dog or two, or even teams of steady spaniels or beagles.

The clumber spaniel became very popular because it is generally mute and does not disturb game ahead, and its relatively slow manner was popular with the corpulent and elderly. Others preferred dogs which gave tongue for wild game shooting, to indicate the line of flight to waiting Guns. Sometimes setters with bells fastened to their necks were trained to beat covert, the warning coming when the bells stopped ringing as the dogs set. In earlier days when faulty firearms made accurate shooting difficult and a bird on the wing a mark beyond the reach of most, the spaniel was relied on to range the wood and drive the pheasant to perch in a tree, whence the wielder of his cumbrous weapon could bring the bird down at leisure.

Where numbers of birds did not warrant a shooting party, the age-old 'maraud' of the owner with his dogs continued. Sadly, the temptation to make profit from every resource has largely done away with all such informality. The closest to this now is the 'hedgerow bashing' in early October when the larger coverts are still too leafy for effective beating. Thus the pattern seen on the great shoots today, of mere skirmishes at the beginning of the season and main covert days from late November on, was well established before the heyday of the battue. This also tied in well with the necessity to provide outdoor amusement for the male guests who concentrated in country houses in mid-winter.

The great Victorian shoots soon established the main rule of pheasant driving — to push them away from home and then bring them back over the heads of the Guns, for

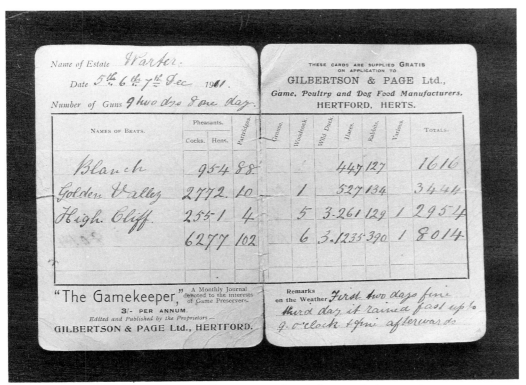

Warter Priory gamecard 1911. The estate produced the record pheasant bag in 1913

pheasants will not fly so freely away from their home covert as towards it. They also worked on the principle that pheasants will commonly run out of thin into thick cover and may easily be made to rise out of the thick cover when driven back again; the return push should be steady to avoid a flush and make sure that all the birds get shot at. Thirdly, they discovered that birds rising out of a covert above the Guns, or out of high trees, will usually rise yet higher and give good shots, but birds flushed from low covert or from levels below the Guns never rise high enough to be interesting. Hence the need to drive birds first into a covert with high trees, or onto ground above the Guns. This has been done with great effect on southern downland where birds are driven out of specially planted hilltop woods, over Guns in the valley below, towards their home territory. Finally it was noticed that when birds were flushed some way from a wood with high trees on the side towards which they were to be driven, they could generally be made to rise high to get above these barrier trees. These would give good shots to Guns posted about forty yards out. Pheasants do not like flying among trees. Men posted as 'stops' could also be used to make the birds rise even earlier and thus achieve the maximum height when over the Guns.

Thus there is never any need to shoot a low, slow pheasant, and no excuse for it. On the other hand, the craze for shooting stratospheric pheasants can be taken to extremes. There is absolutely no point in putting on extreme-range birds for poor or moderate Guns to miss or maim; they should also be put up early enough to get up full steam before reaching the Guns. Birds too difficult to kill soon disillusion a novice Gun, and he will be lost to the sport altogether.

On virtually all the great shoots which I have seen in action, variety of good, testing drives has been as important as putting birds over at a height commensurate with the Guns' ability. It is simply a waste of time to invite guests, no matter how important they are, to shoot very difficult birds of which they have no experience. They will have a miserable time and the host will have failed in his main objective — to make his friends and associates happy.

There is little reason why quality of sport should vary much on a great estate where keepering and rearing are first class. However, failure there is from time to time, more often than not due to one or more generations having failed to maintain the coverts as their forefathers did. When the tallest trees are felled they must be replaced and the undercover controlled to suit game best. Too many owners lack the foresight to consider their descendants.

In some cases there has been considerable re-planting, but the originally ideal coverts may have grown out of shape and sometimes invasive plants such as rhododendron have taken over. Too many mature trees may have blotted out all the light and thus prevented a warm undergrowth. Sometimes, however, lack of perfect covert can be compensated for by the use of artificial boundaries in the form of wire-netting or 'sewin' (sewelling) — a rope with dangling pieces of material which bars the birds' way — kept in motion by 'stops'. Also 'artificial' cover of heaps of brushwood can be laid down at the best flushing points. There are many other tricks of the trade, but on the greatest shoots you will see few in operation and the whole day will seem surprisingly effortless.

Gurston Down consistently shows some of the highest pheasants in Britain

GROUSE

Driven grouse shooting is too well known to need detailed description, but many people do not realise that the object is not only to bring as many grouse as possible over the Guns but also to keep as many as possible on the owner's moor after passing over the butts to make further drives possible on the same day. Here the skill of the headkeeper comes into play, but sometimes even genius is thwarted by the weather, for example when burns are transformed into raging torrents which the beaters cannot cross in the required directions.

Proportionately, probably far more grouse shooters than pheasant and partridge shooters walk-up today because the moorland environment is so pleasing in itself. But the fatigue of walking the heather is not to be lightly undertaken; health and strength are essential, as well as a sixth sense in spotting pot-holes and bogs. Today much of that fatigue has been removed by provision of cross-country vehicles to get Guns into the right area to start, but in the past the weak would use ponies to walk with their stronger friends all day. Some men learned to shoot from them with great skill.

In the mid-nineteenth century the setter was regarded as the best grouse dog, though the pointer was gaining ground among those who used their dogs for partridges as well. Today these dogs are still encountered, but on driven days the scene is likely to be full of springers and labradors.

Discerning keepers soon discovered that there were certain passes, certain places below certain shoulders of a hill, and certain flats along which the grouse were apt to fly when flushed in a certain direction. It was possible to place butts to suit both length of

King George V in the butts at Bolton Abbey

Somerley keeper John Staley controls operations with his 'walkie-talkie'

drive and concentration of birds without need for frequent change. The other essentials were to provide reasonable concealment — sinking the butts if the contours of the land were unsuitable — and to place the butts at an ideal distance apart so that Guns were not tempted to steal each other's birds and no grouse would pass out of range while providing a safe shot.

It is more important to conceal the butts on longer drives off hill ground in Scotland, where birds are brought right off their own territory into totally new country. But on a flat moor in Yorkshire, where there is not enough slope for a half-sunk and drained butt, it would be impossible. And it is not necessary there as the birds can be made familiar with raised butts on earlier short drives. They will continue to approach them without fear if the Guns are well concealed.

The introduction of driving to Scotland did not immediately bring the great bag increases met with in England. A major reason was that much of the higher ground was too rough to drive and the birds simply retreated to inaccessible places when pressed. This meant that the idea of killing off many of the old birds through driving was often defeated. It is even likely that the stock of Scottish grouse decreased over the first fifty years of driving.

Whether it is grouse, partridge or pheasant, driving is the mainstay of the modern scene and, whether or not we rebel against it as being unacceptably artificial, it is the only way in which so many people can continue to shoot game in this relatively tiny overcrowded island.

Joining the Ladies for Lunch

Holkham: lunch at the Barn Plantation between the wars

Even today it is rare for a woman to take her place regularly in the male-dominated shooting line. This is not to say that women are never good Shots; some certainly are and have done exceedingly well, especially in clay pigeon shooting. But the fact remains that, from the beginning of driven game shooting and the birth of the great shooting parties, ladies played little active part and on the whole found spectating boring and uncomfortable. Thus a very structured social occasion was early established, as in J. J. Manley's writing of 1880:

> Partridge shooting has a distinctly social aspect; it is the gathering of friends in country houses, and of a pleasant mingling of classes in the fields — squires, farmers and labourers — all more or less being brought into wholesome contact one with another. To make a good bag is a chief and legitimate object of the sport, but to spend a pleasant day in the fields in glorious autumn weather is by no means a secondary one. It is a sport, too, in which friends join, by accompanying the sportsmen, marking the birds, carrying the game, and making themselves generally pleasant and useful. Nor are the ladies without their share in it; they, too, not only give their benediction to sportsmen who do not get up early in the morning (for which there is no occasion), but often come into the fields to see a little sport, or join the party at the picnic luncheon, for which they have so carefully catered. Without their pleasant presence and aid in carrying out the evening's social programme, a day's partridge shooting would not be complete.

Apart from the boredom and discomfort, the shooting field in general had no appeal for ladies because of its excessively high competitive spirit, especially in Victoria's reign when the need to excel was pushed to the limit. Now that the whole thing is more relaxed, ladies are accompanying their husbands for the entire day much more frequently. Pursuit of big bags, as we have seen, became almost a mania in many areas

— on some estates the whole business was taken so seriously that the ladies were banished for the week, lest they disturb the semi-professional Guns. Diet was strictly regulated and everyone packed off to bed very early. All that mattered was to be 'top Gun' and, not surprisingly, only the top Gun went home happy. Yet when it came to finishing the week with an informal maraud after a few duck or snipe and a marsh pheasant or two, few of these big Guns were interested. Only the true sportsmen turned out early with the owner, and from examination of the game books from many estates it is obvious who the truly dedicated men were.

Today the shooting party, even on the grandest scale, is unlikely to last more than three nights and two days. There is still an overall concentration on weekends, but many weekdays are shot too. Some of the very large estates have sufficient land to take different beats on several days a week, and some of the bad commercial shoots pack different teams in on much the same ground for several days a week. What many failed to realise was that they could not continue to shoot on as many days a week as their grandfathers had, even where a large head of game was reared, because the new generations were not content to sally forth for a small bag, taking all day over it.

THE STATE OF THE GAME.—*Lady Customer.* "How much are grouse to-day, Mr. Jiblets?" *Poulterer.* "Twelve shillings a brace, ma'am. Shall I send them——" *Lady Customer.* "No, you need not send them. My husband's out grouse-shooting, and he'll call for them as he comes home!"

Lady Studd, with her keeper as loader, takes an overhead pheasant at Gurston Down

Many people think that most game shoots take all day over their lunch and that their over-indulgence is gross. Nothing could be further from the truth. One hour is the norm, 45 minutes not that uncommon, 1½ hours is rare. Nor are most shoots flowing with drink as the popular Press suggests. The food is inevitably good, for who would expect otherwise on a day when satisfaction is in the total experience. Yet on the great shoots there is a tendency towards the wholesome, simple, hot dishes secretly longed for by the rich man in his daily business entertainment. Ox-tail or steak and kidney pie followed by apple pie and cream are favourites of men who can afford oysters, steak and champagne at every turn.

There are shoots where the entertaining is excessively lavish, but these tend to be gatherings of business associates on commercial shoots, or at stately homes where a lord has sold a package shooting break. In that event there is the ritualised dinner and gourmet breakfast, in a world which never fails to get the Guns' wives along. This is what the organisers are after — all-round satisfaction and harmony so that the much-valued guests will return with their custom.

In the early nineteenth century a long lunch was no problem as the Guns generally started earlier than now and did not usually shoot for a full day. At Windsor, the Prince Consort did not allow shooting after lunch and Queen Victoria continued the tradition after his death. But by the time she died in 1901 the practice was very old-fashioned and to get in a longer day, lunch was often postponed until 3 o'clock; some keep this timing to this day. Most common, however, is for a lunchbreak at about 12.30 to 1.30 at the main house if it happens to be convenient, or in a nearby tenant farmer's house, the gamekeeper's cottage or a special shoot lodge. It must be remembered that the grouse and partridge shooter mostly has daylight on his side, but the poor old pheasant man on his main days in mid-winter must be on his toes to get all the required drives in.

Lord Ripon drew this moment from the past in one of his entertaining gamebooks

J. J. Manley left this picture of a Victorian shooting lunch:

Let the spot for this important crisis of the day be well chosen. Let it be a regular business, not a hasty snatch of bread and cheese under a hedge, but a well considered and well carried out affair. It is an utter mistake to imagine that cold viands are most appropriate for heated and jaded frames. Hot soups, stews, hashes, or pies and hot potatoes — they will keep hot for hours wrapped in flannel — are most palatable and refreshing in hot weather, on the same principle that hot curry is eaten in India and hot soup at balls.

Let your drink be as cold as possible. A small iceberg enwrapped in flannel is a most enjoyable adjunct to the partridge shooting lunch. Drink champagne, claret, hock or any other light wines, with or without soda water, but, as a rule, eschew beer, sherry, and spirits.

Do not be in a hurry with your lunch, nor afterwards. Take a cigar, lie on your back, stretch your legs, with your heels up if possible, after the sensible American fashion. If the ladies join the luncheon party so much the better, for their presence will prolong this pleasant interlude in the day's sport.

How idyllic it all sounds.

CHAPTER 6

FIT FOR A KING

GIVE GREENER GUNS

There is no better gift than a Greener gun,
an enduring reminder of your discrimina-
tion in selecting the "best,"
affording the recipient a
lifetime's pleasure.

The illustration represents a "high-
grade" Greener Gun
Price **£200**
— but there are other models
ranging from a
Single Barrel Gun at £4-4-0 or a
Double Barrel Hammerless at
£17·17·0 — and we can give
immediate delivery from Stock.

*In the days of the big battues labour was cheap
and gun ornamentation lavish*

The old saying 'looks can kill' is certainly true of a very fine gun. Britain has always led the way in what might be called effective elegance, and this is reflected in the superior investment value of British, particularly English, shotguns. The best are not only fit for a king but have actually been fitted to kings from all over the world. And these fine guns come from a small number of leading British makers, a few of whom have continued in business throughout the entire history of driven game shooting, modifying their weapons to suit technological development and fashion.

The standard game gun on a great shoot is the 12-bore with side-by-side barrels 28in (70cm) long. Most Guns will be wealthy enough to afford a matched pair, though many from old shooting families use inherited guns which have had the stocks altered to suit. In less prestigious shooting — game and clay pigeon — the side-by-side has been overtaken by the over-and-under in which one barrel is placed on top of the other; but such a weapon is still improper on the first-class shoot. Also there has been some movement towards shorter barrels — down to the 25in (64cm) legal minimum — as some people prefer their swifter handling and they are not likely to snarl up in covert branches; but most prefer the greater steadiness of the longer barrels. Standard guns are also now hammerless.

Though gunpowder was certainly invented by the thirteenth century — probably by the English monk Roger Bacon, but perhaps earlier by the Chinese — it was a long time before it was applied to sport. For centuries the gentleman's preoccupation with gamebirds was with hawking. Not until well into the eighteenth century did the shotgun become reliable and efficient enough to attract the leisured classes.

In those wonderful old prints of walked-up shooting scenes we usually see flintlocks in action, but these were very inconvenient. To begin with, all the paraphernalia of muzzle-loading had to be carried by the Gun, and in rain or even on a damp day the powder caused misfires. There was also the 'hang-fire' — the period between pulling the trigger and the shot leaving the gun — caused by slow-burning powder. Such weapons were fairly useless for flying game, unless in the hands of an expert or used on a flock, but for walking-up they got by as most shots were at birds flying directly and undeviatingly away from the Gun.

In about the second decade of the nineteenth century the flintlock was generally replaced by the detonator or percussion gun. A Scottish minister, the Reverend A. J. Forsyth, was the first to patent fulminate for igniting the charge of powder in a gun, in 1807. Many variations were tried, but it was not until the invention of the copper cap with the fulminate in the crown that the difficulty was overcome and the muzzle-loader made about as efficient as it could be. Hang-fires and misfires had largely been overcome, but loading was still too slow to facilitate big bags, unless of course a team of men loaded, say six guns, for their master.

The first efficient breechloading guns of the 1850s provided the spur that great shoots needed. True, the muzzle-loading enthusiast could vary his powder and shot more accurately to suit target and conditions, but the breechloader would not be required to deal with such a variety of quarry in so many different situations. The necessity now was to standardise bores in order to regulate the supply of cartridges — with muzzle-loaders the same powder, shot and caps could be used with almost any size bore; only the wads had to be cut to fit and most shooters had their own tool for this. Thus all the more unusual bores rapidly disappeared, though it is a tribute to British craftsmanship that even original flintlock pieces are still used by a handful of enthusiasts today.

The 12-bore very quickly gained dominance, but most were still fired by external hammers until the 1870s when 'hammerless' models gained precedence. This increased speed of firing; more important, it cut down the number of accidents. But even more rapid firing was to come. First came the cartridge-ejecting mechanism which, even with a loader, was quicker than the non-ejecting; finally came the single trigger to fire both barrels in a selected order and cut out the split second taken in moving the finger from one trigger to the other. Thus the sportsman of the late nineteenth and early twentieth centuries used basically the same type of gun in general use today.

Rapidity of firing was obviously important in 'warm corners' where some of the early feats were quite surprising, especially as each flush or rise of birds usually takes only a few minutes. Sir Frederick Milbank killed 190 grouse in just one drive, shooting with 3 guns loaded with pinfire cartridges and black powder, in 23 minutes. The Earl of Southesk shot pheasants at the rate of over 14 a minute and the Marquis of Ripon is said to have killed 28 pheasants in one minute at Sandringham.

Choking, the degree to which the end of the barrel is constricted in order to regulate

Date Dec 24th	Number.	OBSERVATIONS. 12476
Red Deer . . .		
Grouse . . .		
Partridges . .		
Pheasants . .		
Snipe . . .		
Wild Duck .		
Wild Geese .		
Woodcocks .	15	
Quail . . .		
Sea Fowl . .		
Wood Pigeon .		
Hares . . .	2	
Rabbits . . .		
Various . . .		
Total . . .	17	

Webster & Larkin, 6o, Piccadilly, W.

Typical page from Lord Ripon's gamebook. Perhaps he was dreaming of bigger game, though anyone would have been pleased with fifteen woodcock

the shot pattern at distance, has changed. In Victorian times tight choking to maximise range was favoured, but this was largely a throwback to walking-up. Most guns now have a more open choke for shorter range in the right barrel and a tighter choke (though far less tight than in the past) in the left barrel. Yet rarely is this facility used properly and most Guns stick to firing the barrels in the same order regardless of marks presented. Few Shots are quick-thinking enough to make the choice.

The first percussion double guns cost about £4 in 1850, but the best makes — Purdey, Lancaster, Manton etc — cost 50 or 60 guineas. Today, with rare exceptions, all expensive guns on a great shoot are English; the bulk of sportsmen must put up with cheaper, though thoroughly serviceable, foreign models — mostly Italian, Spanish and Japanese. All must conform to British safety standards and pass proof tests, and there is no doubt that a skilled man could kill almost as many birds with a £200 gun as with a £20,000 one, provided it fitted him properly. Yet, fine balance does not come cheaply, and the man who shoots regularly knows how important it is to have confidence in a gun. First-class English scroll engraving, or whatever, brings pride of ownership and inspires that confidence. On any great shoot you will see a dazzling array of the very finest guns, inlaid with gold, monogrammed and carefully preserved in the finest wood and leather cases; but along with the coats of arms and other indications of privilege will be the little signs which indicate a truly keen shooter. His stock will have acquired that wonderful patina which only age and constant use can bring, and his cartridge bag will be dark-stained and supple, quite unlike the new calf straight from Holland & Holland's window. Nor can a best British gun come straight from the rack — at least a two-year delivery is likely. Auctions make many good guns available, but the buyer must have his purchase fitted — and get the monograms changed.

Development of gunpowder was important too. Not only were faster-burning powders required, but also virtually smoke-free varieties. The old black powders created a terrible smothering fog which prevented the Gun seeing a bolting rabbit or fleeing bird to get a second shot off in time. Superior powders facilitated lighter loads and lighter guns which were just right for making big bags on the great shoots.

There was also considerable experimentation with cartridge cases and a major step forward was the introduction of the waterproof plastic case which prevented the swelling up so common in paper-cased (cardboard actually) varieties. Thus a cartridge today will always pop smoothly into a gun when required, though sadly the plastic is not bio-degradable and many are left about the countryside.

Three guns for Lord de Grey at Studley Royal, 1901

Yet even the finest gun in the world is no good on the greatest shoot unless the man handling it is skilled in its use. On most of the great shoots the owners have had the good fortune to learn from their fathers and friends, but even so they tend to make regular visits to shooting schools to brush up on style. And one thing above all is clear as regards the very best Shots — they appear to have all the time in the world.

Just as one gets to love a gun so too does an old jacket or cap become inseparable — unless your wife gets her hands on it! But, although today it is all right to turn out on most shoots in tatty but loved garments, in the days of Edward VII it most certainly was not. The early Victorians were not hide-bound by fashion in the field, but by the 1850s vanity had got the upper hand. 'Stonehenge' in 1859, on dress for grouse shooting, thought a light, even linen jacket almost indispensable in September when the weather was fine, but on wet and rough days woollen clothing; while nothing was more suited for walking than old-fashioned leather gaiters or leggings.

In 1880 J. J. Manley thought covering for the feet the most important item of all in partridge shooting and that, in spite of all the shooting boots with semi-classical names attached to them and with all kinds of fastenings by means of straps, laces, buckles and buttons, nothing was better than old-fashioned laced boots. Socks were to be of wool, not cotton, well soaped inside with common yellow soap in a state of paste, with which the feet themselves may also be smeared to prevent blistering and chafing. Knee breeches of light material, 'full and baggy at the knees, not like hunting cords, but on the principle adopted by the navvies, who tie up their trousers to give the knees full play, should always be worn — knickerbockers in fact, and below them gaiters of leather or, better still, of coachman's drab cloth.' The shirt had to be flannel and the coat and vest, or better still a Norfolk shooting jacket, had to be of light texture and colour, 'the wideawake of ditto, or substitute for the latter, a straw hat and puggaree'.

Another writer in 1903 emphasised the importance of having a coat with the sleeve let in to permit freedom of arm movement and, 'in really soaking weather, a cap with an all-round brim, so that it leads the water off away from the head, instead of conducting it to soak into the back hair and give you neuralgia.' Also 'it is better that your loader should be too hot than that you should be too cold. A Shetland wool under-waistcoat can be wrapt up in a light mackintosh and the loader will hardly feel the burden slung by a strap over his back.'

Overall, today's shooting men are a tribute to the field in their smart practicality of dress, but there has been a strange reversal of tradition over the last decade. It is now the custom for the 'working man' to dress exceptionally smartly for driven shooting, whereas the richer you are the scruffier you are allowed to be and get away with it. The weather-beaten slept-in look implies that you wear your shooting kit even more than your pyjamas and thus that you really know your business.

CHAPTER 7

SHOOTING, CONSERVATION AND THE FUTURE

Conservation of our wildlife and countryside generally is most significant on our great shooting estates. It is largely by fortune rather than design, but it is an indisputable fact which has been widely recognised by all our national conservation organisations in recent years. In addition, today there is a great deal of direct conservation work undertaken by shooting people entirely for the benefit of our fauna, flora and landscape and which has no spin-off for shooting. This is largely because the sportsman is traditionally a great lover of wild things and, frequently being of a practical nature, is in an excellent position to carry ideas through.

On the coast many wildfowling clubs have wardened extensive stretches of coastline, preventing the slaughter of thousands of protected birds by those who care nothing for the law. They have also reared and released many thousands of duck, most of which have subsequently not been shot; but more important has been their voluntary management of many marshes and ponds for the benefit of *all* wildlife there.

Inland shoots too have done much to help wildfowl through persuading farmers to save existing marshes and ponds and, increasingly, to create entirely new waters in a land which has been excessively drained to maximise agricultural profits. A whole variety of birds and plants — many rare — share these precious waters with the duck and, sometimes, geese. Such work costs considerable money and it is extremely unlikely that many waters would ever have been created or reinstated without the sporting interest.

The contribution of the gamekeeper as a general warden of the countryside has been enormous. A walk around some of the great shoots near towns is a real eye-opener. Carpets of scarce flowers mingle beneath inspiring old oak and beech trees where nightingales still sing. Without that traditional protection those places would be motorbike tracks, littered with soft drink cans and refuse sacks. Piles of rubble would have been dumped in the hedgerows, some of the trees would have been set light to and the deer either driven out or gruesomely killed by savage poachers. All across the country thousands and thousands of private acres are saved from terrible vandalism of this type by our hardworking and thoroughly underestimated gamekeepers.

When game rearing started it was a wonderful godsend for our songbirds in winter. Millions which would otherwise have starved over this last century have been saved by sharing the corn and other food put out for the pheasants. And there are keepers who put out extra food for the wild birds quite regularly.

Fine weather and a fine pheasant for Lord Chetwode at Highclere

(right) Head of the Guinness family, the late Lord Iveagh,
on his famous Elveden shoot
(opposite) Guns draw for pegs at Wrackleford House
Facing the camera is shoot owner Christopher Pope

(above) Retired Elveden headkeeper Ted Barfield
signalling the start of a drive with a horn which has been
used since the nineteenth century. The 1936 Bedford van
still transports Guns around the shoot.
(right) A welcome break and a Pope cocktail between drives
at Wrackleford

It would be difficult to contemplate or even estimate the number of trees and shrubs which have been planted specifically for game over the last two hundred years; it must be many millions. And a very large proportion of our remaining, mature hardwoods continues in safety only because the woods are owned by gameshooters. These prolific reserves are also the haunts of orchids, turtle doves, sparrowhawks and warblers. Mammals, amphibians, reptiles and insects such as butterflies thrive in and about their glades, rides and edges. Beauty and wonder continue where the plough and the combine have been banished.

Even where agriculture flourishes, there is room for wildlife, but there will be more on a shooting man's farm. He is the one who knows the value of hedgerows for game and wildlife, how important it is to leave rough corners for butterflies as well as partridges, and who is prepared to put his pounds up front for conservation. The great shoot owners not only want a healthy countryside now, they also have the all-important incentive to create or preserve something worth handing down to their heirs. Even if they are primarily interested in the landscape of their parks that is good enough because inevitably this leads to the planting of hardwoods rather than those acres of alien conifers which threaten to engulf us and most of our native wildlife. The shrubs which shooters plant are good for roosting, good for nesting in and, more often than not, provide extra food for wildlife in the way of berries and seeds.

It has long been known that woodland edge is very important for game, providing refuges and nesting sites close to open feeding areas. It is therefore much better to have

The late Lord Biddulph off to pot a rabbit

shelter belts and small copses rather than vast, uninterrupted woodlands. The great shooting estates have achieved this admirably and attracted many non-game species along the way. Some have brought great variety to otherwise monotonous landscapes and increased the species list tremendously. And the great estates also provide the big home covert which is the sanctuary for all kinds of sensitive wildlife as well as home base for pheasants, and all this for shooting it through probably just once a year. These are much better reserves than the highly commercial forests, for old trees are left to decay here and there to produce food and homes for fungi, beetles and woodpeckers. Light gets in and the woodland floor glows with spring flowers.

Game crops are frequently planted at the Guns' expense, and these feed all sorts of wildlife as well as the pheasants and partridges. They also provide valuable refuges from predators on otherwise bleak farms.

Of course, what happens on most estates is a compromise between headkeeper and forester. The owner wants both to succeed. He wants his timber to be productive to help pay for the shooting, and in some cases wants the shooting to be good to compensate for the slight sacrifice of timber profits. If game is to flourish the forester must sacrifice his dense block of trees, but if a fair timber crop is to be taken the keeper must abandon all thoughts of tangled brakes with scattered trees enough for shelter and shade, but no more. It is a shame that the old system of coppicing has generally fallen into disuse because it was so beneficial to all interests, though roosting trees still have to be provided.

Pheasant shooting at Holkham. The covert in the background is typical of the many planted specially for sport

All these havens provided by shooting interests are places from which wildlife and plants can filter out to recolonise 'lost' land whenever the opportunity arises. They are also strictly supervised so that predators never reach 'pest' proportions. For example, rats are killed in large numbers, thus preventing great destruction of wildlife as well as of game eggs and chicks. So too are magpies, whose inroads into songbird populations have been well publicised since the species' recent population explosion. And shooting farmers are now being urged not to spray unnecessarily so that insects and thus partridges may have a better chance of survival. This benefits everything, from butterflies to the badgers which root about for worms.

A recent survey by the Standing Conference on Country Sports revealed that, taking woods of less than 10ha (25 acres), 82 per cent are retained as game coverts in addition to other reasons. A similar percentage of farmers and landowners gave game as one of the reasons for new plantings.

The role of grouse shooting in preserving one of our most valued habitats — heather moorland, where many scarce species of bird such as the merlin have their last stronghold — must be emphasised. Grouse must have heather, both young and old, and that same plant is a wonderful host to a profusion of insects which in turn help to sustain birds and mammals of every description. Also the heather uplands are a highly valued landscape in this country where few such wild environments remain. These are hills preserved for the nation, and an increasing number of ramblers visit them. There is no doubt that without the shooting interest virtually all this heritage would suffer.

Sadly, these days the most important factor shaping gameshooting is money, though many of the great shoots are in the fortunate position of being backed by considerable wealth. Without let guns, possibly 50 per cent of gamekeepers would be out of a job.

The 1960s saw the heyday of the syndicate, while the late seventies and eighties have seen a continuing rise of the let day on which most big shoots depend. Commercialism will probably continue to increase, but unfortunately this means that standards often suffer in the search for bigger profits. This is particularly disappointing for the keepers concerned.

If there is to be any long-term future for shooting in this country, sportsmanship must come before profits. Very large bags must be avoided to stem public criticism, and wherever possible more natural methods of rearing should be adopted. Bird-rearing in semi-darkness indoors, and on weldmesh runs, smacks of the broiler system and will continue to invite attack. Hopefully the emphasis will switch back to habitat management.

Owing to the high costs of labour and equipment, many shoots, including the large ones, tend to buy 6/7-week-old poults rather than day-olds or hatch their own eggs. Less labour and capital costs are involved and the gamefarmer bears the risk in the early stages. A single-handed keeper can cover a bigger area for vermin and eventually feed more poults if he does not have to bother with them until July. Anyone with a full-time keeper should release certainly not less than 2,500 poults, and probably as many as 4,000. There is also a very welcome trend towards the Guns taking closer interest in game rearing on almost every shoot.

There has already been experimentation with a 'rent-a-keeper' scheme, in which a

Partridge shooting, when birds were more plentiful, at West Barsham, Norfolk

keeper may be hired out to several shoots. This, however, can lead to problems where a keeper tries to take on too much, and ends up not doing any of the work properly. And if he doesn't produce the goods at the end of the season, friction will result. This idea is unlikely to be of interest to a big or great shoot, but may attract many of the smaller syndicates starting up when they need professional help, especially advice on spending.

As it stands, there is a mass of poor to middle-of-the-road pheasant shooting in Britain which is widely available without recourse to a sporting agent. But very high quality sport is at a premium and the demand for it is increasing among paying Guns, especially those from overseas. With so much pressure there is increasing temptation for many previously private estates to sell a day or two to reduce overheads; yet once the commercial arena is entered it is very hard to find the way out.

Obviously pressure is greatest on southern estates or those with easy access, such as a nearby airport, but as these get booked up agents and Guns have to look further north to more remote regions. Many of the clients for days of 400 birds or more are from America, France and Germany. Later in the season they are joined by Guns from the Netherlands and Belgium, who are satisfied with smaller numbers but very insistent on quality. Some of these are happy to go north because the prices there are often lower for high-quality sport, even though more hand-feeding is needed in such climes.

Many of the great shoots are at an advantage economically in that the proprietors also control the farming, and therefore many services and much food can be provided at cost. But overall in recent years the net cost to a shoot, assuming a 50 per cent recovery, was about £14 to £18 per bird shot. Shoots dabbling in commercialism will charge less, the fully commercial more, and the very high-class ones with elaborate back-up may charge as much as £22 per bird. There is also often an objectionable surcharge clause on 'overs', though there may be a rebate on 'unders' provided it is linked to the numbers of cartridges fired and reasonable weather.

The demand for grouse shooting continues to be staggering. Everyone wants to do it and most carry on once they have tasted the moors. Sadly, this means many moors are overshot and this has certainly aggravated the general decline of the species, though as already mentioned, we do not yet know the cause of this. It is certain, however, that the price of grouse shooting will go up and up.

In 1986 the going rate for grouse was about £40–45 plus VAT per brace, based on the previous year's results. Grouse are very unpredictable though, therefore prices tend to be fixed on a daily rate — usually in January or before. A projected day of, say, 100 brace would be sold for some £4,500. If it happened to be a bumper year and a very good team of Guns went to shoot on a good day, they might get 130 brace which would work out at roughly £34 a brace. But if, as is more likely, it was a bad year and a moderate team of Guns appeared on a very windy day, they might get only 40 brace at £112 per brace! Yet few moor owners will allow a rebate/surcharge clause and the Guns are expected to take pot luck. In 1990 the demand for quality grouse shooting was unabated and leading moors charged up to £75 plus VAT per brace.

Provided the problems of economics and conservation can be sorted out, gameshooting should continue to attract increasing interest from a broad cross-section of the community and therefore be in a strong position to fend off 'anti' attacks. Some great shoots will decline as new owners develop other interests or turn to profit from other sources. Other estates may ascend from insignificance once major new planting schemes come to maturity. Others will rumble on in much the same way for ever. What we don't know is how much fashion, and even politics, will influence the way in which the sport is conducted. At the moment it is in the ascendancy, but any shift in the political wind could let other opinions in and cause considerable disruption, if not curtailment. If such a sad move ever comes about man will be forced yet further away from his roots in the great outdoors and be all the poorer for it.

THE
GREAT SHOOTS

Loading the game wagon at Studley Royal, 1901

CHAPTER 8

EASTERN ENGLAND

Holkham

James Pinnock, head of the Holkham beaters about 1880

By virtue of its light soil and relatively dry climate, eastern England has always provided some of the best British habitat for gamebirds. Thus in the days before rearing and release became established, Norfolk and Suffolk in particular led the way in wild gamebird shooting; there was also a great variety of wildfowl and other quarry species. And later, as shooting became more fashionable, the eastern counties maintained their early lead as access from the metropolis was fairly simple by road and rail. Yet in a more remote part of Norfolk, along its north coast, is Holkham, the great estate on which many subsequent shoots were modelled. There, in the probable birthplace of driven pheasant shooting, lives the family whose passion for sport has frequently been stronger than the attraction of fashionable society. True, there have been many famous visitors to Holkham; but the owners, the Cokes, Earls of Leicester, have never pandered to the court clique as much as other estates and consequently have been able to concentrate on innovation in both sport and agriculture.

Viscount Coke (now 7th Earl of Leicester) began running the estate while his father was still alive because the 6th Earl was ranching in South Africa and rarely came home. When I asked Lord Leicester what he thought money could not buy for a shoot he replied: 'A great feeling of anticipation when one goes out, simply through the tremendous history and ambiance of the place.' And Guns I have spoken to agree that it is a privilege to be at Holkham.

The family's fortune was founded by Sir Edward Coke (1551–1634), Lord Chief Justice to James I. Much of the old Norfolk family's wealth came through astute investment in land; but the great hall we see today was built by Thomas Coke (1697–1759), who was created Earl of Leicester in 1744, though his title died with him. The estate went to Wenman Roberts, a nephew by marriage, and it was his son, Thomas William Coke, who became 1st Earl of Leicester of the second creation in 1837, and for services to agriculture earned the enduring title 'Coke of Norfolk'. Whereas most of the great landlords were content to leave farming the land to their tenants, Coke undertook the farming himself and inaugurated annual sheep shearings to which farmers came to exchange ideas.

Thomas William died in 1842 aged eighty-eight, his stability and far sightedness having facilitated steady growth in sporting interest. For example, the park has existed in the form we see it in today for well over 150 years and is the result of intermittent planned planting during the eighteenth and early nineteenth centuries. Thus it reached perfection in the early years of this century when all the broadleaved trees attained maturity and the great battues reached their zenith.

The Cokes were fortunate in having a clean sheet to plant upon, though they did not have the wealth of rough heathland peculiar to many parts of Norfolk such as Sandringham, with heather, hollows, little copses, birch plantations and pools of water where wild pheasants live naturally. Holkham's strongpoint was the massing of the woods around the park, a lay-out which offers optimum conditions for game which can forage peacefully in its central grassland, and find abundant shelter in the broad woods by which it is belted — unlike many grass parks which are unhelpful in game preservation, being too sparse in forage and shelter, thereby forcing the pheasants to feed outside their bounds. Scotch pine is abundant in the woods, with plentiful oak, both deciduous and the evergreen *ilex*, which is also in the park itself.

The arrangement of Holkham's coverts was simple enough, its claim to distinction being the immense scale on which it was planned. The 9-mile-long wall contains 3,000 acres (1,220 ha) of woods and farmland as well as traditional parkland, where pheasants feeding in the open always have cover nearby. Along the whole north front is a great fringe of marsh, with dykes down which the pheasants love to wander, while the great lake is a major attraction to wildfowl.

In the Edwardian era a planned and continuous programme of regular felling and re-planting should have started to replace trees in decline, for without this the splendour of any park will disappear in a single generation. But because of two world wars, the slump of the inter-war years and further depression after World War II, such a programme did not commence for another seventy years. Today Edward ('Eddy') Douglas Coke is still faced with the problem of over 400 acres of over-mature wood in

Feathered hats and handlebar moustaches at this early Holkham shooting party

the park, and most single specimens and small groups have reached the ends of their lives. It will take thirty years to replace these once fine trees because too much felling too quickly would create unnatural and unsightly gaps in the landscape.

Fortunately Lord Coke is interested in both conservation and shooting and aims to provide for future generations. Born in 1936, he took over the shoot in 1973 when Lord Leicester became unwell, but he was already active in running the estate. In 1968, his first winter, he planted 13,000 trees, 70 per cent of which were hardwoods, mostly oak. He is very pleased to have planted well over 100,000 trees in the first ten years, but points out that in the early days of the estate 50,000 trees a year were planted for twenty years! He is quick to emphasize that 'this lovely archetypal English countryside is due entirely to sporting interests; shooting and conservation plantings are synonymous'; but without doubt the woods producing the best shooting on the estate are those in which the cover is more natural.

Following the magnificent example of the Earl of Leicester who made land available for the Holkham National Nature Reserve in 1967, Lord Coke does all he can to encourage wildlife and mitigate the impact of modern farming. Of the estate's 25,000 acres (10,120 ha), he himself farms some 4,000 acres (1,620 ha) direct or in partnership and there are about 30 tenant farmers with an average holding of 400 acres (160 ha), though some have considerably more. Cereals and sugar beet are the main crops and there are 1,600 acres (650 ha) of commercial hardwoods. He has removed a few hedgerows during his tenure, but regards a 30-acre (12 ha) field as 'big enough'. Some 16,000 acres (6,480 ha) are shot over and a little maize is planted specifically as game cover, though the large acreage of sugar beet grown outside the park is of great benefit to gamebirds.

To help conservation, in 1984 Lord Coke stopped spraying headlands and hopes to persuade his tenant farmers to do likewise. He reduces the rents of tenants for keeping hedges 8ft (2.4m) high and in good order, ideally with a wide base to provide cover, breeding sites and food for wildlife. He does not fill in ponds, often leaves dead trees standing to help species such as woodpeckers, and vast areas of nettles are left for butterflies. Two-thirds of the estate lies within an Area of Outstanding Natural Beauty and 4,000 acres (1,620 ha) form part of the largest National Nature Reserve in England and Wales, administered jointly by the Nature Conservancy Council and the Holkham estate. He is very keen on opening up the countryside for everyone; the park has unlimited public access on foot. The house itself was one of the first to be opened to the public. In the eighteenth century it could 'be seen any day of the week, except Sunday, by noblemen and foreigners, but on Tuesday only by other people'.

Lord Coke took up shotgun shooting at the age of twenty-five when he came over from South Africa, where he was a keen rifle Shot. He still stalks in Britain. He has no interest at all in bag numbers or poor birds and stresses the importance of fellow Guns being 'kindred spirits'. And like most of the great shoot proprietors he also likes roughshooting, walking the marsh alone for a snipe or pheasant. He does not hold or buy any shooting away from Holkham and uses a pair of 1908 hammerless Cogswell & Harrisons, with 30in barrels, made for his grandfather.

Not surprisingly for a Norfolk man, Lord Coke is very interested in the full range of quarry species. He has been a member of the British Association for Shooting and Conservation (BASC) for a very long time, is President of the Wells & District Wildfowlers' Association and the Burnham Overy & Burnham Norton WA, which he founded. Today both wildfowling clubs are allowed to have special days on which the geese are driven off the lake and culled. Feral greylags have been increasing in the area and pinkfeet have been making something of a comeback after a long decline, not to mention the Canadas — probably the largest flock in the country.

Lord Coke's idea of a great shoot 'must be one with impressive surroundings. I have shot very high birds in the Fens, but that is not stimulating country.' His thoughts turned only to Elveden.

Today Joe's Stop (Marlpit Clump) probably produces the highest birds, but at the turn of the century Scarborough Clump certainly had a reputation awesome enough to scare the faint-hearted away. The ground to be beaten formed one continuous covert and the object of the first day's shooting was to drive every pheasant, if possible, into Scarborough. It was a long business and there was always the fear that pheasants would not run forward. But no one knew better than Lord Leicester how to make pheasants obey; it was said he could drive them into his billiard-room! Half of Obelisk Wood and the five clumps between it and the great boundary coverts would already have been driven into the area to be shot over, and marked with crosses on a plan. The start, where Guns joined in the main business, was also marked, and the point of the final flush was shown by a dark patch with square dots representing the Guns.

A broad drive ran through the covert and there the Guns would amuse themselves knocking over the hares and an occasional rabbit as they tried to cross the ride, but no pheasants could be shot until just before reaching the Clump. But soon Scarborough Wood would be reached and then the place for lunch, also marked on the map. But the Guns and beaters kept their places and ate their lunch standing, for unlike most shoot owners, Lord Leicester took the sport extremely seriously and regarded lunch as of minor importance. Talking was discouraged, sitting not recommended and alcohol not provided. Despite this it was the one shoot to which everyone wanted an invitation. Thankfully, lunch is no longer a spartan affair, though a nice tradition continues in that raw onions are still eaten from Lord Leicester's original tin.

After lunch was the critical time of day at Holkham. In front of the Guns, within a space of perhaps 4 or 5 acres, would have been at least 1,000 pheasants. Would they be 'kind' and go into the 'stop' over the road, or would they be awkward and break back over Guns and beaters? But over lunch the birds, too, had a much-needed rest and were thus more inclined to oblige. The order would be given to shoot cocks going back and make plenty of noise. That part of the wood on the left of the road would then be beaten, but no Guns drawn from the right for this purpose. Birds would be seen crossing the road, running and flying like a swarm of bees going into a hive. Then they were all in the Clump and the keeper of the beat, for whom this was the great day of the year, must have felt deep relief and satisfaction.

George V (centre), with cigarette holder, joins a shooting party at Holkham

Beating was over, and it remained for a single keeper to flush the birds out over the Guns as gradually as possible, while stops held firm on the far side. The Guns were posted three deep and if the back row was not the place of honour, at least it was where the shooting was most difficult. After a period of this gradual flushing, the whole line of beaters drove the Clump through to the Guns to put out remaining birds. Thus the day's sport ended.

At Holkham, where there has always been a large proportion of wild birds, the simplicity in rearing methods has been characteristic of a favourable soil. At the turn of the century the four principal beats were in the woods surrounding the park. On three of these beats just 700-800 pheasants were reared. Each keeper put down 1,100-1,200 eggs and expected to hatch 85 per cent, hoping to turn out 80 per cent into the coverts. No incubators were used and many of the hens were set in the woods near the keepers' houses. When the birds were hatched the coops were placed in drives in the woods and generally moved twice a day. Under this system disease was rare.

Much earlier, in the 1820s, Holkham had one of the few lady gamekeepers of the nineteenth century. She was Polly Fishbourne whose flashing eyes and close-cropped hair are said to have spellbound the cattle as well as the men. She once saved a man from a bull which was goring him; apparently it backed down because it had a sore memory of the time when she shot it in the muzzle as it threatened to charge!

Holkham's gamebooks run consecutively from 1793, providing a marvellous insight into the whole history of British gamebird shooting. Today's crack Shots with their best breechloaders stand on organised drives with Burnham Thorpe, Nelson's birthplace, in the background. But the famous admiral was never a popular guest at Holkham because he had the very dangerous habit of carrying his muzzle-loader around at full cock. Nelson obviously had a liking for game, though, as he was among those who took it away. For 3 November 1797 the register records: 'To Sir Horatio Nelson 6 partridges, 1 pheasant and 1 hare'. As everywhere at the time, game was a much valued resource and, while the books did not at first bother to list the Guns, they always detailed game disposal.

Bags were very small then but Guns went out on many more days. The very first entry records just 4 partridges shot on 2 September 1793, though on the 7th the bag was 54 partridges and 3 hares, and on the 14th 7 partridges, 1 hare and 25 rabbits. In that first recorded season between 2 September 1793 and 7 February 1794 the estate bag was 1,349 partridges, 358 hares, 589 rabbits, 262 pheasants, 114 woodcock and 136 snipe. Those were also the days of a more catholic diet and entries such as '1 landrale' shot on 17 September 1796 were common. The traditional sporting interest in natural history also began very early: 'November 18, 1795 — 1 swallow seen'. This one was not bagged, but later many rare and unusual species of bird were taken for the remarkable collection which is still preserved at the hall.

Whatever they were shooting, Lord Leicester's keepers were certainly noticeable, for towards the end of the eighteenth century, after a visit to Locks the London hatters, he invented the billycock so that his men might be distinguished from 'lesser' mortals. Today Holkham's nine keepers still wear these hats which have also been adopted by city gents and are more popularly known as 'bowlers'.

As everywhere, the early emphasis was on partridges, though there was an exceptionally high pheasant bag on this estate in the early nineteenth century. The bag for the season 1853–4 was 3,325 partridges, 3,116 pheasants, 3,251 hares, 161 rabbits, 102 woodcock, 154 snipe, 154 duck, 36 teal and 30 various. In 1885, 8,100 partridges were shot, but the peak bag seems to have been 8,512 in 1905–6; in that record season were also shot 4,064 pheasants, 4,428 hares, 464 rabbits, 94 woodcock, 37 snipe, 9 duck and 72 various. Such a dramatic increase in partridge bags was undoubtedly due to the advent of driving.

Throughout this century partridges have declined but pheasants mostly increased; in 1911, 5,700 pheasants were bagged, but the peak was nearly 8,000 in 1970. The bag for 1946–7 included 1,366 partridges and 2,322 pheasants but, reflecting the changes in agriculture, a decade later the bag had just 115 partridges and 2,422 pheasants.

Woodcock, in the nineteenth century, were present in greater numbers than today. Though concentrations are larger later in the season in western Britain, it is through Norfolk that many of the migrants come. At Swanton Wood, Melton Constable, in Lord Hastings' time (1860), a record bag of 105 'cock in a day was made. Swanton was considered the best cock covert in England, and one at Sandringham second, but Holkham was among those in contention. Not surprisingly therefore, the Holkham gamebook for the last eight years of the eighteenth century records the shooting of 996 woodcock, while 181 were shot in the season 1818–19. Examples of recent bags are 408 in 1976–7 and 244 in 1985–6.

Having a right-and-left at woodcock is remarkable enough but to kill two with one

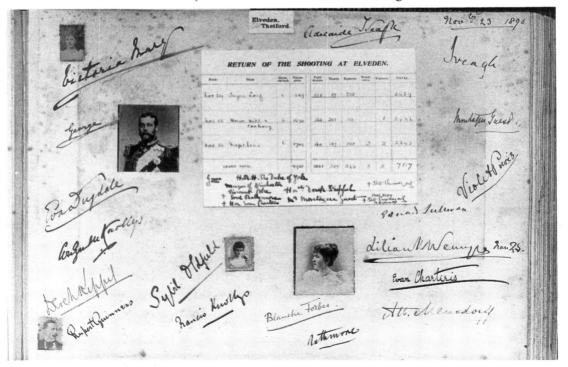

Viscount Coke obtained these signatures of Guns and guests for his Holkham gamebook when he was shooting at Elveden in 1896. Included are the Duke of York and Lord Iveagh

shot is even rarer, especially with a muzzle-loader. But that is just what the famous sculptor Sir Francis Chantrey did at Holkham on 20 November 1829, despite the handicap of having only one arm, though some reports say he had only one good eye. However, he was so delighted he carved the birds in marble and his work is preserved among the treasures at Holkham.

Hares were always an important part of the bag and 1,215 were killed on 19 December 1877; just five days after this, 1,039 were put in the larder. On both occasions there were eleven Guns. The record hare year was 1911, when 8,173 were killed.

Variety in the bag has always been an attraction at Holkham; not just the normal wildfowl either. One morning in 1901, before covert shooting, some of the younger and more enthusiastic members of the house party went out flighting and bagged thirty-four golden plover, though many more were lost in the hurry to get home for breakfast. Such a bag would be remarkable today, but even the goldies seem ordinary compared with one Egyptian goose and one wild turkey in the bag for 1 February 1957.

Golden plover (4) were also among the bag of 7 November 1905 when 1,671 partridges, 10 pheasants, 26 hares and 2 rabbits were killed by 8 Guns on the Warham beat (2,000 acres (810 ha)). This was then Britain's record partridge day bag, and guests included Prince F. Dhuleep Singh. There were 20 drives, the best of which yielded 168 partridges. On four consecutive days that week the party shot a total of 4,749 partridges, yet in 1797 as few as 80 partridges in a day had been thought remarkable for Warham beat.

Typical page from the Holkham gamebooks. Viscount Coke collected these signatures at a Sandringham shoot in 1897. The Guns included the Prince of Wales and the Duke of York

There have been many other remarkable performances at Holkham. For example, Mr Coke killed 80 partridges for 93 shots in 8 hours on 7 October 1797. He was often said to be the very best Shot in England, being 'so capital a marksman, that, as he inflicts death whenever he pulls the trigger, he should in Mercy forbear such terrible Examples of his skill'. Another story subsequently discussed in the smoking room ad infinitum concerned the England v Scotland match between Lord Kennedy and Mr Thomas William (later Lord) Coke. The wager was decided in October 1823 when Mr Coke killed 192 partridges at Holkham whereas Lord Kennedy, who had selected Monreith (Wigtownshire) for his ground, managed only 187.

But noble guests had to be wary of accidents in the field, as a remarkable story of 1800 testifies. On 8 January that year Lord and Lady Andover were members of a shooting party, but at breakfast that morning Lord Andover announced that he would not be going shooting. On being pressed, he admitted that his wife had dreamt that, while he was out, his gun had exploded and killed him. Later Lady Andover felt guilty and persuaded her husband that her mind was not at ease and that he should go after all, so he set off at midday with his dogs and a servant.

He had not managed to locate the main party when at about 1.30pm the dogs pointed and he went towards them, cocking his double-barrelled gun. However, one of the dogs sprang at the birds and as Lord Andover called it, he handed his gun to his man. Unfortunately, as the dog was being scolded the gun in the servant's hands went off and Andover was struck full in the back, near the shoulder. He was still alive when Lady Andover saw him at Creake Farm, but the shot had entered the lungs and he died in his wife's arms two days later.

Unlike the 2nd Earl of Leicester, who is said to have been so disdainful of fashionable visitors that he even refused to shave for the impromptu arrival of Queen Alexandra, the present Lord Coke is decidely hospitable. There are important guests still, including the Duke of Kent, Lord Buxton (every year) and Lord Strathmore; but on the whole the nucleus is of local Guns. One of the finest Shots who visits now is Hugh Van Cutsen, but both Lord Coke and headkeeper Preston agree that the finest Shot they have ever seen was the 5th Earl of Leicester. In his heyday in the fifties and sixties he stood well behind the line and cleared up the very high pheasants missed by guests. Lord Coke is very closely involved with the running of the shoot: 'I was out at six with a keeper checking traps this morning.' And on the night before a shoot he always liaises with the keepers to decide on the venue.

James Preston can remember the 700-bird days but the average is 200-250 now. And in these times of financial constraint he has his own beat to run as well as supervising the other eight keepers. Yet this estate is almost unique in having resisted the tide of commercialism so well. Only some five days are let, in 1985 at a cost of about £2,000 per day, bringing an exceptionally small total in relation to the enormous overheads and so the shoot makes a big loss. Paying Guns were always from the USA, but in 1985–6, for the first time, two days were let to the French.

The Duke of Marlborough is a fine and elegant Shot
Blenheim: fashion in the field

A pheasant retrieved at Holkham

The concentration is still on wild birds, and no eggs, poults or birds are sold; just 1,000 birds are bought in. Before 1984 they were day-olds, but that became very uneconomic and that year they changed to six-week-olds. They all go into the park. No partridges are bought; eggs of redlegs and greys are picked up for incubating, only a few being left because the parents find it very difficult to raise a full brood on a modern farm; those in the underkeeper's care have a much greater success rate. Preston fondly remembers days of more sympathetic agriculture: 'You can't see an anthill now.'

Not surprisingly, poaching has not been a great problem in this remote corner. Preston's main chores are getting the birds together with so much woodland about and so much natural food to encourage straying, the acorns of the evergreen oak being particularly attractive. There are also such large distances to cover. Preston says the job is hard enough now and is amazed at how all the work got done in the days without vehicles. But with labour cheap, more men were once employed — for example, the current twenty to twenty-five beaters is just half the old quota.

Predator control remains important at Holkham, and a special effort is made to get rid of the grey squirrels, which are relatively new to the area and pose a threat to the vast areas of young trees. Lord Coke pays a bounty on grey-squirrel tails. Pigeon are shot under a £5 permit, but the proceeds of about £300 per year have been donated to the Game Conservancy. Most of the rabbits are gone now through myxomatosis and habitat change, but the estate is obviously good for wildlife as the endangered otter is still found there.

At Sutton Scotney, Richard Cowen re-loads while marking a shot partridge down
(inset) Ex Eagle Star Chairman Sir Denis Mountain helping to pick-up at Sutton Scotney

Signatures of guests and gamecard for Holkham, 8-11 December, 1896

On a shoot day outside the park there are usually 5 drives in the morning and 3 in the afternoon, but in the park 4 and 2 respectively as the drives are longer. Shooting normally starts at 9.30 and ends at about 4pm. Just 7-8 days are shot in the park now, where there are 3 keepers. Each keeper on the estate has about 2,000 acres (810 ha) to look after.

A typical day begins with assembly outside the hall with the magnificent lake in the background. Guns draw there for pegs but later Lord Coke is very attentive in fine-tuning his guests' positions so that they get the most out of the day. And in between drives he is thoroughly happy working his dogs in helping to pick up. He is definitely a spaniel man 'because they are more sporty, have no hesitation in entering thick cover such as bramble, and are always working.' There is always much talk of the weather because, being chiefly a wild bird shoot, this can spell success or disaster. For example, when I was there in December 1985 the concentration was on cocks, which made good sense as it had been a very poor breeding season and wild hens are always the best mothers. Actually, Lord Coke told me that he is going over entirely to cocks only. 'The time to catch them is at the *beginning* of the season when they are not so wily. At the moment people have it all wrong.'

This was one of the very few great shoots visited where the birds were every·bit as good as expected, yet everything was achieved without fuss or ceremony and there was enormous fun. With men like Lord Coke at the helm of our great estates — Holkham employs eighty staff direct, not to mention the tenant farmers — we have little to fear for the future of shooting. Here we have someone who genuinely wants to continue farming in an efficient and pioneering way but also maintain an important place for shooting as an active and enjoyable part of our heritage. He recognises the dangers though: 'Antis are mostly uninformed and therefore tend to make emotional judgements. We will probably never reach the extremists. Our greatest bulwark is getting as many people as possible involved.' It is to this end that many local people are invited to shoot every year.

However, Lord Coke does suspect that rearing may be banned eventually, 'and there could even be a quota system'. Certainly, if such drastic moves are to be avoided, it will be due to owners like Lord Coke, who is as interested in letting local naturalists put up owl nest-boxes as he is in game habitat.

Merton

Due south of Holkham, in the East Anglian heartland near Watton, is the famous Norfolk shoot of Lord Walsingham. Drastically altered and cut in size, the estate retains little of its former glory, its shooting history having burgeoned and faded in accordance with the fluctuating fortunes and enthusiasm of its owners.

The de Greys (Walsinghams from 1780) became squires of Merton in the mid-1300s when one of them enterprisingly married the heiress, but the shooting records, in the form of large leather-bound gamebooks, run only from 1821–88 and 1929–83. Sadly the records covering 1889–1928 were destroyed in World War II during the Army's occupation. Fifteen tons of nineteenth-century and later estate records were stored in the old dairy at Home Farm; the thatched roof collapsed, the rain got in and all were ruined.

But there is one earlier record preserved in perfect condition — a small paper-covered book which details game shot in 1780–1.

	Pheasant	Partridge	Hare
Sept	—	145	28
Oct	25	85	20
Nov	20	55	31
Dec	26	39	27
Jan	16	21	21
Total	87	345	127

In addition, 20 wild duck were shot from October on, plus 6 woodcock. For rabbits there was 'no account kept but near to 80'.

The main Merton gamebooks are unusual for the meticulous way in which every item of game had its disposal logged, indicating just how highly the 'crop' was valued, though much of it was given away to deserving cases. In fact the early gamekeepers were little more than game harvesters and for many years were left to do most of the shooting for the table, especially early in the season, when the 'boss' had little interest in sport. In 1821–2 keeper James Watson (the nominal headkeeper who died in 1834) appears to have done all the gameshooting, but he went out frequently for very small bags:

	Pheasant	Partridge	Hare	Rabbit
Sept	2	66	26	12
Oct	16	45	18	12
Nov	7	33	11	18
Dec	13	31	20	6
Jan	1	28	14	29
Total	39	203	89	77

In addition 3 wild duck were shot in January, 6 woodcock from November on and 7 snipe in November.

On the first day of the season, 1 September, Watson went out on the Sturston beat where he shot 2 partridges, 1 hare and 2 rabbits, all of which were disposed of to the Rt Hon the 3rd Lord Walsingham at Worthing, Sussex. Sadly, he burned to death in a fire in his London house shortly afterwards. Game was despatched fairly quickly all around the country, for example to Lady Langham at London, Sir William Wraxhall at Cheltenham and Mrs Methuen at Southampton.

Merton headkeeper 'Old' Watson died in 1834

On 16 December 3 pheasants were 'taken from two poachers', and 2 more on the 28th. Also that month, '6 hares were caught in the rabbit nets and too much injured thereby, and by the dogs, to turn loose again'. On 29 December 1 hare was 'boiled for the dogs being unfit for Mr Fox as intended'.

On 28 February 1822, the first of very many species of wildfowl and other lesser known birds was shot for the table — 1 'dunbird' (pochard). Also between the end of the 1821–2 season and 31 August 1822, the keeper shot 27 hares, 120 rabbits, 2 woodcock, 12 snipe and 12 wild duck. The next month contains the earliest record of gentlemanly interest in sport when on 30 September Captain Methuen joined Watson on the Tottington beat to shoot 28 partridges and 1 rabbit. On 1 October the officers of the Royal Dragoons (the recently deceased 3rd Lord Walsingham's old regiment at Canterbury) were sent 12 partridges, while a teal was shot on 2 November and next day sent down to the 4th Lord Walsingham at Richmond (he was Archdeacon of Surrey) along with a pheasant, hare, 4 rabbits, 2 woodcock and 3 snipe.

On 24 January 1823 a hare was given to the guard of the Thetford mail coach, the first of many entries over the years which reveal the great number of craftsmen and professionals whose goodwill helped to make the estate tick. Game, especially hares, was given to an amazing total of fifty-eight vocations ranging from clockmaker, charcoal burner, sweep, ditcher, bonedealer, postman and station master, to surveyor, auctioneer, schoolmaster, lawyer and veterinary surgeon, not forgetting the policeman and exciseman. The needy were not forgotten either. On 2 April, 16 hares went 'to 16 poor persons at Tottington', followed by 17 next day 'to 17 poor persons at Merton'.

The first record of one of the de Greys shooting is that of 13 October 1828 when the Honourable Thomas shot 2 hares and 2 rabbits. The main name in the record now is Israel Buckle, the keeper appointed in 1835 who did so much of the estate shooting over many years, often joined by the Honourable Brownlow de Grey in the 1830s. With their interest, and later that of Mr B. de Grey, bags started to rise. Israel Buckle died in 1873, his son John having become acting head about 1865.

Woodpigeons and waterhens (moorhens) were first recorded in the bag in October 1831. And while much of the ordinary game was consumed in the house, the more unusual species such as pigeon and moorhen, snipe and plover were almost always sent to Lord Walsingham, if he was away. The keepers continued to go out many days on their own, shooting all types of quarry. In December 1835 the first fieldfare and lark were shot by Buckle and went to the cook at the Hall. They were obviously enjoyed as many followed. By this time sportsmen were doing most of the shooting but Buckle had it to himself in late December and January, and in some years right through September. And he shot partridges and pheasants as well as vermin. In the late 1830s the daily bags were still small, with three or four Guns getting just a few birds each, but shooting on many days.

The very first entry for Lord Walsingham shooting is 12 November 1839 when he shot 14 pheasants, 16 hares and 2 rabbits with R. H. Wrightson, the Hon George and the Hon W. de Grey, the total bag being 32 pheasants, 63 hares, 9 rabbits and 1 woodcock on Sturston beat.

In the 1840s bags started to rise. On 22 November 1842, 8 Guns killed 350 head: 180

*Merton headkeeper Israel
Buckle died in 1873*

pheasants, 117 hares, 51 rabbits and 2 woodcock. Beaters killed 210 hares in
Buckenham Plantation on 25 November 1843. There were many hares to dispose of
that month, but Robert Roper didn't get his because he stole some wood. Neither did
Robert Cunningham as he 'trapped wild ducks'. The pattern of eight or nine Guns for the
big days of the season was already established. And with more and more game to
dispose of, it was sent all over the country and even abroad, as well as to dealers. For
example, in December 1844, six pheasants were to go to Robert Duff in Paris 'to be
forwarded immediately'.

Charity continued in January 1846 when 6 hares were given to 'six men at ditch in
garden'. There was more culinary experimentation on 30 September when Henry
Erskine, in Lord Walsingham's party, shot a swan, but it didn't go into the Hall until 8
October. Ptarmigan, blackgame and grouse were being sent to the Hall from northern
estates, and the surplus of ordinary game from Merton was mostly being disposed of in
large quantities to dealers or hoteliers. For example, on 13 November Mr Farmer of
Brandon took 200 pheasants and 230 hares, and on the 16th another 100 pheasants. A
considerable amount of game, however, was sold privately, frequently to nobility in
London, the gamebooks often recording that carriage had been paid in advance, by
cheque.

It was the age of collecting, before photography and legislation did away with
the need for, and possibility of, forming great displays of natural objects. There was also
interest in ordinary game as decoration. In December 1846 therefore, 2 pheasants, 4

partridges and 1 rabbit went 'to the care of Mr Reid, Bird Stuffer, Doncaster'.

On 3 October 1849, 5 pigeon went to the Hall 'for a pie', and on 19 November 8 Guns made a large bag of 216 pheasants, 56 hares, 17 rabbits and 2 woodcock. Appetites were still keen in 1850 when, on 15 November, 6 birds were consigned to the big kitchen 'for partridge cutlets'. And the swan shot by Buckle on 9 December was fairly well hung when it went to the Hall on the 18th.

French partridges must have been a novelty in 1852 because in January a pair were sent to Mr Reynolds of Thetford for stuffing. September was productive, with many personal daily bags of 40–50 partridges to various de Greys, and even keeper John Buckle on his own. On 7 December, that magical 100 pheasants were bagged for the first time; the 8 Guns included Lords Walsingham, Sheffield and Churchill. Six partridges, 66 hares and 13 rabbits took the total to 185. On the 21st another 113 pheasants were in a bag of 278 to 9 Guns on Cardigan beat, and on the 23rd a further 168 among 282 head. Also in 1852, the following remarkable entry was made for December 29: 'Hon Thos de Grey with a stone — 1 pheasant on Merton beat. Number of shots fired — about 36'. To this there is an addendum signed 'Walsingham 1899': 'Thomas (VI) Lord Walsingham's first pheasant — roosting on the walnut tree (since blown down) near the back yard gate.'

The following year six pheasants and four hares were allocated to the rent-day dinner, an annual event that dined on game for years to come. In February, eighteen snipe went to the Hall 'for a pie'. Sandpiper and shoveler were added to the menu in March, and on 30 September Buckle shot the first of small numbers of quail which used to occur from time to time. In January the following year the first golden pheasant was tasted. Today they are well established in the wild at Thompson and Merton where they are protected.

In 1856 the keeper was still allowed to shoot much of the game. In fact, that September John Buckle shot all the partridges — 638 on 24 days with bags varying between 6 and 43. Bags had continued to grow steadily: the season's partridge tally rose from 251 in 1834–5 to 1,399 in 1857–8; for the same period pheasants rose from 191 to 2,412 and hares from 654 to 2,395. Also in 1856 'two pots of jam' were sent with 3 pheasants and 3 partridges to 'Hon T. de Grey at A. F. Birch, Eton College, by Great Western Railway'.

There were more culinary delights in 1857 when 219 plover eggs were gathered in April, and on 21 September 2 haunches of venison, 12 partridges, 2 hares and 6 rabbits went to the Watton dinner. Pheasant and partridge bags were often over the 100 per day now and large quantities of game were consigned to Mr Luckie in London. The following year a turtle dove was shot and eaten, along with one rail in September and a heron in October. September's partridge bag was 1,212. Between March and May 1859, 303 plover and 399 French partridge eggs were harvested. That year some game was already roasted before being sent down to the Hon Thomas de Grey and Reverend A. Birch at Eton College; for example, they had six partridges on 3 October. On 12 October keeper John Buckle was shot at by a poacher and 'badly wounded'. The aggressor was sentenced to eight years penal servitude.

The year 1860 saw a strange 'order' fulfilled when, on 5 January, 2 owls and 2 turkeys were despatched, along with 30 pheasants and 10 partridges to the Lady Kenyon, Gredington, Whitchurch, Salop by L&NW Railway. Plover and French partridge eggs continued to the table and many were sent down to Lord Walsingham in London. Even the eight 'dottrell' shot by Mr de Grey on 22 August were eaten in the Hall. Grouse were now coming down from the celebrated Blubberhouse Moor in Yorkshire. That year also saw the first entry of that subsequently universal word 'various', used to describe the bag of vermin and odds and ends — as bags grew there was less time to enter many of the little details. On 27 December the elusive 200 bag was passed with 219 pheasants to 6 Guns in Merton Wood along with 1 partridge, 41 hares, 4 rabbits and 1 woodcock. On Christmas Eve the Hall took in 4 pheasants, 4 partridges, 2 hares, 4 rabbits, 5 snipe, 4 wild duck and 5 teal — what a marvellous feast they must have had. But 25 larks and 1 wild goose were on the holiday menu over the 1862 Yuletide.

The first really important party of Guns came on 29 October 1862 — seven of them

Headkeeper John Buckle in the late nineteenth century

including the Earl of Leicester from Holkham and the Duke of Wellington, both for the first time. On 7 November came a sharp reminder of the penalties for breaking the law when Robert Roper, one of the Stanford cottagers, poached another hare and was 'to be expelled shortly'. Twelve *grouse* were shot by Buckle at Merton in August 1863 and on 7 September just 3 Guns bagged 170 partridges, 47 hares, 13 rabbits and 1 pigeon. Other large bags followed, including 224 partridges on 22 September and 233 on 16 October; only small numbers of French partridge were shot.

A big step forward came in 1864 when, on 7 December, 575 pheasants were in a bag of 729. The eight Guns included the Lords Walsingham, Digby, Southampton and Mount-Charles, and this really got things going for the first royal visit in 1865. An unsuccessful day's hunting awaited the Prince and Princess of Wales on 13 January, but the shooting bag of 597 next day included 514 pheasants. Apart from the Prince of Wales, the ten Guns included Lord Leicester again, Lord Colville and Lord Suffield. The elusive 1,000 bag was passed on 20 December 1865 when 8 Guns shot 893 pheasants out of a grand total bag of 1,062. Fortunately, gamedealers Garners of Brandon were able to take 600 pheasants on 23 December and a further 400 on the 26th. January 31 1866 brought the estate's first 'cocks day' when just Lord Walsingham and the Honourable T. de Grey shot ninety-nine.

Famous game Shot and wildfowler Ralph Payne-Gallwey Esq made his first appearance in the Merton gamebooks on 4 December 1867. The estate was now a major stop in the sporting circuit, but it was still pleasant to record all the unusual incidents of country life, such as on 20 April 1868: 'A nest with four young woodcocks nearly in full plumage found in Birch Wood'. More notable was the entry for 22 August: '1 pheasant to Hon T. de Grey by cricket ball'. In November he was joined for the first time at Merton by Lord Ashburton, whose Grange estate in Hampshire was to become one of the leading shoots of all time.

The royal party was back in 1870 and the race was on to put up the biggest show for the Prince of Wales who was now ensconced at Sandringham. On 22 November the Guns also included Harry Chaplin, whose name was to pop up in all the leading gamebooks over many years. The 548 bag included 464 partridges and on the following day the 1,231 count featured 1,068 pheasants, followed by over 500 head on both the 24th and 25th. The Prince of Wales obviously liked game because he was subsequently sent 60 pheasants and 40 partridges at Sandringham.

The 5th Lord, Thomas, born 1804, son of the Archdeacon, was a QC and ran Merton 1829–70, planting many coverts and making his son's famous career as a Shot possible. Sadly, he shot himself in 1870. Nobody knows why, but it could have been a mistake while cleaning a gun. Next winter 'Lord Walsingham was in California during the shooting season' and very little happened at Merton.

However, next season the shoot was in full swing again with the first visit, on 30 January, of one of the most celebrated Victorian big Shots — the Maharajah Prince Dhuleep Singh, whose nearby Elveden shoot was to acquire similar fame. That day he and Lord Walsingham demonstrated their great love of the sport and obvious enjoyment of each other's company in shooting a really mixed bag, the like of which has come the way of only a very few people — 9 pheasants, 21 partridges, 2 hares, 2 rabbits,

3 woodcock, 5 snipe, 19 wild duck, 20 teal, 2 pigeon and 2 larks. Interestingly, Dhuleep Singh took back to Elveden 4 wild duck and 8 teal.

Dhuleep Singh's appetite for Merton was obviously whetted as he was back on 11 November 1873. The 9 Guns included the Prince of Wales and they shot 436 partridges and other birds; on the 12th the same party bagged 604 pheasants, 182 partridges, 300 hares and 71 rabbits, and on the 13th, 333 partridges and 108 pheasants. But all this was merely an appetiser for the big day on the 14th in Merton Wood when the bag was 1,568 pheasants, 12 partridges, 249 hares, 43 rabbits, 6 woodcock, 8 pigeon and 4 various — a total bag of over 2,000 with the pick-up. When the Prince of Wales went back to Sandringham next day he took 20 pheasants, 12 partridges and 6 hares, and the 5 men with him were given 10 pheasants. On 9 December, Lord Carnarvon, another giant from shooting history, paid his first visit and completed the circle of friends who, with Dhuleep Singh, Lord Ashburton and Lord Walsingham at their centre, would go on to make many remarkable bags on many great estates. The same day the well known Shot and author Archibald Stuart-Wortley paid his first visit.

Next royal visit was that of the Duke of Cambridge on 16 December 1875. In two days the bag was over 2,201 pheasants, 372 partridges plus various other game — the Duke took 10 pheasants, 8 partridges, 2 hares and 3 woodcock back to London. In 1876 the Maharajah showed his continuing love of wildfowl when, on 29 January, he took back just 4 teal. In subsequent years he must have had enough gameshooting elsewhere for he generally came back to Merton only to shoot duck with Lord Walsingham who also enjoyed fowling. On 18 December 1878 Walsingham shot 8 teal and 89 other duck (48 mallard, 1 goosander, 1 goldeneye, a gadwall, 7 wigeon, 18 pochard, 8 tufted, 2 scaup, 2 shoveller and 1 smew), as well as 10 pheasants, 1 hare, 2 woodcock, 5 snipe, 5 pigeon and 13 various; and on 19 December another 70 (63 of them mallard) plus 13 teal.

There followed a steady stream of noble and influential visitors, but not too many of them were regulars, indicating shooting as a social entertainment rather than a way to build friendships. But Lord Walsingham's enthusiasm was undiminished and he frequently shot alone, as indeed did his heirs. For the big occasions the routine was to provide guests with a good partridge day followed by a mighty bash at the pheasants. And throughout, the records include everyday incidents which give such a marvellous insight into the interests of a bygone age — 16 January 1881: 'Severe frost saw 25 wild swans (hoopers) pass over Merton SE to NW 3.15pm. Walsingham.'

The USA (via Liverpool) was the destination for two pheasants on 7 January 1885. Somebody over there must have been very fond of high game, unless the birds were packed in ice. Lord Walsingham was really after the duck again that year when, on 26 January, with Lord Ormathwaite, he shot 128 plus 2 snipe, 28 teal and 1 bittern. Sir Ralph Payne-Gallwey was back in October. On the 12th, with just Lord Walsingham, he bagged 23 pigeon and 1 wild duck. What enthusiasm when they had just enjoyed four consecutive 100-plus partridge days at Merton on 7–10 October. It is not surprising that pigeon shooting increasingly drew Lord Walsingham's attention, for the bird was becoming more common as farming provided it with varied and regular food supplies. Yet some days he went out for just one bird.

More unusual guests were to come — H. Rider Haggard the novelist on two big pheasant days in 1887 and, oddly, Mr Partridge and Mr Pheasant the same year. Sadly the gamebooks are missing from 1888 to 1929, but there are other records. These show that by 1877–8 the season's bag had risen to 5,223 pheasants, 3,067 partridges, 1,728 hares, 2,197 rabbits, 51 woodcock, 22 snipe, 75 wild duck, 54 teal and 80 pigeon.

The 6th Lord Walsingham, Thomas, was the one man said to rival Lord Ripon as the greatest Shot who ever lived, but his enthusiasm for sport brought financial ruin. He made shooting history by killing 1,070 grouse in a day at Blubberhouse, at the rate of $2\frac{1}{3}$ birds per minute, firing 1,510 cartridges during 20 drives and twice deliberately killing 3 birds in the air with 1 shot. He used a pair of light Purdey hammerguns, fired black powder and at the end of the day had no suspicion of a headache; in fact that night he sat up late playing cards. He was also a remarkably brilliant man, a first-class scientist and one of the best entomologists of his day. Wentworth-Day records: 'When I was a boy he used to stay at my old home at Wicken in Cambridgeshire and go out at night to catch moths on the fen arrayed in a moleskin coat, a snakeskin waistcoat, and a cap made of a hedgehog's skin with the snout pulled down as a beak and a pair of artificial eyes in it.' He was a keen ornithologist, and as well as forming his own collection he bagged all the hummingbirds for the British Museum of Natural History using dust shot to minimise damage to the birds. And on 31 January 1889 he made one of the most incredible individual mixed bags of all time — 39 pheasants, 6 partridges (5 grey, 1 red legged), 23 mallard, 6 gadwall, 4 pochard, 1 goldeneye, 7 teal, 3 swans (male, female and cygnet), 1 woodcock, 1 snipe, 2 jack snipe, 1 woodpigeon, 2 herons, 65 coots, 2 moorhens, 9 hares, 16 rabbits, 1 otter, 1 pike (shot) and 1 very large rat — total 191 head.

Rich when he inherited, he was bankrupt when he died. His fortune went mainly in the lavish manner in which he ran everything connected with sport or science. He also suffered a great loss when Walsingham House, which stood where the Ritz Hotel now stands, was demolished and a residential club built on the site. Of bad design, it was a failure and Walsingham lost £¼ million over the venture. He was also robbed by agents, one of whom shot himself. The London property had to be sold in 1912 along with the two Yorkshire estates, for in spite of his three estates he had stretched himself too far. The Prince of Wales didn't help either, for when he took the Merton shooting in the 1890s within a single year he had exhausted the wonderful wine cellar which had been systematically built up over many generations. Fortunately Merton was not sold off because it was subject to an entail restricting inheritance to particular heirs. The 6th Lord spent the last seven years of his life abroad and died in 1919, but he had had a remarkable run.

Among his greatest contributions to shooting were his two books *Shooting — Field and Covert* and *Shooting — Moor and Marsh* which were published by Longmans, Green & Co (1885) in the immensely popular Badminton Library; his co-author was his old friend Sir Ralph Payne-Gallwey. In the former, Walsingham described the driving of Merton's woods in great detail, even with a plan; but he was also sensitive to the wider aspects of natural history, a good example being his analysis of the contents of pigeon crops from Merton:

Contents of Crops of Pigeons Shot at Merton, Norfolk

Date	No	No of acorns	Other kinds of food	Weight of contents of crop (oz)
8 Dec 1885	1	33	44 beech mast	
	2	39		
	3	31 (large)		these
	4	33		were
	5	33		not
	6	40		weighed
	7	34		
	8	37		
	9	42		
	10	24	quantity of barley	
30 Dec 1885	1	50		3.25
	2	36		2.75
	3	46	17 haws and some turnip tops	3.25
	4	19		2
31 Dec 1885	1	32 (large)		3.75
	2	29		2.50
	3	60[1]		3.75
	4	47		3.25
	5	51		4.50
	6	49	quantity of barley	3.75
	7	41	quantity of barley	3.25
	8	13	quantity of barley	1.75
	9		194 holly berries	2.25
30 Jan 1886	1		turnip tops	1
	2		turnip tops	1
	3	43 and a quantity of pieces of acorns	turnip tops	4.50
	4	20 (very large)	turnip tops	3
	5	40		2.75
	6	43		3.25
	7	13	turnip tops	2.25
	8	7	rush-seeds, barley and turnip tops	1.75
	9	3	clover leaves	1.25
	10	63[2]		4.50
	11		buds of oak and turnip tops	1.75

[1] Not common acorns, perhaps from evergreen oak   [2] Common acorns

The sixth Baron Walsingham of Merton (1848–1919)

He also took his duties as landlord and host very seriously. If a visitor arrived for Merton on a third-class ticket he was firmly bundled into a first-class carriage by the guard at Thetford. 'No friend of his Lordship's goes anything but first on this line', would be the cry, 'He's one of the real old Norfolk "gintry" and his friends will have the best.' Feudal in his devotion, at the age of seventy-six he would shoot all day, audit the books of the village hall at night, open a concert, sing two songs and dance with his own kitchenmaid. It was his pet boast that he believed himself to be the last man in Norfolk who drove about in a family brougham. He would gallop the brougham through the arch of the clockhouse in front of the hall. The clearance was inches. The coachman would dismount and give him the reins. The scratches still on the stone bollards evidence the tight turns required to follow the circle of the drive to the front door.

This wonderful old aristocrat has faded into history, but many of the marvellous names he created or used linger on at Merton: for instance Mad-house Plantation named after the fourteenth-century building which once housed local lunatics and was later used for shoot lunches. The ruins are still there. Then there is Wayland Wood (sold to Norfolk Naturalists Trust in 1976) — an 80-acre (32 ha) covert said to have been the spot where the Babes in the Wood were lost — where the keeper's cottage was very properly known as Cruel Uncle's House. The Cardigan Covert commemorates the Charge of the Light Brigade at Balaclava, which took place in the year of planting. The Prince of Wales is a square covert planted in the year of Edward VII's birth, and the Redan was planted in 1855 and laid out in exactly the same shape and measurement as the famous Redan at Sebastopol. The Waterloo Covert commemorates the famous battle, and Shaker's Furze is where there was once an encampment of Quakers.

John, the 7th Lord, born 1843, was also an avid shooter. He remembered the early hard-walking days with affection, when sport took precedence over comforts: 'Then ensued lunch, not a bad part of the day's work; lunch, just right, sufficient and not too luxurious, topped up by a glass of cherry brandy to give an impetus to the afternoon cartridge. There were no cocktails in those days.' But he was also a practical man and, not surprisingly, cost-conscious. His pre-World War II estimates of the costs of rearing are interesting. Much of the estate was wild ground covered with heather and bracken, interspersed with coverts, ideal for the breeding of wild pheasants, the soil being light. It was therefore unnecessary to buy eggs, and a great initial expense was avoided. The boundary eggs were collected and placed under hens — no incubators, no luxuries. But the figures do not take into account the keepers' wages.

Cost of Rearing 5,000 Pheasants
1 February to 1 August

	£	s	d
600 hens bought in Feb at 2s 3d each	67	10	0
125 sacks of maize, whole and ground	59	7	6
27 sacks of barley meal	17	11	0
10 sacks of wheat	6	10	0
25 cwt of biscuit meal	25	0	0
20 cwt of best greaves	20	0	0
25 cwt of best game rice	20	0	0
11 cwt of Chamberlin's pheasant meal	13	4	0
2 sacks of hempseed	3	0	0
2 bushels of linseed	1	2	0
2 sacks of dari seed	2	4	0
1 sack of fine oatmeal	0	18	0
	£236	6	6
Per contra: 600 hens sold in August at 1s 3d each	37	10	0
Net cost	£198	16	6

The story of Merton in the twentieth century is of many lettings, including Sir Mike Edgar, Sir Abe Bailey, Mr H. G. Latilla and Sir Bernard Docker.

Yet, despite general recession, and under tenant organisation, shooting at Merton continued to thrive after World War I and reached a second heyday in the 1930s. The bag for the season 1929-30 was 7,223 head — 4,858 pheasants, 657 partridges, 216 hares, 1,131 rabbits, 69 woodcock, 21 snipe, 136 duck, 9 teal, 76 pigeon and 50 various. The largest day-bag was 354 when a syndicate was in operation, Lord Walsingham shooting just a few days with friends. Royal patronage continued with, for example, the Duke of Kent and Prince Arthur of Connaught on 18–19 November 1935. The two days yielded 863 and 840 pheasants, rising to 988 and 950 after the pick-up. That season's bag was 9,453 pheasants, 2,847 partridges, 280 hares, 2,593 rabbits, 56 woodcock, 5 snipe, 110 wild duck, 26 teal, 1,482 pigeon and 167 various — grand total 15,687. Sir Abe Bailey and friends had some of the shooting.

On 28 January 1939 Mr Chamberlain, Sir Hugh Ellis and Lord Granard joined the Guns, but it was the end of the good old days with the outbreak of war. The bags speak for themselves. In 1938–9 there were 7,030 pheasants and 902 partridges shot, in 1946–7 the totals were 114 and 30. The game books record a sorry tale of woe:

In 1942 the greater part of the estate, comprising the whole parishes of Tottington, Sturston and Stanford, and some parts of Merton and Thompson,was requisitioned by the War Dept for a battle training area; whereupon Sir Bernard Docker gave up the shoot. What was left was rented by the late Mr H. G. Latilla, and for several seasons thereafter was shot by him in a desultory fashion. At the end of the War, despite pledges previously given to the contrary, most of the requisitioned land was not released, but was acquired to the extent of 7,500 acres by the War Dept under a compulsory purchase order (just £25 per acre).

The family estate had shrunk from 34,000 to 1,500 acres (13,760 to 610 ha) in 100 years. The present Lord Walsingham (the 9th), born 1925, took over the estate in 1954. In 1968 he retired from the Army and started with just 300 acres (120 ha) in hand. He sold more farms, retaining the shooting and in some cases the leases too so that he could farm the land. The shoot is thus now 3,500 acres (1,416 ha). So far he has been able to rent back just one field from the Army at £40 an acre per annum. In 1985 the shoot was let at around £10,000 per annum on a 5-year lease and Lord Walsingham had no hand in its running, describing the three syndicates run by the Army on the purchased land as 'inefficient from the sporting point of view'. He himself has never much cared for shooting and doesn't now take part, but his teenage son seems to have inherited his great uncle's eye. The famous Shot's hammer Purdeys are still in the family.

Despite the war, the shooting has slowly built up again under the syndicate system, though partridge shooting on the whole shared the general national decline from 1950 as agriculture swept away most of the habitat and introduced so many chemicals. Hares too have declined dramatically through farming practices. The following indicate the trends for the main quarry bags.

	Ph'sant	Pa'ridge	Hare	R'bit	W'cock	Duck	Teal	Pigeon
1956–7	1,176	11	139	15	43	2	1	4
1970–1	2,880	65	45	71	41	74	28	186
1974–5	4,121	154	37	85	52	66	6	63
1982–3	5,003	29	6	50	54	117	12	123

On the other hand this shows how pheasants are relatively easily catered for.

The game book continues to comment on the wildlife and social life of the estate. On 31 January 1952 a great grey shrike was seen in Merton park by A. Jessup, 'a well-known local naturalist'. Meanwhile day-bags had tumbled back to those of the eighteenth and early-nineteenth centuries. On 31 January 1953 there were just 70 pheasants in a 92 bag, but: 'This wild, cold day gave a very sporting finish to the season, but before morning the gales had become the tragic disaster of the East Coast floods.' In 1954 myxamatosis was observed among rabbits on about 7 October and by mid-December they were virtually extinct but 'several adult Reeves pheasants were seen in the winter and they are thought to be established'. Although in the season 1955–6 it was 'three years since we were able to shoot any partridges', pheasant bags picked up, with two of 182 and 224.

In 1959–60 'various' were mostly high-flying waterhens and for the first year since the war bags topped 2,000. In February 1960, Isaac Pratt retired, 'having been a keeper on this estate since 1913, apart from his years of active service in World War I. The estate and family owe much to this fine old servant for his loyalty, integrity and skill. H. Belham appointed'. In November and December 1960 operations were 'seriously curtailed by foot and mouth', but field trials were being held regularly again. The weather featured prominently in 1962–3: 'It is feared that the long frost has killed nearly all the woodcock. January 19 was the coldest day I [Lord Walsingham] remember shooting on: the wind actually drove me out of the open into the Carr.'

Another farewell came in 1965–6: 'John Bacon, our very highly valued old warrener and mole-finder, retired, aged 87, after 20 years loyal service. He only gave up because the doctor wouldn't let him ride his bicycle.'

Most of the land lost was breck, which was chiefly suitable for roughshooting. The heart of the pheasant shoot, the central spine of Merton Woods, remains, but was neglected for many decades. There was no cropping for about a hundred years and no thinning between 1917 and 1968. Then an organised programme of regeneration began, to help both forestry and shooting. Fringes were left and the minimal clear felling was much exceeded by new plantings of hardwoods in nurse softwoods carefully sited to create new drives or improve others.

Thus the Merton shoot is now basically a business rather than a family interest with, in addition, 1,500 coarse fishing day tickets for Thompson Water let each year. In fact, Lord Walsingham's view of the future of British gameshooting is coloured by economics: 'I see it commercially exploited to yield what income it will; and patronized by sportsmen engaged during the week in jobs unconnected with the land seeking natural surroundings and expensive company at the weekend.' Lord Walsingham's father was one of the founding members of the Norfolk Naturalists Trust, the oldest such trust in Britain, and the conservation interest remains very strong today: 'It is traditional for the Merton Estate to lead in conservation and I am told that it stands out from the air as an oasis of mixed woodland and arable.'

Like most estate owners, Lord Walsingham supports controlled public access to the countryside, believing that if reasonable access is not conceded, unreasonable access will be seized. He led the way in opening Peddar's Way through Merton Park in 1978. Of greater concern has been the spread of the roe deer, some fifty or so now inhabiting the 400 acres (162 ha) of woodland. Because of these, without 4ft (1.2m) growtubes it is impossible to grow any young trees at all.

The men who now shoot Merton are mostly businessmen from about forty miles around, and in 1985 they had to pay about £350 a day or £4,500 per annum for the privilege. Legal & General and Fisons Pension Fund now own some of the land shot over. Today there is just one keeper and 10,000 day-olds are bought in; eggs are traded for poults, and there are 10 release pens in the woods and 30 feed points. Only pilot numbers of partridges are put down. This programme facilitates eighteen driven days (fortnightly), and there are two for duck.

On top of everything, Merton Hall was drastically reduced in size by fire in 1956, yet, despite a whole series of major setbacks for the estate, the shooting continues. A business it may be, but sound provision for the future is being made through habitat planning and there is no reason why, with the real enthusiasm of a future heir, Merton should not recapture much of its sporting magnetism.

SANDRINGHAM

Sandringham, just north of King's Lynn in Norfolk, was bought by the Prince of Wales (later King Edward VII) specifically to develop for shooting. His passion for the sport was to rub off on future generations of the royal family but, as time has gone by and public attitudes towards pursuits such as shooting have changed, a lower profile has become necessary. Never again are we likely to return to the days when a monarch was the great pivot around which the whole of fashionable shooting society turned. Our present Queen does not shoot but her great enthusiasm for working and training gundogs is well known and she frequently picks-up while other members of the family shoot. And, in spite of anti activity, the British royal family is a significant force in the fieldsports world, with Sandringham very much a country retreat where they generally go to shoot and relax after Christmas, often all members being present at a Boxing Day shoot.

Today there are sixteen staff in the game department at Sandringham. The concentration is on habitat management over some 20,000 acres (8,095 ha), including 3,000 (1,215) farmed in-hand and a country park. Prince Philip, whose love of shooting is well known, has said 'Conservation and shooting are the same thing. You won't get wild pheasants unless you get good habitat and that is good for conserving all forms of wildlife.' Much valuable cover has been retained primarily for the shooting interest, including water meadows and rough margins. In addition, many hardwood trees have been specially planted.

In bygone days when there was great reliance on wild stock, there was bound to be

Sandringham 1937: King George VI, Her Majesty Queen Elizabeth, Lord Wigram, Princess Elizabeth (now HM Queen Elizabeth II) and Tim the labrador

variable sport according to how kind the weather was in the breeding season. Thus when it became important to ensure a good supply of birds for guests who wanted big bags, rearing and release was significant. By 1900 some 12,000 pheasants a year were reared on the estate. When Edward, Prince of Wales, bought Sandringham for £220,000 in 1861, he even had Wolferton station specially built to bring guests as near the house as possible. The estate was then just 8,000 acres (3,240 ha) but its game potential was excellent and he was most anxious to provide good sport for the already established great landowners who were pioneering driven shooting all around him. There was a great deal of catching up to do to get on a par with estates such as Holkham and Merton.

Edward converted and enlarged the unattractive house but retained its character as a home rather than a palace. Though the grounds favoured both pheasant and partridge, there had been years of neglect and most of some £300,000 spent on the estate went in developing the shooting. Lord Walsingham wrote of Sandringham in the 1860s: 'There was a lot of change — the coverts were scanty, the cultivation poor — the stock of game very limited, and the woods ill-adapted for that system of beating which has become the hall-mark of the well-driven pheasant.' But in the following decade, chiefly under the guidance of Lord Leicester, Edward made great plans, and by the turn of the century Sandringham was among the leading shoots. However, at first high pheasants were not so fashionable and thus Edward's plantings were often done without regard for the aerial course a bird would follow. It is said he actually opposed any manoeuvre which might result in elevating the pheasants, since this might depress the bags.

Headkeeper Jackson was appointed in 1871 and remained in post up to World War I, thus providing great stability. One of his main tasks was to ensure that all the estate staff knew when a shoot was to take place as no work on the land was allowed the day before for fear of disturbing the game. On the day of a shoot no machinery ran and only beaters were allowed on the roads. Like a general, Jackson rode up and down on a brown cob, directing the beaters and the flankers with their red or blue flags. They wore smocks and red hatbands to distinguish them from peasants who might try to join in the fun. The keepers wore the royal livery of green and gold.

Like Lord Rendlesham before him and Dhuleep Singh and Lord Walsingham after, Edward was unsuccessful in trying to breed red grouse (1879) and introduce game not indigenous to Norfolk, including the Virginia quail.

The seriousness with which Edward took shooting can be gauged by his practice of keeping all the clocks half-an-hour fast, as Lord Leicester did at Holkham. The idea was to get an extra half-hour's shooting on the dark winter days because the gentleman Guns of the time were reluctant to alter their established hours.

Jackson was despatched to Baron Hirsch's enormous Hungarian estate to study the way in which huge partridge bags were made. Subsequently Sandringham was among the pioneers of the remise system, designed to concentrate all the birds into 20-acre (8ha) areas to make driving easier through minimising scattering. Yet, despite all improvements, it was chiefly royal association rather than sport which made Guns eager to be invited to Sandringham. Big bags were inevitable, but birds flew much better at many estates and in greater quantity at a few others.

Edward, however, made sure there was plenty to eat. Lunch was generally taken outdoors at the beginning of this century, often in a marquee. If the ladies came down it was fairly sumptuous with two hot dishes and cold lobster salads or chicken mayonnaise. If the weather was bad, shelter would be taken in one of the estate cottages. A special lunch-room built onto Wolferton station was used whenever there was a big rabbit shoot at the nearby warren.

Considerable use was made at Sandringham of the beautiful heaths — many of which are now gone from Norfolk — in bringing both pheasants and partridges to the gun. Birds would be driven into rough country and directed back over the Guns towards the home woods, sport being improved by placing the Guns in the lower levels which frequently adjoin the heaths. This ground is good for partridge driving because when birds have been driven into it they do not run together again as quickly as in roots or any other shelter. Thus a steady stream of birds is provided rather than large flushes. With its excellent insect food supply, it is also a first-class breeding ground for both pheasants and partridges. Standing water is plentiful in the dips for both game and wildlife to drink, and patches of bog are havens for snipe.

At the beginning of the 1870s some 7,000 head were killed annually, and by the end of Edward's reign this had been quadrupled. Shooting was concentrated into four weeks, the principal two being those which included the King's and Queen's birthdays — 9 November and 1 December. On 4 November 1986 3,114 pheasants were shot, yet some said Edward abhorred the idea of records, and discussion of numbers was discouraged, entertainment for his guests being his prime motivation.

One of the most astonishing records from Sandringham is the Marquis of Ripon's killing of twenty-eight pheasants in one minute, no doubt with the aid of at least two loaders and using double barrels. Yet safety and etiquette seem to have been important too: the adage in the gunroom reads 'Better a pheasant missed than a pheasant shared'.

Large partridge bags were made, a day's bag of 1,300 in the exceptional season of 1904 being among the biggest. Edward was among the Guns but his skill was variable and never in the front rank.

Unlike Edward VII, King George V was regarded as one of the finest Shots in the land, but his quarry was very limited and shooting mostly of a formal nature. He fired his first shot out of a small, single-barrelled muzzle-loader, the same gun from which his father, Edward, his brother the Duke of Clarence, Edward VIII and George VI all fired their first shots. The tradition continued down through the family and the gun is still preserved at Sandringham.

George VI was keener to get variety of quarry and this Sandringham has always provided in quantity, being in a favourable position to receive migrants such as woodcock, geese and duck. He was an exceptional and enthusiastic Shot and, like his father, keen to get involved with the planning of shoot days. His grandfather Edward, however, had left this detail to an equerry. Love of shooting never left him and he died in his sleep just a few hours after he had been rabbit shooting at Sandringham. A quiet man, always at home with the peace and wildness of the Norfolk estate, he established the pattern for future sport. The ceremony and great occasion were gone for ever. Today there is no pomp. The accent is on providing reasonable numbers of sporting birds for a private family shoot, while allowing room for nature within the constraints of economic land use.

ELVEDEN

G uinness is good for game' might well be one of the slogans of the giant brewing company, for when the Guinness family purchased the Elveden Estate in 1894 their great wealth and interest turned what was already a first-class shooting estate into one of the greatest of all time. But, as everywhere, the extent of shooting has wavered in accordance with the whims of each heir and been further complicated by the interruptions of war and the government's view of private land as a national resource.

Elveden lies on Suffolk's northern edge just below Thetford and measures some 8 miles (13 km) in both directions, with a circumference of some 30 miles (50 km). It comprises 22,918 acres (9,275 ha) and the 11,207 acres (4,535 ha) of this farmed by the 4th Earl of Iveagh form Britain's largest single arable unit. There are larger arable businesses, but not at one site. And here we have a double coincidence because not only does this farming enterprise put Lord Iveagh (Arthur Edward Rory Guinness) in his own empire's best-selling *Guinness Book of Records*, but also that famous annual was started primarily to settle disputes about record-breaking performances of game-birds, following heated discussion on a shoot!

A manor existed at Elveden as early as 1086, because it appears in Lord John Hervey's translation of the Domesday Book for Suffolk. It belonged to the Abbot of Edmundsbury (Bury St Edmunds) who later granted it to one of his tenants. On the Dissolution of the Monasteries it was forfeited to the Crown, but in 1550 granted to Sir John Cheke. It then passed through several families to the famous admiral Viscount Keppel in 1768. He built or re-built the manor house on the site where Elveden Hall now stands. Legend has it that its library was given a floor like the deck of a ship and left open to the sky so that the admiral could pace up and down as if on board his flagship. That room, now covered, and the old dining-room, are the only parts of his house still standing.

Elveden's shooting history really starts in 1786 when, on Keppel's death, the estate passed to his nephew, William Charles, 4th Earl of Albermarle. He subsequently let the shooting to the Duke of Bedford. There is, however, an earlier record of shooting in the area. The light soil was always good for partridges and it is recorded that near Thetford in 1737 'Mr Robinson and his company shot near a thousand birds', but we don't know what period this was over. Rabbits too already abounded and were highly regarded as a source of meat.

The area was almost entirely wild heathland, sandy breck, acres of heather and vast expanses of bracken dotted with gaunt woods of Scots pine and fir. The very dry soil was seen as a bar to cultivation — it could be blown away so easily — and it was not until the planting of belts of fir and pine began in the 1840s that things improved, at the same time warming the soil and providing extra cover for game. But Albermarle did farm part of his estate. Arthur Young, in 1804, stated that the Earl at Elden (as it then was) 'has drilled upon a very great scale, and his Lordship's crops at this commencement of his husbandry have answered his expectations.' One of his friends and advisors was the celebrated Mr Coke from Holkham. Shortly after that English agriculture slumped dramatically, Elveden reverted to a purely sporting estate and the little farming that was done was for the good of the game, and under Albermarle the estate had an excellent sporting reputation. Charles James Fox was a frequent visitor and described it as the best sporting manor for its size in England.

Albermarle sold for £30,000 in 1813 to William Newton, a West Indies merchant who at least continued and enlarged the plantations. He appears to have been a keen sportsman, and his game books, kept continuously from 1821 to 1863, show a steady improvement in the bags almost up to his death. His record season was that of 1858/9 when the bag was 3,300 partridges, 2,273 pheasants, 954 hares, 184 rabbits and 38 woodcock.

The next occupant of Elveden was a giant of shooting history, in every sense of the word — the Maharajah Dhuleep Singh of Lahore, known locally as the 'Black Prince', the former ruler of the Punjab, who erected a large and elegant mansion in Indian style. He was, at first, a favourite of Queen Victoria and his reign at Elveden from 1863 was to put the estate in the first division of socialite shoots. He had been brought to England as a child after the occupation of his territory by British forces at the end of the Sikh war. The British government paid him a large sum in compensation and it was from this that trustees bought Elveden from Newton's executors along with the adjoining property of Eriswell.

An indication of the poor agricultural value and returns from Elveden can be gathered from the *Domesday Book of Landowners* issued by the government in 1873. The Maharajah was shown as owning 14,615 acres (5,915 ha) of which the rentable value was only £4,755 17s. The Reverend Robert Gwilt, 'squarson' of Icklingham which has since been incorporated into the Elveden estate, owned 1,952 acres (790 ha) of rentable value £1,246 15s.

Dhuleep had little interest in English farming and was happy to indulge in the life of luxury provided for him. But he was kind, and at Christmas a pair of rabbits was sent to every household on the estate and considered a great treat. He also attended the annual

party and sports day at Chamberlain's Hall Barn, Eriswell, where the most popular event was the greasy pole with a sovereign at the top. Dhuleep came from a naturally sporting race and his diverse interests included falconry. He trained several Icelandic gyrfalcons to take the big hares on the open heaths around Elveden.

On 8 September 1876 Dhuleep killed 780 partridges to his own gun for just 1,000 cartridges. He stood at the apex of two broom coverts and the birds were repeatedly driven over his head. Most were wild and the bag would almost certainly have been much larger had the hand-reared birds not disappeared through lack of cover when a tenant farmer cut a huge field of seed clover only two days before. He very seldom went out for less than a hundred brace of birds to his own gun and was a typical exponent of the big-bag system. Yet he knew the habits and natural history of all game intimately and that of the partridge in every detail from the day of its hatching to the day of roasting. He consumed vast quantities of game and other foods provided at hundreds of lavish shoot lunches and, not surprisingly, in later life became grossly fat, often shooting from a stick.

Dhuleep's two sons Freddy and Victor were in the big time too. On 23 September 1895 they bagged 846 partridges before lunch and then had to stop because they ran out of cartridges. On 17 December, 1,006 pheasants were brought down in 46 minutes at Elveden's Contract Drive (Albermarle beat). On 5 November 1912 Guy Fawkes was celebrated with one of the biggest combined bags of pheasants and partridges ever made in Britain. The gamebook entry reads: 'Wet weather, SW wind, Sugar Loaf beat, 5 Guns — HM The King, Viscount Vallectort, The Hon Sir Derek Keppel, The Hon Henry Stonor, Viscount Iveagh, 1,122 cocks, 1,285 hens, 806 partridge, 18 hares, 13 rabbits, 4 various. Total 3,248. 179 Old Part'gs, 257 French Partridges. Shooting was delayed ½ hour owing to rain. Good show of game.' Dhuleep's bag in a good season was 9,600 pheasants, 9,400 partridges, 3,000 hares and 75,000 rabbits! He shot with three double-barrelled muzzle-loaders, and had two loaders who wore blue-and-green coats and waistcoats.

Headkeeper Turner, who served the estate from the age of eight in 1876 until his death three weeks before his planned retirement at the age of ninety-five in 1963, recalled many details of that remarkable period. He remembered the hand-reared partridges being fed on rice, rabbits, eggs, a special meal and ants' eggs in moderation — too many were said to harm young. 'When the young birds were moved out they were partly fed on buckwheat, cut when nearly ripe from pieces set specially and put down in small bunches. Broom coverts were set for shelter and for driving when it became more popular.' Oats, lupins and rye were also sown for cover and feed. Broom was cut off as low as possible each year as the pheasants ate a lot of broom seed. When large numbers of pheasants were reared broody hens were used for hatching. Food then was just hens' eggs, rice and great cakes of greaves that had to be chopped up with an axe, cooked and dried off with meal. At four weeks the birds went on to boiled wheat and split maize, and after being put to cover gradually went on to dry corn. Elveden's

Thomas Turner began working for the Elveden estate when he was eight and died as headkeeper in 1963, aged ninety-five, just three weeks before he was due to retire.

Prince Victor Albert Jay Dhuleep Singh (1866-1918), whose father, the Maharajah, turned Elveden into an important shoot

first incubators were very crude, open-topped wooden boxes with black tin water containers and paraffin lamps beneath. To alter the heat the lamps were turned up and down. They were really only good for drying birds off after hatching or a chill.

The birds were almost better fed than the servants for when things were bad in the early days Turner's parents had eaten rye bread and their chief fuel was the local fen turf. Wages were then 10s a week for a married man, and the large families had to be maintained on food such as bread, salt pork, potatoes and wheat. Turner's father was a shepherd on the estate. In the 1880s, when he was just thirteen, Turner himself was beating from 9.30am to 6pm. When sixteen, he started to assist one of the keepers for just 12s a week and was twenty-one when he was promoted to underkeeper.

In the 1880s financial problems began to overtake Dhuleep Singh, just as they had Lord Walsingham at Merton. Entertaining in the lavish style could not be carried on indefinitely without a large income to compensate for not farming the land in a business-like manner. Matters came to a head when the government refused to increase the Maharajah's pension and to return the famous Koh-i-noor diamond which had been confiscated from his family and presented by the East India Company to Queen Victoria. Consequently he left for India where he hoped to start a revolution in the Punjab, but he was stopped at Aden. Russia refused to help him so he went to live in Paris, where he died in 1893, but not before regretting his hostility towards England and again accepting the Indian government pension. He lies buried in Elveden churchyard with his wife and two sons.

Towards the end of Dhuleep's life, agriculture had taken another tumble and for some years Elveden, in a sorry state, was run by trustees and bailiffs. After the Maharajah's death the trustees sold pheasant eggs and the shooting was let to syndicates who shot the pheasant cocks, partridges and ground game only, though hens too were shot on the outskirts. Hot eggs were gathered, placed under hens and the chicks hand-reared to keep the hens laying as long as possible. The latter were caught up towards the end of the shooting season and some sold. This regime continued until enteric wiped out 1,000 poults.

But the estate was about to be saved by the remarkable Edward Cecil Guinness, who had become 1st Earl of Iveagh in 1891. Born in 1847, the fourth in line of the Guinness dynasty, although a younger brother, he was the man who made the Dublin brewery — founded in 1759 by his grandfather, Arthur — world famous by floating it as a public company for £6 million and creating a business empire which has never looked back. The Earl needed a home to entertain the society to which he had been admitted, so he purchased Elveden in 1894 and set about its enlargement and glorification. And he lost no time in inviting persons of influence to shoot — the Duke of Marlborough in December that year when 'pheasants rose uncommonly well'. The 1894–5 bag was a record 24,731, comprising 7,524 cock pheasants, 7,576 hens, 1,978 partridges, 679 hares, 6,778 rabbits, 74 woodcock, 29 snipe, 13 duck and 80 various. This might be compared with the 1984–5 bag of 19,043 head — 6,226 cock pheasants, 4,976 hens, 569 partridges, 1,013 hares, 1,527 rabbits (1,423 to warreners), 195 woodcock, 4 duck, 4,293 woodpigeon and 240 various.

The gamebooks have been well kept throughout this century. One of their special features is a column for wind, which can do so much to make or break a day's sport. The statistics are also wonderful 'ammunition' for researchers. For example, through analysis of the Elveden records the Game Conservancy has been able to show that hare and rabbit populations are directly proportional, a very important factor when so many people are worried for the future of the hare population.

The parish and village of Icklingham — except for a few hundred acres — were added to the estate in 1898, the lower part of Wangford at the turn of the century and, with Lakenheath Warren, the estate grew to 25,000 acres (10,120 ha). There were wildfowl and snipe in the marshes at Wangford, where Lord Iveagh created good duck ponds. And every sector had its special name which continues to this day, including Napthen's beat, named after a headkeeper's son who was killed by poachers.

Lord Iveagh built a duplicate of the Maharajah's mansion nearby, then connected the old building with the new by erecting a massive central block rising high above them and capped by a copper dome. The block contained a fabulous marble hall encrusted with intricate Indian designs from floor to roof, around whose two immense Renaissance-style fireplaces the Edwardian house parties gathered. There was also a new water tower as large as Big Ben and a whole new servants' wing; Elveden village was rebuilt and 6 miles (9.6 km) of roads constructed across the estate to smooth the way for the new motor cars.

All modern conveniences were adopted including a private telephone line to maintain contact between estate and Hall, post sockets being provided into which a

Elveden 1901: miles of road were laid down specially to accommodate the new motor cars

portable instrument could be plugged. This fired the imagination of one Canadian journalist who went to watch George V shoot. The phone sockets were only along the main road but the Canadian's report stated: 'Every covert is connected up by a system of telephones to aid the bird-seekers. When game is flushed and missed by one Gun, it is possible immediately to telephone a nearby shooter to be on his guard.' Later Lord Iveagh heard that the journalist was working for a periodical trying to boost telephone sales!

The Earl did not buy Elveden to farm it. He had no need to turn it into a sharp business. When tenants were bought out it was primarily to avoid any arguments about shooting over the land. In fact, as on many estates, the farming continued to be entirely subsidiary to shooting. And as the shoot's reputation grew, regular Guns included the Prince of Wales — as Edward VII he stayed at Elveden every other New Year, alternating with Chatsworth — and the Duke of York, afterwards George V.

Everything continued on a grand scale with 70 men in the game department alone — 24 liveried men, 30 warreners and 16 horsemen, wire-fence men etc. Parties of 8 or 9 Guns were served by some 100 beaters, over 20,000 pheasants were reared every season and it was a poor day if less than 1,000 birds were killed; 1899 was the record year for the nineteenth century with 103,392 head including 21,053 pheasants. The record partridge season was 1902–3 when 5,979 were shot. House parties of twenty or thirty guests were the rule, with the many servants inside the house joined by those the guests brought. Most parties lasted from Monday to Friday, as the weekend habit had not yet developed. Guests generally arrived by rail, the ladies with a huge number of boxes to accommodate many changes of clothes. Royalty would be met at Thetford station by a carriage with postilions and a guard of honour supplied by the local yeomanry, the Loyal Suffolk Hussars. It was some time before motor cars became reliable enough to replace carriages, and there was always a spare following the King in case his vehicle broke down.

It was inevitable that an ever-expanding popular press would attack such privilege, and even before World War I large estates like Elveden were criticised for perpetuating 'The Land of the Pheasant — A Manless Countryside' (*Daily Mail,* 1909). But with the onset of war, there was a new attitude to national self-sufficiency. Elveden too contributed to the war effort. The Army requisitioned thousands of acres, the first tanks were on trial there and much game land was ploughed up. Naturally war put an end to the big shooting parties and they would never be revived again on such a scale, but although pheasant rearing was temporarily abandoned the birds had to be shot and smaller shoots with good bags continued each season.

Very large bags and even royal parties resumed after the war, but everything was less formal and the standard declined as gentlemen of leisure who could afford to shoot in the week were replaced by younger men who worked in city offices and could only get away at weekends. Nonetheless, in the mid-twenties a hot lunch was still served by footmen in the famous tent and an army of keepers and beaters turned out in uniform.

For Elveden the biggest change came in 1927 with the succession of the 2nd Earl, who did not have the same enthusiasm for shooting and immediately set about reclaiming land at 500 acres (202 ha) a year. Naturally the headkeeper resisted the dominance of farming, but when in the early days of silage-making Turner complained to Lord Iveagh about the slaughter of young pheasants taking cover in the lucerne, he got little sympathy. Other land was let to the Forestry Commission, who smothered many thousands of acres of Breckland with coniferous plantations, excluding most game and wildlife. In World War II a large area of Lakenheath was taken for an aerodrome and today this remains a US airbase (sold to the Air Ministry and leased to the USAF). In the 1930s Lord Iveagh asked H. W. Bunbury to form a syndicate over part of the estate as he did not have time to do justice to the shooting. This eased the

Edward VII (centre with beard) reigns over a shooting party at Elveden

financial burden but Guns had to be invited by the Guinness family and there were no substitutes. The system of part family shoot and part syndicate lease has continued ever since.

The game department's long-standing opposition to agriculture was effectively silenced, at least for the duration of the war, by the first ploughing Order served on Lord Iveagh in 1939. Some 6,000 pheasants had been reared for the 1939–40 season and it had also been a very good wild pheasant year so it was advisable to reduce the stock; 21,170 pheasants were killed. In 1940 those keepers too old to join up were mostly put on farms to relieve the labour shortage, so there was little opportunity to keep vermin down, but even worse was the damage caused by the Army. They pulled up some 25 miles (40km) of rabbit netting and piled it in huge dumps along the main road so that most of it was stolen. This allowed tanks to manoeuvre, but also the rabbits which tucked into all the crops. And with so much disturbance it was a miracle any game survived at all. Troops took eggs to eat and poached sitting birds. The only consolation was that the tanks kept the rabbits out of some areas.

Elveden Hall was taken over for a brigade HQ and many British and American officers were invited to shoot throughout the war, the former being mostly family friends stationed nearby — one Gun was the Duke of Gloucester, who was stationed at Elveden for a short period. The Americans were not very good at driven shooting but more effective when some were allowed to roughshoot certain areas. They excelled at shooting rabbits from the bonnet of a Jeep, but the dangerous practice of using powerful bows and arrows had to be discouraged.

Lord Iveagh was undaunted by the Army's mess at the end of the war and set out to clear the camps, tin huts, concrete roads, barbed wire, tank tracks and latrines which defaced the park. And of course all the rabbit fencing had to be replaced. There were 11 keepers and 12 warreners at the time, among 311 people on the estate payroll. In the first year after the war he put up twenty-six houses for staff. He also turned into flats the stables, gun-rooms and boot-rooms at the Hall and the King's post office which had handled the mail when King Edward VII stayed there. Lord and Lady Iveagh lived in the gardener's cottage and the magnificent Hall was mostly shut up. Shooting entertainment was out and food production for the nation was the new preoccupation. Nonetheless, they still killed 8,000 wild pheasant a season as the soil was so good for them. Yet all this nearly never happened because an American sentry shot at Lord and Lady Iveagh as they were driving through the park during the war. The real tragedy had been the death of Lord Elveden, heir to the estate, while on active service in Holland in 1945.

Today there are just 3,819 acres (1,545 ha) of unreclaimed heath so their significance to nature conservation is great. The 4th Earl (born 1969) is very interested in wildlife as well as shooting and his staff do everything they can to accommodate organisations such as the Royal Society for the Protection of Birds. The same estate which in 1994 produced 8,673 tonnes of grain, 50,200 tonnes of sugar beet and 28,900 tonnes of vegetables and sustained 850 ewes and 7,500 pigs, has a place for endangered species such as the stone curlew (the once-common Norfolk plover). Recently it has been recognized that the planting of game crops such as kale and maize are probably of

A guard of honour for Edward VII arriving at Thetford Station en route for Elveden

value to stone curlews, fewer than two hundred pairs of which remain in England, perhaps half on farmland.

Most of the old marshes have been drained now and other areas afforested, including where Dhuleep Singh shot his record bag of partridges. Yet there is still plenty to interest the Nature Conservancy Council, who co-operate in the management of Sites of Special Scientific Interest. There are a few public rights of way on the estate but access has not brought great problems. Permits were originally issued to anyone wishing to watch birds or study the flora and fauna, but eventually there was concern over the large numbers involved so permits are now generally restricted to research workers.

The fluctuation of the rabbit population has provided a valuable opportunity for ecological studies and there has been a forty-year research programme on grassland. When the rabbits disappeared through myxomatosis and habitat change there was nothing to keep the tree seedlings in check and windblown seed has caused considerable natural regeneration and loss of the much valued, old heath habitat. Now, if trees do re-establish they are managed for five or six years, then cut for Christmas. Rabbit numbers are nothing like they were, though there are still periodic build-ups and a full-time warrener is employed. Some 2,000 a year are taken, compared with 13,000 sold in 1974 alone. Night-shooting in February is particularly effective, but most of the big old heathland warrens have gone under the plough. In 1921–2 an amazing 128,856 rabbits were shot and killed. There has also been a special bracken

Elveden, 1951. Headkeeper Turner keeps a watch for rabbits while the late 2nd Earl of Iveagh and Lady Iveagh look at the agricultural changes which made the estate famous

research project, for where there are no trees bracken has been smothering the natural grass of Breckland.

The age-old conflict between farming and game departments well-nigh disappeared in 1972 when Bill Sloan, as the estate's general manager and agent, was employed to run both, his background being in farm management. Bill said that 'Each department is regarded as a profit centre. We are not running a philanthropic organisation but as long as the game department breaks even it is regarded as a capital asset. The farms do not charge for crop damage by game, but in return the game department has to control the vermin, though one might say this is expensive vermin control.' Bill Sloan retired in 1992 and was succeeded by Mr E. F. Boyt. Mr J. W. Rudderham has taken over the running of the game department and has emphasised the estate's commitment to game and conservation. Ted Barfield retired as headkeeper in 1993 after 37 year's service.

There has been virtually no hedgerow removal on the estate. On the contrary, planting of windbreaks has continued — chiefly lines of Scots pines — and beneath these there certainly remains plenty of good cover for nesting partridges. The present policy in tree planting is for one-third hardwoods to two-thirds softwoods. Trees are very much a crop, but their importance to game is 'very much a consideration'. Trees are no longer scarce items in the area as a whole, for north-west of the estate are 56 sq miles (145 km²) of Thetford Chase and to the east 7,000 acres (2,830 ha) of the King's

Forest. Not surprisingly, deer have spread considerably and must be culled. Ted Barfield told me Prince Michael shot his first roe deer there in the late seventies — 'I remember it well because he rested the gun on my shoulder.' Fallow, red and muntjac also occur.

Today the shooting of the estate is approximately 14,650 acres (5,929 ha) to the family syndicate, 4,000 (1,620 ha) let to Lakenheath Rod & Gun Club as a rough shoot, 3,000 (1,215 ha) to the Forestry Commission (who let the shooting to others), 1,500 (610 ha) to the Barnham Tenant Farmers Syndicate, 900 (365 ha) to the West Eriswell Syndicate and 430 (174 ha) to the Codsen Hill Shoot. Days are let only on the family part — twenty-eight including nine cocks-only days. Farmers and businessmen take them on a birds-shot basis.

There are now 6 keepers on the estate, bags average 180 pheasants plus 30 various on a total of 40–50 days, including those let. 1976 was the last year when partridges were shot successfully, Barfield having no hesitation in saying that the prime culprit for the decline is the run of cold, wet springs. Straying is a great problem with the English partridge; the last time some were put down a number were shot 23 miles (37 km) away! However, there is renewed interest in wild partridges and pheasants and duck, initiatives taking place to improve their habitats. Each beatkeeper works under the supervision of Jim Rudderham.

Five thousand pheasant chicks are put under gas brooders and 3,000 under 'electric hens'. Also 1,000 poults are put in the care of the trainee. The worst enemy has always been the weather. Apart from that, with the increase in forestry the fox is number one pest, then the stoat and crow, grey squirrel and rat. But Barfield pointed out that 'at least we don't have to buy any slug pellets as there are enough young pheasants to eat them all: the land is light anyway.' Over the ten years to 1984–5 the season's bag for the whole estate averaged 12,044 pheasants. A growing problem has been the pheasants

King George V arriving at Elveden for a weekend's shooting

themselves, for as the concentration has been on reared stock the birds have become heavier and Barfield said they do not fly so well as they did twenty-five or thirty years ago — a special worry on flat land.

There are still some nice traditions which conjure up the estate's colourful past, including blowing the same hunting horn as was used in the Maharajah's day to start and end drives. There is also the splendid 1936 Bedford van still used to take the Guns from drive to drive. The 3rd Earl could remember 800 gutted rabbits hanging up in it one summer after the war, and 'someone had to open the door to let the air in'.

Famous guests in recent times have included Deputy Prime Minister Lord Willie Whitelaw, ex-Prime Minister Sir Alec Douglas-Home and King Constantine of Greece, a good Shot.

The 3rd Lord Iveagh succeeded to the title in 1967 on the death of his grandfather, his father having been killed in World War II. Considering his wide business interests he managed to shoot quite frequently — about ten days a season. Not only was he chairman of the Guinness parent company and chairman of Guinness Ireland Ltd, but he was also a member of the board of the Bank of Nova Scotia and director of a number of Irish and Canadian companies. He was a member of the Irish Senate 1973–7 and held many honorary positions with wide interests in medicine, agriculture and horse racing. He was also closely involved with the promotion of Charolais cattle in Ireland, where he farmed and lived most of the time when he was not in an aeroplane.

He took up shooting through his 'own inclination' and liked it for 'a day in the open air together with the enjoyment of the sport'. As with most shoot owners, he believed that gameshooting will increase in popularity and regarded the views of antis as 'misplaced' but was 'very happy that people have their own convictions'. He believed that the popular press did generally convey the wrong image of shooting to the general public and the only change in the law he would like to have seen was one to allow gameshooting on Sunday after 10am.

I saw some very good wild birds at Elveden and much enjoyed the relaxed atmosphere. The January pheasants were more than good enough for the Guns and the dozen or so woodcock we encountered left none of their number behind.

The young 4th Earl, who succeeded to the title on the death of his father in 1992, is a very good and enthusiastic Shot, being out most Saturdays during the gameshooting season. His younger sister (Lady Louisa, born 1967) shoots with a 20-bore and his brother Rory Guinness (born 1974) killed his first two pheasants in a snowstorm with a .410 shotgun when he was just nine. So the future of Elveden's shooting looks assured and in good hands.

The fabulous contents of Elveden Hall were auctioned by Christie's in the 1980s as Lord Iveagh could not foresee living in the house again, and 'wanted others to have the opportunity of enjoying the works of art'. Thus the treasures are gone from this magic place where the Maharajah once entertained kings of England and where the US Army Air Division planned World War II bombing raids on Germany. There are no plans to sell it and I have the sneaking feeling that Lord Iveagh enjoys the brooding presence of the place where Dhuleep Singh's ghost can watch and make sure that sport at Elveden retains its great tradition.

Another good partridge killed over Sutton Scotney's high hedgerows

SIX MILE BOTTOM

Today Six Mile Bottom Estate, near Newmarket, Suffolk, has an excellent pheasant shoot, but originally everything was planted specially for partridges, and pheasants were regarded as inferior. In fact before the partridge's great decline after World War II, Six Mile Bottom and Holkham had been regarded as the two best partridge shoots in Britain, following the break-up of the Grange estate in Hampshire. Most of its success was attributed to its Victorian owner, General John Hall. During his tenure no partridges were shot before Christmas and the distinguished soldier claimed that the five concluding weeks of the season were well worth the waiting.

General Hall's theory was that the land lay quieter in January, the birds drove better and came more singly off plough-land than out of roots. Opponents might argue that partridge shooting should finish by Christmas as the birds begin to pair in early January and the best and strongest young birds do so first. But General Hall countered this by saying that no birds at all had been shot before January anyway. The best land would be shot over only once and with many of the birds paired they would tend to come over in couples rather than packs. An example of one of these good late weeks is that of 26–29 January 1869 when the partridge bag was 419, 532, 606 and 442. For such days the General collected all the best Guns of the time, his task made easier because late in the season he could be more certain they would not be engaged elsewhere.

Once thus established, the shoot continued to attract all the big Shots, and royalty too in every decade since the Duke of Cambridge rented the shooting following General Hall. Edward VII had a bit of trouble there when, as a guest of Sir Ernest Cassell, he shot a beater, though the latter was not killed. And in 1921, when Felix Cassell was shot in the face, the shooting was cancelled for the rest of the year. At that time the estate was 8,211 acres (3,323 ha), including Hare Park of 1,118 acres (452 ha), with 7 partridge beats and just 2 days pheasant shooting. George V continued the royal tradition and well known Guns in the late twenties included Lord Coke, Sir Harry Stonor and Neville Chamberlain.

Big bags were sought of course, and in 1930 a special effort was made to achieve a new partridge day record. On that memorable 25 September only 20–30 brace were taken on the first two drives and the estate owner, Capt R. F. C. Cunningham-Reid, said to the headkeeper: 'Coot, you're like a cricket team without a captain.' The eventual bag was 1,418 partridges, 56 hares, 5 rabbits, 8 pigeons and 12 various — total 1,499. That season's total bag was 2,642 pheasants, 6,639 partridges, 1,348 hares, 1,592 rabbits, 133 pigeon and 53 various — total 12,407. The big, arable fields were in excellent heart with high hedges and belts planted specifically to give good birds.

(above) Dallowgill owner Godfrey Bostock with his keeper outside Lord Ripon's original shooting box
(below left) Godfrey Bostock grouse shooting with Mrs Bostock and loader
(below right) Mrs Barbara Hawkins, who has her own Yorkshire moor, grouse shooting at Dallowgill

At the end of that season Charles South took over his father's beat, having worked as an underkeeper since 1921. Later he became headkeeper and retired in 1973 after twenty-three years in that position. He remembered how George V had his own red stick and markers for each stand.

> In those days there were two sets of beaters with twenty-five in each accompanied by three keepers. They carried red or white flags and received about 12s a day. There were usually twelve drives but sometimes up to sixteen. The King came only when Lord Milton had the shooting. For lunches there were two marquees — one for the Guns and one for the loaders, keepers and dogmen. We had half a loaf, a pork chop and a few pickled onions each.

Although he always preferred to work with partridges, South's contribution to the pheasant shooting was considerable and the present proprietor, Noel Cunningham-Reid (born 1931), who took over from his father in 1952, named a drive 'South's Drive'.

The thirties were the heyday of partridge shooting at Six Mile Bottom, 4,104 being in the 1935–6 total bag of 18,280 along with 4,029 pheasants, 2,002 hares, 6,371 rabbits, 8 woodcock, 1,732 pigeon and 34 various. In General Hall's day hares had been quite insignificant, the numbers not having built up along with the acreage under the plough.

The Duke of Kent shot in 1938, when bags of 400-plus partridges were being achieved, but today there are only one or two partridge days — from early October. George VI, too, was a visiting Gun.

As partridges began their long decline, pheasant rearing accelerated. The insect food on which partridge chicks so depend was drastically reduced as fewer tenant farmers kept sheep and the need for artificial fertilizers began. South blamed the use of sprays in particular and recalled of earlier days:

> There were millions of insects then, from fleas to butterflies, not to mention frogs and skylarks all over the place. I always remember one day when at the end of a drive the beaters sat on a pile of dried pigs' manure — there were heaps of it all over the fields then — and within minutes they were smothered with fleas. Also you could hardly sit down without getting covered with ants. Now there are only a few in the churchyard.

Shooting continued through World War II, though on a reduced scale and with many military Guns. One guest then was Sir Tommy Sopwith. But after the war there was very little game left as poaching had been so prevalent.

Lord Mountbatten of Burma, who had been a regular guest since 1935, was among the Guns on the record pheasant day of 26 November 1960. When Guns were feeling it after lunch, Noel Cunningham-Reid said to South: 'Where can we go so that we don't get too many?' South had to reply, 'Nowhere Sir', yet only 4,000 had been reared that year. High Gun of the day was Lord Brabourne (Lord Romsey's father) with 337; Noel Cunningham-Reid was second with 335. The bag was 1,425 pheasants, 17 partridges, 21 hares, 1 rabbit, 9 pigeon and 2 woodcock — total 1,475.

The Duke of Edinburgh was there on 13 November 1975 when the bag was 466 pheasants and 16 partridges, and Prince Charles on 31 January 1970 when 453 pheasants were shot, returning on 20 December 1974 for a day of 438 pheasants and 14 partridges. Other well known Guns in recent decades have included Prince Bernhard of the Netherlands (1984), King Constantine (in 1983 on two pheasant days of 1,022 and 950), the Honorable Angus Ogilvy (1982), the Duke of Kent (1980), Mr R. C. Rockefeller (1979) and Prince Richard of Gloucester, not to mention many barons and counts and foreign royalty such as the Maharajah of Jaipur. The Duke and Duchess of Devonshire had two small days in 1952.

Over the years the estate has hosted coursing meets, but there have been big hare shoots in February with bags of several hundreds. One unusual entry in the game book is that of 6 October 1936: 'Hawking — Lord Howard de Walden took 1 pheasant and 8 partridges in Hare Park.'

The weather has been kind enough to permit a mini partridge revival in some years — for example in 1976 when 1,000 were killed, the best day being 310. Noel Cunningham-Reid told me these were about 50 per cent greys and 50 per cent redlegs, although there were ten times as many greys as redlegs on the ground, 'because most people don't know how to shoot greys'. He took up shooting when he was sixteen and finds grouse shooting the most fun. He also does a bit of rabbit and pigeon shooting. 'I have twenty guns of all bores and use them all on about fifty days a season!' He sympathises with the anti movement and envisages 'increasing social and anti-blood pressure on shooting'.

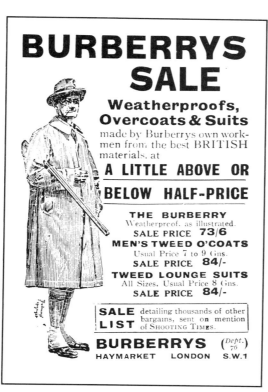

After taxation complications the reduced 7,000-acre (3,240 ha) estate has cut back on its shooting in recent years, from a peak of some 40 days to about 10 let days costing £12 per bird in 1985. The Guns, chiefly American and Dutch, bring vital income to the mainly cereal-growing estate. In recent years the exchange rate has given them exceptionally good value. There are 3 keepers who, in the 1984–5 season worked for a bag of 7,326 head including 6,300 pheasant, 88 partridges, 893 hares, 6 rabbits and 1 woodcock. Only pheasants are put down and day-olds are bought. Some 25–35 days run twice a week from November. As to who shoots now, I asked Noel Cunningham-Reid if he has any eccentric guests and his reply was 'Most'.

MIXED BAG

As already mentioned, eastern England has always been one of our finest gameshooting areas, and there are far too many excellent shoots to discuss in detail. Those described so far reflect general trends, but the following have made their mark in many ways.

The claim to be the birthplace of partridge driving lies in dispute between **Chippenham** (Cambridgeshire) and **Heveningham** (Suffolk), where it had been introduced by crack Shot Lord Huntingfield by 1845. Suffolk also lays claim to the red-legged partridge introduction, most historians attributing the act simultaneously in 1770 to the Marquess of Hertford at **Sudbourne Hall** and Lord Rendlesham at **Rendlesham** (both Suffolk). The latter once ran to 20,000 acres (8,090 ha) but was much broken up and largely taken over by the Forestry Commission. Sudbourne too was broken up but, as with so many estates, later owners tried to reassemble the sporting rights.

Six thousand partridges off 18,000 acres (7,280 ha) was considered a fair year's total at Capt Prettyman's **Orwell Park**, near Ipswich, in 1911 when 300 brace was a good day. But on the Earl of Ellesmere's 5,500 acres (2,225 ha) at **Stetchworth**, Cambridgeshire, heavy soil which stuck to the partridges' feet was a great problem at that time. Nonetheless, half the land is light and sandy and in 1907–8 as many as 2,598 partridges were killed — 2,180 off the light land. Headkeeper Hersey thought the heavy land 'not worth the keepers' wages'; however, he did think it worthwhile to mark eggs with a rubber stamp to counter stealing. Now the Duke of Sutherland is said to shoot an average of 1 pheasant per acre off an increased estate of 6,000 acres (2,434 ha) with 3 keepers. No rearing has taken place since the war — a marvellous example of good predator control, habitat management and conservation of the wild breeding stock.

Melton Constable's Norfolk woodcock under a November moon always set the pulse racing, as did an invitation to Captain Henry Birkbeck's 9,000 acres (3,640 ha) at **Westacre** — the third largest estate in Norfolk after Holkham and Sandringham. A keen conservationist, High Sheriff Capt Birkbeck has recently planted many miles of hedges and left many fields unsprayed.

Euston, the Duke of Grafton's estate near Merton and Elveden, is chiefly known for the Euston System, which is to help increase wild pheasant and partridge numbers. Because of this system some 4,000 to 7,000 birds were killed there annually at the turn of the century despite no hand-rearing at all. The eggs are taken as they are laid and replaced with 'bad' eggs which have been saved from the year before and boiled. The removed eggs are set under hens or otherwise incubated and, when they have reached the chipping stage, are returned to the natural mother (or nests with small clutches) who finishes the hatching and knows no difference. It is advisable not to remove any eggs until at least four have been laid, and imitation eggs should not be used. This system achieves a much higher survival rate as it is rare for a partridge to bring off a large brood (up to twenty-five) successfully, especially on a modern farm where insect food is scarce.

During Mr Pearson-Gregory's long tenancy up to 1912, a bag of 807 partridges and over 1,000 pheasants was made in a day. But some of the most remarkable days were those when some 600 pheasants plus 600 partridges were bagged, with no hand-rearing at all. Many such were obtained on the West Farm at Barnham, where the famous 'Sheep-walk' is. The great days continued through the thirties. For example the 1936–7 head count of 14,352 included 9,214 pheasants, 4,037 partridges, 485 hares, 340 rabbits, 75 woodcock, 34 duck and 167 various.

The 'Black Prince' Dhuleep Singh is said to have shot 1,000 rabbits at **Cockfield** (Suffolk), and then rolled in the heap at the end. Sir Charles Blois (born 1940) who took over in 1968 when part of the estate was sold to his brother, continues the fine tradition, though admits to having been anti until about seventeen. This is a fine example of a private Suffolk shoot where the number of keepers has decreased from three to one but where consistently good bags of 80–100 partridges and 100–200 pheasants are achieved on 4,000 acres (1,620 ha), 3,500 (1,416) being shot over. The season's bags now average 2,000 but the gamebooks, which start in 1829, reveal years of 3,200 partridges and 3,000 pheasants.

The Cockfield keeper who retired in 1976 after living on the estate all his life, can remember being paid about 22s a week to look after 800–1,000 acres (325–405 ha). The farmer paid 10s an acre rent to the landowner and let the warrening rights for the same figure to the keeper who then paid the rabbit catcher 36s a week to catch rabbits. The owner even charged the keeper for warrening rights on unfarmed land.

Today, 1,200 acres of the estate is a Site of Special Scientific Interest (SSSI) and National Nature Reserve. Sir Charles writes:

> As part of the agreement with the NCC [National Conservancy Council] we are obliged to kill as vermin all the species killed as such on a normal shoot. They are as keen as we are to restrict the access by the public to the reserve — permits going only to those whose access will benefit the NCC. Their work to restore footpaths is much greater than ours. We are all aware that a minority of over-enthusiastic birdwatchers do more harm to wildlife than almost anything else apart from wild predators. The only conflict here is sometimes when the NCC wants to work in game-sensitive areas in the shooting season. The reason for initially encouraging the reserve was to control trespass. They have fenced off large areas and the NCC signs are better respected than "Keep out — Private".

The best all-round Shot to have visited Mr David Cock's shoot at **Roffey**, Dunmow, Essex, is Guy Moreton; well known visitors have included Prince Rainier of Monaco.

On this 1,100 acre (445 ha) shoot they have never failed to bag more than they put down, but twenty years ago they shot more than twice the number put down. One of Mr Cock's favourite shoots is that of Colonel Sir John Archibald Ruggles-Brise at **Finchingfield**, Essex. A sporting bachelor, Sir John has made over most of his 2,500 acres (890 ha) to his nephew.

The importance of good habitat has been clearly shown at Mr Henry Edwards' **Hardingham** shoot, near Norwich. A relatively ordinary Norfolk farm shoot in the early 1970s when it relied largely on reared birds, it involved the Game Conservancy in a planting scheme and now shoots ten times the original bag while rearing the same number of birds!

To conclude eastern England's remarkable story, mention must be made of sporting artist William Garfit's shoot at **Hauxton Pits** near Cambridge — a fine example of what can be created from virtually nothing. Born in 1944, in 1968 he took over just 78 acres (31.5 ha) of derelict gravel workings which are surrounded by houses, main roads and factories; yet he enjoys five even-bag driven days there with up to twelve quarry species on one day, in pleasant well-planted surroundings. He keepers it himself with just two part-time volunteer keepers, and over 1,000 head a season have been killed. Will sees variety as one of the hinge-pins of a great shoot. An average day of 104 head comprises 65 pheasants, 20 mallard, 5 woodcock, 4 pigeon, 1 snipe, 1 goose, 3 moorhens, 1 coot, 1 jay and 3 rabbits.

None of Will's land is farmed, though it had been before gravel extraction 1940-68. It is all gardened for game and wildlife, with 44 acres (18 ha) of willow woodland, 10 acres (4 ha) of fisheries, 14 acres (6 ha) of specimen trees and 10 acres (4 ha) of marsh. There is a very high population of breeding migrant warblers and 112 species of bird have been recorded, including osprey, purple heron, shrike and rare waders. There is also a wide range of botanical and entomological life including four species of orchid, rare moths and the only incidence in the county of certain species of moss.

Some 400–500 seven-week-old cock poults are bought in and all the early duck eggs are picked up and incubated in a helper's sitting-room. The change to cock poults was made because they give a better return (65 per cent over 5 years compared with 50 per cent cocks and hens). The stock of hens is now wild and thus a bonus. With mixed cock-and-hen days the tendency was to shoot out the wild hens and have only tame hens at the end of the season.

The shoot has provided much fun too. Will remembers 'the day old Ken stoked up the Tortoise iron stove in the Nissen hut for our midday drink break. It made the chimney red-hot and set fire to starlings' nests in the roof. Guns and beaters made a bucket chain to the nearest pond while Ken doused the flames from a ladder.' Then there was the beaters' day when 'Bob the rat man shot a mallard driven from his front but was surprised to find a greylag goose dead at his feet as it had come from behind and flown into his shot — much to the amusement of all, especially as I'd asked people not to shoot the greylags. He's still known as "Greylag Bob".'

CHAPTER 9

CENTRAL SOUTHERN ENGLAND

Lord Carnarvon and entourage at Highclere, 1901

The counties of Dorset, Wiltshire and Hampshire have a great sporting history, but when it comes to shooting Hampshire is supreme and even rivals Norfolk. It was there that William of Normandy, at a convenient distance from his capital, established the royal hunting ground of the New Forest. But bow-and-arrow gave way to shotgun and today the Forest shoots are just some of many which continue the sporting greatness of this region with widely varying habitats. From the high downs in the west and north to the great central partridge strongholds and the steep, hanging woods of the south, there are birds to suit everyone.

The famous Colonel Peter Hawker followed his dogs on the stubbles of Longparish, near Andover, and punted after geese on the Solent throughout the first half of the nineteenth century. He wanted no part in large bags and would go out all day, even in pouring rain, for one pheasant. After marching up and down for hours with his muzzle-loader, he frequently returned home triumphantly with forty partridges on a pole.

Since then, this region has become densely populated and gameshooting is necessarily highly organised. It has changed immensely, but let us see what has happened to some of those great estates and consider other, rising, stars which point the way to the future.

BROADLANDS

Lord Romsey with his gundogs at Broadlands

The fish and fowl Jacobean-style interior woodcarvings, commissioned by Palmerston to represent the fruits of the estate, remain entirely appropriate at Hampshire's Broadlands estate as the present owner, Lord Romsey, is as keen on fieldsports as his distinguished ancestors were. But whereas Viscount Palmerston (1784–1865), Britain's outspoken Victorian Prime Minister, took some eight hours to travel down by coach or horse to Broadlands each weekend before the coming of the railway, Lord Romsey's shooting guests are quite likely to arrive by helicopter.

Romsey Abbey owned the original manor and area known as Broadlands before the Norman Conquest, and on its surrender to Henry VIII after the Dissolution of the Monasteries it was leased to John Foster, steward of the abbey. Edward VI granted it to his uncle, Admiral Sir Thomas Seymour, who sold it to Sir Francis Fleming in 1547. His daughter married Edward St Barbe and for 117 years the property remained in the St Barbe family. Sir John St Barbe left it to his cousin Humphrey Sydenham in 1723, but Sydenham, ruined by the South Sea Bubble, sold to Henry Temple, 1st Viscount Palmerston, in 1736. The work he started, carried on by the 2nd Viscount and Capability Brown, in landscaping, clearing and planting much of the estate, had considerable bearing on future sport.

Broadlands already had royal connections; James I stayed there as early as 1607. But it was after Lord Louis Mountbatten married Edwina, daughter of Wilfred Ashley (Lord Mount Temple of Lee) who owned the estate from 1907 to his death in 1939, that royalty featured regularly among the shooting guests. The late Lord Louis, Earl Mountbatten of Burma, victim of an assassination in 1979, was a most enthusiastic Shot and visited many other shoots, though he was never as adventurous as Lord Van

Temple who once saw a pike in the river and shot it. A well-loved man, Lord Louis inspired great loyalty among the keepers. His famous headkeeper Harry Grass recently remarked: 'Just give me half an hour in a room with the devils who killed him.'

Lord Romsey told me that the shoot was quite small in the 1940s and 1950s but 'when my grandmother died my grandfather was worried that he might be rather lonely and decided that building up the shoot might be one way to ensure companionship.' In the late fifties and early sixties bags were still only in the region of 150 to 200. In 1960, 600 pheasants were shot in November and 600 in December; the Duke of Edinburgh was a regular visitor then. The big build-up to 700-bird days came in the late sixties; the big day in 1968, with part paying Guns and part family, brought just under 1,000 head, but was beaten in 1969 with 1,200 on a double-gun day. The 1968-9 bag was 2,800 head; in 1969-70 it was 5,500 and in 1970–1 9,000 — a really steep climb.

The Prince of Wales was there on the very big day in 1970 when, as Lord Romsey said, 'birds flew very well' and 10 guns achieved the magic 2,000:

> Everyone had worked hard to reach that memorable number. There seemed to be nothing left to achieve in terms of bags. So when I took over I changed the whole philosophy of the shoot, especially when Grass retired. I wanted to do away with Broadlands' reputation as a blunderbuss shoot, grandfather's huge monolith.

Up to the 1960s there were usually only six Guns and everything was laid out with this in mind; but today, with twenty-one days let, the standard eight-Gun pattern is mostly adopted. But a cash input has long been necessary — Lord Louis always had two to four paying Guns. Lord Romsey: 'We now shoot many more days to balance the books. Our target is to try to cover all costs.' On the first fully let day in the 1977–8 season the bag was 545. Two days were let to the Earl of Westmorland, who had Norwegian guests.

In 1979–80 Lord Romsey had five days and seven were let, two to French syndicates:

> We shot 7,800 pheasants and very little else — just 26 wildfowl, for example. There had been a total decline of the wildfowl shoot but now we shoot some 600–800 fowl on the river and stillwaters, and they are all wild. We are well-placed with the Solent nearby. This provides some excellent sport and I mix this up with pheasant days at the beginning of the season.

Now the estate is working hard on conservation and habitat improvement. For example, agro-sprays are more strictly controlled as Lord Romsey would 'like to see hares become a minor problem again'. Now they are scarce, though as recently as 1960, 332 were shot. Wild partridges remain scarce — 1947 was the last time they were shot successfully. But reared birds are now yielding good bags. In the 1985–6 season, when they put down 75 per cent English and 25 per cent French, there were five partridge days including two of 100 brace, whereas in the 1982–3 season they shot just 139 partridges, along with 7,200 pheasants, 716 duck and 16 hares. Since then hares have not been shot.

A turning point came in the 1983–4 season — the biggest year, when the bag was 9,500 pheasants, 640 duck, 200 partridges; day bags averaging 400–500. With new headkeeper Bill Webb, Lord Romsey decided to change the entire pheasant stock to get better birds; with many years of inbreeding and cosseting, the existing ones had become grossly overweight and slow. Therefore birds were brought in from the renowned shooting areas of Norfolk, Wales and Yorkshire and already Guns have remarked on their greater speed and lightness. Further development became possible in 1985 when 1,500 acres (610 ha) of the 6,000-acre (2,430 ha) estate came back in-hand after expiry of a lease. Now Lord Romsey is continually experimenting with drives, even on royal days; in fact Her Majesty The Queen and Prince Philip were there in the 1985–6 season.

There are now four full-time keepers and one trainee — more than there have ever been. In 1955–6 the shoot cost just £1,400 with three keepers but the turnover is now over £100,000, with let days in 1985 costing £15 per bird including VAT. They put down some 20,000 pheasants, with a preference for black-necks, plus 2,500 partridges. The aim now is to provide smaller days than in the past, with perhaps 300–500 pheasants or 100–200 partridges, and the accent is on quality. But as there are more shoots now – average twice a week — the seasons' totals are up, the record being 11,500 head. This estate is unusual in that its total bag is now larger than ever before.

The estate is run very much on commercial lines today and everything must show a profit to pay for the enormous overheads. Consequently there is current expansion of all sporting resources, including provision of fishing and shooting holidays, with the

One-time Broadlands head-keeper the late Harry Grass (left) thoroughly enjoyed working for the late Earl Mountbatten

Game manages to flourish at Broadlands despite a constant stream of visitors

accent on overseas revenue. However, Lord Romsey does not provide accommodation in his house, unlike so many other stately homes: 'We have a holiday in the winter whereas Lord Normanton at Somerley doesn't, and the Marlboroughs at Blenheim are lucky in that paying guest Guns have become their friends.'

Poaching has been a considerable problem in this area with large centres of population nearby and high prices paid for pheasants and deer. The estate has one particularly famous poaching case from 1822 when Charles Smith was hanged at Winchester for shooting one of Lord Palmerston's keepers while he was watching game. The case was subsequently seen as symbolising the age-old struggle between oppressed peasants and the privileged classes, especially when Smith was given two headstones! One inscription recorded his death as a martyr, suggesting that he was in the right; the other, correcting this many years later, emphasised the capital crime of attempt to murder. Oddly, history was nearly repeated in the 1980s when a poacher shot at and wounded keeper Bill Webb, but in this case the punishment was more lenient and fortunately Bill Webb recovered well for, to quote Lord Romsey: 'I wouldn't say we are one of the top ten shoots in the country, but I would say that Bill is one of the top ten keepers.'

Born in 1947, Lord Romsey (Norton Knatchbull), whose mother Patricia became 2nd Countess Mountbatten of Burma on the death of Lord Louis, has worked as a television and film producer. His father, Lord Brabourne, has an excellent shoot at

Mersham Hatch in Kent. Lord Romsey started shooting at the age of twelve when he was given a 28-bore for his birthday, and now his favourite quarry are Spanish partridges and English duck. He also enjoys a little roughshooting: 'We always have a shoot at Christmas — great fun — a knockabout shoot — really rough, including moorhens, and they certainly need to be controlled.' His guns are Purdeys and Holland & Hollands, and the qualities he considers necessary in a good Shot are 'concentration, hunger, speed and good eyesight'.

Although Lord Romsey sees the future of shooting in Britain as being 'at risk politically', he is at least doing his best to harmonise the activity with other interests. He is very interested in nature conservation and belongs to the Hampshire & Isle of Wight Naturalists' Trust as well as the Farming & Wildlife Advisory Group. 'We have planted nearly two miles of new hedgerows and filled in many gaps. We will add to this until we have restored the optimum habitat for game and wildlife. I am pleased to say that English partridges are nesting here again, and last year seven coveys were counted.'

THE GRANGE

The Grange, 1901. Typical team of Gun, loader, cartridge boy and picker-up

Before The Grange, near Alresford in Hampshire, was split up earlier this century, Lord Ashburton ran one of the most celebrated shoots in Britain. It belonged to the age of huge bags and attracted all the big Guns, but has now faded into obscurity. Ashburton himself was one of the leading Shots of the day and regularly vied with Guns like Walsingham, Dhuleep Singh and Carnarvon for top spot on all the best estates.

Towards the end of Victoria's reign, Hampshire overtook Norfolk and Suffolk as premier partridge county and The Grange led the way with that Napoleon of keepers, Marlowe, at the helm. Marlowe was so highly regarded that even Lord Northbrook's keeper, Fifield, from the shoot next door, came over for advice, and he was an older

Plenty of birds at the Grange in 1901, when competition with neighbouring estates was fierce

At the turn of the century Lord Ashburton was at the centre of shooting society

man. Lord Ashburton's father had brought Marlowe over from Buckenham in Norfolk, where the natural conditions are better for partridges, so the achievement of The Grange was all the more remarkable. First consideration was to treat partridges as superior to pheasants. Then egg-stealing and poaching were rigorously controlled with an underkeeper assigned to map and watch every nest on the estate. Vermin destruction, too, was very important for the big bags were entirely of wild birds.

When in October 1887 at The Grange 4,109 partridges were killed over four days the shooting world was astonished; the seven Guns included HRH The Duke of Cambridge, the Duke of Roxburghe and Lord Walsingham. Lord Ashburton never expected to see such numbers of wild partridges again. The Grange had beaten Holkham's 1885 record of 3,392 over four days. Not surprisingly, they were even accused of cheating, yet all was due to good management called the 'Assisted Nature' system.

At The Grange every hedgerow and bank was watched for the least sign of a rat or weasel, and all the year round there were some thirty baited traps to every hundred acres. Also every sitting partridge was treated as a living incubator with each clutch adjusted to the desired size, those in dangerous places being moved to mothers where disturbance was at a minimum. Marlowe seems to have discovered the very important fact that a partridge must not be disturbed during the first twenty-four hours of sitting, but after that 'management' may begin. Sometimes birds will even allow eggs to be placed under them without moving.

The Grange did get further big bags, but World War I brought the good days to an end. From then on anything very labour intensive was on a shaky economic footing and it was not long before the great partridge decline began, the famous manors being further overburdened by increased taxation. Shooting continues at The Grange, but on a small, private scale rather than as the nucleus of high society.

These three pages from Lord Carnarvon's personal gamebook record the all-time three-day record pheasant bag (also, at the time, the one-day record), which was achieved on his own Highclere estate in 1895

HIGHCLERE

Unlike The Grange, Lord Carnarvon's Highclere shoot, on the North Hampshire Downs south of Newbury, has retained the star rating which it acquired towards the end of the nineteenth century. The 6th Earl, the extrovert character whose father was famed for his discovery — with Howard Carter in 1922 — of the tomb of Tutankhamen, remained a keen Shot until just two seasons before his death in 1987, and now his son (formerly Lord Porchester) continues the great sporting tradition of the Herbert family.

From AD 749 Highclere was the principal of many residences of the powerful Bishops of Winchester, and the renowned William of Wykeham rebuilt the mansion in the fourteenth century. Under Edward VI the Crown took possession and granted it to the Fitzwilliam family, but eventually the estate was inherited by the Honourable Robert Herbert in 1706. He was succeeded by his nephew Henry who was created earl in 1793, the title Earl of Carnarvon being a revival of one created in 1628 and held by a son-in-law of the 4th Earl of Pembroke.

Henry Herbert became Lord of the Manor in 1769. He cleared away the farm buildings which surrounded Highclere and constructed the large Dunsmere Lake. And by clever planting of trees and shrubs he not only made Highclere Park a place of renowned beauty but created an appropriate setting for a great shoot. He also enlarged and improved the house.

The 2nd Earl succeeded in 1811, continued to develop the park and was largely responsible for the vast plantings of azaleas and rhododendrons. Upon his death in 1833, his son Henry became the 3rd Earl and it was he who conceived Highclere Castle as it stands today, in later life devoting himself to its reconstruction. His architect was Sir Charles Barry, the man who designed the Houses of Parliament. While the work was being carried on between 1839 and 1842 a huge feudal fireplace and walls 16ft (5m)

Date. 27 Nov.	Number.	Highclere Wood & Redpoles. OBSERVATIONS.
Red Deer		Same guns.
Grouse		a great quantity of pheasants
Partridges	5	in both woods, a splendid
Pheasants	1700	show of game in the walk.
Snipe		In Redpoles —
Wild Ducks		H.V. Come 2nd time
Wild Geese		7PS 18½
Woodcocks		A 150?
Quail		H.C. 60
Sea Fowl		D.& 70
Wood Pigeon		Self 14½
Hares	1	...00
Rabbits	1702	
Various	16	
Total	3424	

A. Webster & Compy. 60, Piccadilly. W.

Date. 29 Nov.	Number.	Beeches OBSERVATIONS.
Red Deer		Prince V.D. Singh
Grouse		Prince F.D. Singh
Partridges	6	Earl de Grey
Pheasants	2811	Lord Ashburton
Snipe		J. Rutherford
Wild Ducks	2	+ self.
Wild Geese		1200 pheasants killed at
Woodcocks		the beeches corner. the
Quail		most wonderful show of birds
Sea Fowl		I have ever seen anywhere
Wood Pigeon		This total of pheasants
Hares		beats any day ever
Rabbits	969	previously shot + H.
Various	15	Total 10807 week R. 3...
Total	3803	Is also ...

A. Webster & Comey. 60, Piccadilly. W.

thick interlaced with secret passages were discovered. At the time the Earl lived at the beautiful Milford Lake House, from where many shooting parties still set forth.

In the season 1895–6 the Earl really set out to make record bags. Competition was so intense that his headkeeper used to contact the headkeeper at The Grange nearby to find out what they had shot at the end of the day, only to gloat if the Highclere bag was bigger. And over the three days 26, 27, 29 November 1895, Lord Carnarvon's party excelled.

By extraordinary good luck I was able to study Lord Carnarvon's personal pocket gamebook for that season, it having gone out of the family at some time in the past. It clearly shows what an incredible amount of time and energy leading Shots of the day devoted to shooting. To begin, Lord Carnarvon spent the whole of August at Delnadamph, north of Balmoral, and shot grouse on 12 days with bags ranging from just 6 to 106; his companions included Prince F. Dhuleep Singh and Prince V. Dhuleep Singh. The party returned to Highclere to commence partridge shooting on 2 September and by 10 December there had been fifty-one days at the 'little brown birds', many of them with just Lord Carnarvon, Lord Ashburton and Dhuleep Singh shooting. Pheasant shooting began with odd small bags on partridge days, and by the time it ended on 27 December the longtails had been in the bag forty-five times. Lord Carnarvon also shot in France that season.

The headcount for that all-time record three-day bag late in November was: pheasants 1,160, 1,700, 2,811; partridges 5, 5, 6; hares 42, 1; woodcock 4; rabbits 2,362, 1,702, 969; wild duck 2 on the last day; various 7, 16, 15 — total 10,807. The Guns were the brothers Dhuleep Singh, Earl de Grey, Lord Ashburton, Harry Chaplin and Lord Carnarvon, with J. Rutherford replacing Chaplin on the last day. The 26th at

Rabbit forward for Prince Victor Dhuleep Singh at Highclere, 1901

Laying out the bag

the Grotto was 'Rather a disappointment as regards rabbits on the Hill Peppingham and Warren but the wood full of game'. Highclere Wood and Redpoles (later Red Pool) on the 27th brought 'A great quantity of pheasants in both woods and a splendid show of game in the walk in Redpoles'. The 29th was at Beeches. Carnarvon wrote: '1,200 pheasants killed at the Beeches corner, the most wonderful show of birds I have ever seen anywhere. This total of pheasants I believe beats anything ever previously shot and the total 10,807 head for the 3 days is also I believe a best on record.' The Beeches stand had taken just 45 minutes!

Over 1,000 pheasants were shot on several other days that season. Also, on 19 October Lord Carnarvon and Prince Victor Dhuleep Singh on the warrens beat shot 3,082 rabbits, 6 pheasants, 5 partridges and 1 various — an incredible 3,094 head to two Guns. Lord Carnarvon fired 1,880 cartridges and Prince Victor just under 1,800; the former killed 1,559 rabbits, the latter 1,523. The total for the season was 32,354 head. The estate was then 9,000 acres (3,640 ha), of which the heavily wooded part adjoining the park was good pheasant cover and the rest good for partridge driving. Remarkably, the 1895–6 season was the first in which the new Earl had any reared birds, his predecessor having allowed the shoot to go back.

Much of the Highclere success in producing not only large quantities of birds but also plenty of testing targets was attributed to the new headkeeper, Henry Maber, who came from the Duke of Grafton's shoot at Euston. The 6th Earl recalled Maber as . . .

a big, florid man, a true countryman steeped in all the wisdom of his art, who rode a stout cob to enable him to cover the thousands of acres of the estate to supervise the multitudinous duties of the keepers. His language, while respectful, was colourful and direct. One morning, my father had begun to discuss the placing of the Guns when he cut in to say: 'Excuse me, m'Lord. Before you go any further I'd like you to get the lee side of me. Mrs Maber told me my breath didn't smell very sweet this morning.'

On another occasion we were walking up Lime Avenue and had just reached a particular beech when we spotted a young gardener, Digweed, who was acting as a stop. However, at that moment he happened to be relieving nature against a tree. 'Now Digweed', Maber roared, 'you turnip-headed gardener, stop that there dung-spreading and keep on tapping.'

Henry Maber was succeeded in 1923, by his son Charles, who improved many of the drives and taught the 7th Earl to shoot. He was a great character and much admired for his knowledge of shooting and the countryside. Sadly he was severely gassed in World War I while serving with the Machine-gun Corps, and in World War II he was a Lieutenant in the Home Guard. His son Basil, who still lives at Highclere with his mother, has just retired from life-long work as Senior Scientific Officer at Porton Down and regularly assists the 7th Earl on shooting days. The present headkeeper, Eddie Hughes, was born and bred at Highclere and has been a keeper on the estate since leaving school, apart from eighteen months when he worked his his brother.

For the 6th Earl the best event of 1911 — infinitely more fun than being a page at the Coronation — was being given a 16-bore, single-barrelled, non-ejector by his father. At first he was only allowed out accompanied by Maber, but when he was considered responsible he suddenly found himself on a stand alongside the famous crack Shot, the Marquis of Ripon:

> He was a very jealous Shot and he turned to me in his reedy voice, almost a falsetto, and said, 'Dear boy, I will give you one shilling for every head of game you shoot today.'

The effortless style of Lord Ashburton in 1901

Prince Victor Dhuleep Singh waiting for a Highclere drive to start, 1901

During the day I managed to shoot thirty-seven head and his Lordship paid me two gold sovereigns. However, there was an incident during the day that depicted the old man's character. A cock flew across him, at which he fired both barrels and missed. More by luck than skill I managed to kill it but one thing old Ollie loathed was having his eye wiped by anybody, least of all a 12-year-old boy. Nevertheless, he turned to me and said dryly, 'Well done, dear boy, well done.' But for the rest of the day he shot everything that appeared likely to come anywhere near me.

But the 6th Earl had plenty of encouragement from his godfather, Prince Victor Dhuleep Singh, and Victor's brother Freddy, who were frequent visitors.

Victor was a man of huge proportions, always immaculately dressed in spats. He had both barrels full choke and I often stood in admiration at the accuracy of his shooting which enabled him to decapitate low pheasants. Apart from his two loaders, His Highness would always take along a boy whose job was to carry a wicker seat, into which the Prince would slump, as no ordinary shooting stick would bear his weight. He was a tremendous eater and I recall a luncheon when he so filled his plate with curried eggs that the sauce overflowed onto the tablecloth. Once my father put at his disposal a pony and cart in order to carry him from stand to stand, but when he hoisted himself into the seat after lunch there was a resounding crack and one of the shafts broke. This almost dislodged the footman who was sitting in the monkey seat but, having overcome their initial shock, the whole party roared with laughter.

Sadly, the curse of Tutankhamen seemed to come true when the 5th Earl was bitten by a mosquito in Egypt in 1923 and died of blood poisoning. Unfortunately for the 6th Earl, although he inherited Highclere under the law of primogeniture, he was left with little else to pay the death duties. Much had been left to his mother, including all the

The 6th Earl of Carnarvon shooting at Highclere in the 1930s.(right) Major Murray Graham and Lord Cochrane at Highclere in the 1930s

bloodstock, the 5th Earl having set up the Stud Farm in 1902. But the 6th Earl refused to give Highclere up. Instead he sold off some of the paintings and jewellery. Yet he still had to sell the 12,000-acre (4,855 ha) Bingham estate in Yorkshire and some silver plus some of the outlying and least attractive parts of Highclere, cutting it down to 6,000 acres (2,430 ha) — 5,500 (2,225) today.

Slowly life returned to normal but all expenses were critically examined and when shooting resumed it was with a paying syndicate of four Guns. That lasted just three years as the Earl became more devoted to his horses, but in the thirties day bags were still often around 800 to 900.

World War II brought problems. The downs and Stud Farm paddocks had to be ploughed up to grow a succession of food crops and the woodlands were ravaged to provide pit props and larch for making landing craft. Re-planting started in 1947 under a dedication scheme.

The 6th Earl entertained many celebrities on Highclere shoots, including the Duke of Edinburgh, the Prince of Wales, Lord Soames, Harold Macmillan and the owners of many fine shooting estates such as the Duke of Marlborough and the Duke of Roxburghe.

Today the estate is effectively run by the 7th Earl, whose interests are widespread, not the least being racing manager to Her Majesty The Queen since 1969. Born in 1924, he has held many important positions connected with horse racing and breeding, local government and agriculture. He was a member of the Forestry Commission 1967–70, of the Sports Council 1965–70 and the Nature Conservancy 1963–6. His contribution to the general welfare of fieldsports has been enormous: founder Chairman of the Game Research Association 1960–7 (Vice-President 1967), member of the Game Conservancy since 1967 and, most importantly, Chairman of the Standing Conference on Country Sports. Of perfect character to promote the popular image of fieldsports today, he has done a great deal to unify the fieldsports world, to develop its potential for people from all walks of life and cultivate close relations with the conservation movement.

The whole of Highclere estate is designated an Area of Outstanding Natural Beauty, and the present Earl, as President of the Hampshire & Isle of Wight Naturalists' Trust, is very concerned with conservation. There are two SSSIs on the estate — Burghclere Beacon and Old Burghclere Lime Quarry. The former is a dome of chalk grassland crowned by an Iron Age hillfort at the northern margin of the Hampshire chalk plateau, the scrub element of which is nationally important; a wide range of aspect and soils is associated with varied plants and grasses. The disused limeworks exhibits various stages in the succession, from bare chalk of the steep quarry sides through chalk grassland to scattered and dense scrub. The site is valued for its invertebrate fauna, including the scarce small blue butterfly, as well as its plant life. The 7th Earl regards public access to areas with beautiful views as vital, but emphasises the need for good management and signposting.

The present Earl took over the running of the shoot in the 1984–5 season, that being the first in which his father was too ill to shoot. Bags have been averaging just 5,000 in recent years. Yet the shoot is very much in the ascendancy in terms of quality birds and atmosphere, and paying Guns are from all walks of life. Sadly, that scourge of shooting men, tinnitus, prevents Lord Carnarvon from accepting many shooting invitations but he still manages to get in some 20 days per season. He uses 30in Purdeys with pistol grips and is a very fine Shot, completely unhurried and elegant.

Lord Carnarvon, with ears protected, awaits the action at Highclere

The shooting is now let except for family days around Christmas and some partridge days. Day bags average 250–350 pheasants and 50–90 brace of partridges, and the host places the Guns. The 6th Earl always deplored drawing for pegs, saying that this hit-and-miss method could result in some very disappointed guests. Placing Guns at every drive ensures a fair share of the shooting for all. Three keepers find the worst predators to be crows on partridge eggs and foxes on sitting pheasants, with the occasional owl attack on poults. Partridge shooting commences mid-October and pheasants mid-November.

Highclere retains a magical air, the mysterious palace brooding over some 1,200 years of sport and history. The beautiful hanging woods and contours allow the birds to come over like dive bombers, and those I saw streaming from Heaven's Gate certainly lived up to expectations. Around the house it was as if time had stood still. The old game larder was still there awaiting yet another bag at the end of the day, the rusty hooks on woodwormed beams, row upon row up to the ceiling; on them a single hen pheasant, a jay and a squirrel from recent days, and pinned on the wall a few names of local people with orders for pheasants.

Lady Carnarvon does not shoot or hunt, but fishes in Wyoming as she comes from the ranching family of Wallops in Wyoming, who are distant relatives of the Herberts. But the two sons, Geordie and Harry, are keen, and there seems little doubt that they will continue the wonderful sporting history of Highclere into the twenty-first century.

BEAULIEU

Chiefly known for his interest in vintage cars and the National Motor Museum complex at Beaulieu, the 3rd Lord Montagu is also an enthusiastic Gun who presides over an estate with much to offer the sporting world. Born in 1926, he succeeded in 1951 but started shooting when he was ten. For him the attractions of shooting are 'being in the countryside, watching all wildlife and vegetation, being away from work and pitting one's skill against nature'. But there has been more here than pheasants to attract members of the Royal Family and other celebrities to shoot throughout this century and the last. Superbly situated along the Beaulieu river and the Solent, the estate is a natural haven for wildfowl, and the variety of these, along with good partridges and pheasants, makes this one of Hampshire's most exciting venues.

The estate, now 8,000 acres (2,830 ha) — 4,000 (1,620) shot over — 1,500 acres (610 ha) having been sold in 1958, has been in the Montagu family since the Dissolution of the Monasteries. But it was King John who gave Cistercian monks the site of the Abbey of Beaulieu and the manor belonging thereto. It was customary in the thirteenth century for both kings and abbots to own sporting estates, the first for the love of the chase, the second because fish was a religious necessity, followed by stronger meats when fasts were over; and the choice of the south-eastern New Forest could hardly have been bettered for variety of fish and fowl. Then, over some 10,000 acres (4,045 ha), there were all the blessings of fine agricultural land plus sea trout from the river; bass, mullet and oysters from the estuary; pike and perch from the 70 acres (28 ha) of Sowley Pond; duck from the marshes and game from the woods.

A good stock of *wild* pheasants was regarded as the root of Beaulieu's success at the turn of this century, many generations of birds having developed maternal instincts far superior to those of hand-reared stock; as many as 3,500 were shot in one season's bag of 5,000. Also, the long boundary of water has always acted as a natural retainer of game and a barrier to poaching. There were then 3,500 acres (1,416 ha) of woodland, with two sections of over 700 acres (280 ha) each, though this did make some drives very long and the number of beaters required excessive — up to 50 plus 50 stops!

The woodcock bags have been good too. In the 1880s, 33 were killed on one day and over 20 on several others. The 1899 bag was 146 — as many as the totals from some very famous Scottish and Irish woodcock shoots. The varied bag is shown in the figures for 1900: partridges 1,544, pheasants 4,045, wild duck 342, teal 57, snipe 70, woodcock 44, rabbits 6,439, hares 451, wild turkeys 18, pigeons 394, plovers 19, various 75. Wild pheasants usually outnumbered reared by 3 or 4 to 1. In 1896, 692 partridges were killed on 1 day and nearly 1,000 brace over 4 days. The wild turkeys brought off quite good-sized broods in most years and flew surprisingly well. But, as the Honourable John Scott-Montagu MP wrote in 1903: 'The covers at Beaulieu do not naturally lend themselves as a rule to high pheasants, and it is only by ingenuity and considerable care in cutting wide rides that the pheasants have been made to fly really high. There are, however, a certain number of open heaths and broom and gorse patches which are very suitable for this purpose.'

The Honourable John also began the family interest in cars and in 1903 wrote authoritatively on their early use for sporting purposes. When shooting wildfowl on the stubbles, a sport which takes place late in the evening, 'for the return journey a motor car is a much more speedy and comfortable means of reaching a late dinner or supper

Motoring pioneer The Hon John Scott Montagu and party at Beaulieu in 1903

than an ordinary carriage. Also, on rainy and windy nights the motor car can wait close by and not catch cold, as a pair of horses would do.' And for grouse shooting: 'It is obvious that the motor car will become more and more valuable to remote lodges where stations are at great distances.' On partridge days cars would not be worried by flies as horses were and 'lunch baskets can be stowed away beneath the seats, to be brought out to form a table for the meal.' After five years' experience he recommended a 'fairly fast car for the Guns, while another stronger and heavier vehicle is reserved for the loaders and keepers, who can start a quarter of an hour earlier in the morning and follow the guests home in the evening.'

Game carts, too, were his concern: 'Where only two or three hundred head are killed per day, a one-horse van with cover is quite sufficient. At Beaulieu we have one of these which answers its purpose very well for small days; but for bigger days, when from 500 to 1,500 head are killed, more elaborate arrangements are necessary. A two-horse van is then required.' And all game carts 'should have broad bands on the tyres' to prevent them cutting up the drives.

The present Lord Montagu shoots on about thirty-five days each season using a single-trigger Purdey 12-bore with pistol grip for most. The estate's fishing is let and he enjoys the occasional sea-fishing trip. His ambitions are to go goose shooting and have a left-and-right at woodcock, and the best Shots he has encountered are ex-world motor racing champion Jackie Stewart and Tony Ball, partner of land agents Strutt & Parker.

Of the 37 days shot each season on the estate (3 separate shoots) just 2 were let in 1985 to parties of 9 Guns at a cost of £2,200 each day. None of the land is in-hand, but none of the twelve tenant farmers retains the sporting rights. Bags now average 200 pheasants plus 15 partridges per day and there is 1 keeper for each of the 3 shoots. Shoot 1 puts 5,000 six-week-old pheasant poults straight into release pens. Shoot 2 has 4,000 day-olds reared under electric hens to 4–5 weeks, then straight into the field under gas and to release pens at 6 weeks. Shoot 3 follows this plan with 4,000 birds. French partridges are preferred to English for their easier rearing. Fox and stoat are the worst predators, but mink are also on the list. Bags have shown a 65 per cent return in recent years, when seasonal totals have averaged 6,000 head.

Not surprisingly, Lord Montagu believes that limited public access to the countryside should be encouraged but stresses that education is very important. Beaulieu has received awards for outstanding contributions to heritage education and Lord Montagu is chairman of the Historic Buildings & Monuments Commission. Conservation remains important and management of the shoot habitat at Beaulieu has done much to encourage wildlife. There are still 2,000 acres (810 ha) of woods and the North Solent Shore Nature Reserve covers 1,000 acres (405 ha), clearly demonstrating how shooting and conservation can coexist to mutual advantage.

SUTTON SCOTNEY

This famous Hampshire shoot, in the heartland to the north of Winchester, provides a classic example of the old saying 'If you look after the partridges the pheasants will look after themselves.' This was always good partridge country, but it was J. Arthur Rank (later Lord Rank) who gathered up the pieces and created one of the greatest partridge manors of all time.

Arthur Rank bought Sutton Manor and its 3,000 acres (1,215 ha) from Colonel Miles Courage of the famous brewing family in 1934. Gradually he acquired neighbouring estates, including Lord Northbrook's Northbrook Farm and West Stratton and Micheldever. Land purchases were complete in 1946, leaving the Ranks with 14,000 acres (5,665 ha) owned, but 15,000 acres (6,070 ha) shot over including a parcel rented from a neighbour.

In the Edwardian era the Earl of Northbrook's Stratton had been a noted partridge manor of some 5,000 acres (2,025 ha). The nesting ground was natural with a few belts planted and much of the land cultivated. Rearing only took place when nests were cut out in mowing, but eggs were changed around frequently between nests on the estate and with neighbours. Any eggs taken in were placed under hens and then under a sitting partridge when they 'billed'. Rats were the worst vermin — in the year to 1 March 1911 keepers killed 11,961; but owls were strictly protected. The Earl was adamant that 'it is undoubtedly bad for partridges to have too many hares or pheasants on the ground'. The number of French partridges was small and did not interfere with the greys. Partridges were fed only in severe weather and not shot after Christmas. In the best season, a bird to the acre was killed. On 13 October 1908, 7 Guns killed 1,066 partridges over the Station Road belt leading from Micheldever Station to East Stratton and on 2 October 1915 another 7 killed 1,042 but one Gun was late and received the normal punishment of missing the first drive.

In the thirties Arthur Rank set about bringing his estate up to something approaching the glories of the old Grange (pages 152–4). The undulating ground had large, mostly arable, fields bounded by thick hedges, belts of larch, spruce and fir and by higher belts of beech, and this combination made for high, fast partridges and an ideal partridge shoot; but J. Arthur Rank was still expanding his estate and still busily planting up specially for the game. There were, however, some wild pheasants — about 1,000 being the average season's bag.

Previous to Arthur Rank's occupation the shoot had been mostly shot by syndicates who had left a small unhealthy stock. Bags were 2,319 in 1935, 3,087 in 1936 and 2,152 in 1937. The Euston System (page 144) was still used on some beats. Hungarian partridges had been tried without success and to ensure a change of blood, eggs were now exchanged with friends in Scotland. In addition to the new belts, two or three remises of about 2 acres (1 ha) were put down on each beat for shelter and winter feeding, and a special mixture containing vitamins A and D used. The remises were planted with a variety of corn including barley, maize, dredge corn, millet and dari and this seems to have enabled birds to winter well.

Corn featured significantly in Arthur Rank's personal life too. He entered his father's milling business before World War I, enlisted during the war and ended up as a captain in the Royal Artillery, being specially released just before the end of hostilities to organise women's labour in the mills. He continued in the mills after the war and his particular business was animal feedstuffs. Rank was a staunch Methodist, lay preacher and Sunday School teacher. In the early thirties he decided the finest way of propagating the teachings of Christ was to use 'talking' films. This led to his creating the major film industry which became the Rank Organisation, but he also became chairman of Joseph Rank Ltd, which under his guidance became Rank Hovis McDougall. Throughout all this he retained a keen interest in shooting.

Lord Rank was an excellent Shot. In fact he had a partridge shoot at Tichborne Park for five years before he took over Sutton. He used 20-bores (two pairs in case one broke down) and in later life 28-bores. His 20-bores are still used by his grandson. Lord Rank did not have any sons, but his daughter Shelagh kept him company on shoots, and today uses very light Churchill 12s with 2in chambers. Joint Master of the HH for five years, she married Robin Cowen, who first went to Sutton in the thirties and was Lord Rank's agent there for many years. He told me of one January many years ago when Lord Rank was shooting with his brother-in-law and partridges were never shot after December. 'In the pheasant drive a screaming partridge flew over the brother-in-law, who promptly shot it dead. At the end of the drive my father-in-law asked who had shot the partridge — "I said no partridges!" The brother-in-law replied "I did, it was suffering from disease." "What sort of disease?" asked my father-in-law. "Galloping consumption", came the reply.'

One of Lord Rank's regular guest Guns was Sir Brian Mountain, whose father had also shot there. The Mountain family's involvement with Sutton, Eagle Star and the Rank Organisation was to prove significant as Eagle Star purchased 12,000 acres (4,855 ha) of the Sutton estate in 1975 when the Rank family had to pay considerable death duties. Eagle Star's chairman and managing director, Sir Denis Mountain (recently retired), continued the traditional shooting link with Sutton as a guest of Robin and Shelagh Cowen, but Eagle Star still runs a good shoot on their part of the estate.

Eagle Star now lets about twenty days at Sutton to American, French, German and British Guns at an approximate cost of £4,000–£5,500 per day. The company has also been active in its support for nature conservation, best known being its sponsorship of the wardening of the sea eagle project on the Isle of Rhum in association with the RSPB.

There were six beats and the Cowens retained the Home Farms and some of the best shooting. All their four sons are good Shots but the two daughters shoot little. Shelagh is an excellent partridge Shot and these birds are Robin's favourites too. He is on the Steering Committee of the North of England Grouse Research Project, the family having a 1,600-acre (650 ha) estate at Glanton, Northumberland, where they set aside an area specifically for wild flowers, plus land in Yorkshire and Lancashire.

There was no letting at all on the Cowen section at Sutton, where love of the sport always took precedence over size of bag. The pheasants are all wild and the Cowens never shot them till November or even December. The only time Robin removed any hedges was 'When the bloody DoE stuck roads through and I had to sort out the mess';

The Hon Shelagh Cowen lets her labrador cool off after work at Sutton Scotney

but he did plant many. From the mid-sixties, following the general decline of wild stock, partridges were reared — two-thirds were chukar-cross because they are easier to manage and give very good sport, and a third were greys. They were shot from the end of September to Christmas. The Cowans shot some 13 to 14 days each season, the average bag 1975–85 being 3,000–5,000 head (including partridges 1,238–2,038 and pheasants 1,137–2,964). The highest bag of wild pheasants was 515 on 8 January 1971.

Some 9,000 acres (3,640 ha) of the Eagle Star section are shot over, the whole being let to tenant farmers with a mixture of cereals and just 400 acres (160 ha) of woodland. Here, too, management of habitat for shooting has benefitted wildlife and plant life generally. Five keepers rear partridges on an open-field system using bought-in day-olds. This is supplemented by the headkeeper rearing from picked-up eggs — both partridge and pheasant. The partridges put down are greys. Some 25 days are shot between late September and the end of January, a good bag averaging 400. With four separate beats four consecutive days can be arranged for overseas visitors and there is usually a break of two weeks between shoots on one beat. Business guests are entertained on at least two days. The bag on this Eagle Star section has steadily improved since 1976 and in the 1984–5 season was as follows: pheasants 3,211, partridges 5,564, pigeons 70, various 32, hares 2, rabbits 2; total 8,881 head. But in 1976 hares had been 649 and rabbits 74.

When I joined Sir Denis Mountain and the ex-Private Secretary to the Queen, Lord Charteris, on a Cowen family partridge day in October, the atmosphere was that of an old-fashioned private shoot. Jovial, ruddy-faced Sir Denis is a good Shot and his interest is shared by two sons and brother Nicholas. He likes shooting 'for the fresh air and working the dogs. If anyone said come and pick up for the day I'd be there like a shot.'

It was a pleasure to watch good Guns on this friendly shoot. This was exciting stuff with little warning of the birds' approach on drives from behind tall hedges, though keepers and beaters did sometimes whistle to indicate a bird going forward. No pheasants were to be shot, but many a splendid curling longtail came forward despite the exceptionally bad breeding season just past, indicating just what fine heart this shoot is in and confirming the maxim of partridges first.

In 1987, the Rank/Cowen family sold Sutton Manor Farm, which was the last remaining piece of the original estate. Eagle Star continued with their shoot on the major part of the estate until 1991 when, under the financial restrictions of the day, they felt unable to continue to run the shoot in the traditional way. Since then the Eagle Star section of the estate has been let out in four beats either to farm tenants or syndicates. However, Richard Cowen, one of Robin's sons, still has the shoot on the Manor and Newdown section (1,650 acres, 650 ha) of the estate and continues to run it in the best tradition, as it was under Lord Rank.

SOMERLEY

Like that other great New Forest property, Beaulieu, Lord Normanton's Somerley has never lost the reputation it acquired in the nineteenth century as one of the best all-round shoots in the country. The one big difference today is that the 6th Earl, Shaun Agar (born 1945), has literally opened his doors to commercialism. Foreign Guns come not only to enjoy the excellent sport, but also to stay in the stately home and savour the whole experience as Lord of the Manor.

'The coverts at Somerley have a great share in that sylvan beauty which the vicinity of the New Forest unfailingly suggests, and are at the same time exceedingly well laid out for showing the pheasants', commented *Country Life* magazine in 1902. And there were the delights of the Hampshire Avon, 'a fat stream flowing through placid pastures', to provide sport in the form of salmon and 'a very fine lot of wild duck'.

It was the splendid wildfowl shooting, developed through a system of 'gazes' or 'blinds' which brought Somerley to early attention. Much depended on favourable weather and competent, considerate Guns who did not loose off at the first opportunity, preventing birds dropping within range of all. Ideally there would have been rain before the shoot, enough to fill the river but not enough to flood the meadows dispersing the duck and making a quiet approach virtually impossible. This should be followed by hard weather; then on the actual day strong wind, low cloud and a little sleet or snow. Worst would be a calm, bright day on which duck rose too high. A portion of the bank, 200–600yd (180–550m) long and known to be a favourite duck haunt, was screened by putting up a high post-and-rail fence a few feet from the bank and filling it in with greenery such as fir and gorse. The gazes were constructed in this so that the Guns could enter without being seen by fowl on the water. The fences actually attracted the fowl, too, as they provided shelter from the wind and seclusion.

It was essential for Guns to approach the gazes simultaneously, usually by synchronisation of watches when well out of sight; there were even marker posts at which each Gun should be by certain times. Once it began, the shooting would be incessant for about ten minutes before Guns moved on to the next stand and thence to the third. These were called the Upper, Middle and Lower Stands and there were seven gazes in each, Guns working up- or down-stream according to wind direction. An afternoon shoot might well follow one in the morning, and the pick-up was done both by boat and by walking the bank. On 3 December 1913, with such a system, Guns bagged 145 wild duck (mallard), 50 wigeon, 32 teal, 1 pochard, 7 snipe, 121 coot and 11 various — 367 head. On 16 February 1926, 137 teal were in the bag of 197 duck, among 232 head. The record snipe day was 104 on 4 August 1931 to 3 Guns — one of the best snipe bags ever — in an impromptu shoot over meadows bordering the Christchurch Avon. One of the pickers-up was Lady Georgina Agar who claimed to have 'a wonderful nose for finding dead birds in obscure places'.

Somerley's excellent gamebooks run from 1828, the estate being owned by the Baring family until the Agars purchased it in 1780. At first the shoot's game element was very small, almost on the rough side, but now it is predominantly a gameshoot with wildfowl on the small side. Duck numbers on the river now are down, as there are so many other waters to entice them away following arrival of the local gravel extraction industry; wildfowling probably peaked just before and just after World War II. Yet, with local motorway construction, gravel extraction has provided a valuable source of income for the estate. In the days of the 5th Earl (died 1967) it was very much a covert shoot with hardwoods and rhododendrons. Now the rhododendrons have been cut back and much use is made of game crops 'which father never used to do. Now, of course, we fly birds back home to get extra height'.

Headkeeper John Staley came from Windsor in the mid-seventies. He succeeded the very distinguished keeper George Cole, who was at Somerley 1938–40, returning after the war to become headkeeper with four beatkeepers in 1946. Cole left in 1973 to become headkeeper for Sir George Meyrick at Bodorgan, Anglesey. It was then decided to expand and go commercial. Now some 29 days (25 pheasant and 4 duck) are let, chiefly to American interests, including engineering companies servicing North Sea oil rigs, a helicopter company and a real estate company. They all fly Concorde and must have high earnings as in 1985 Somerley pheasants cost £12.50 each plus VAT and bags averaged 200–400. But altogether some thirty-two days were shot on the 7,500-acre (3,235 ha) estate (3,000 acres (1,215 ha) shot over) in the 1984–5 season. The sold days included four syndicate days but this side of things is being wound down as Guns find it hard to keep up with the cost and Lord Normanton is having to subsidise this heavily. He does reserve a couple of days for friends though.

On commercial shoots the big attraction is that Guns stay at the house with Lord Normanton. One American Gun likes it so much that he has been coming for nine years, bringing parties with him. They like to shoot two days — Friday and Saturday — and usually come over for one or two weeks, during which time they take in about four

Lord Normanton briefs the Guns at Somerley on a let day. Note his Range Rover registration

shoots. Somerley also takes Austrians, Germans, French and some Italians who buy a rough day in January when they like to walk around. The Normantons now regard many of these people as friends, which is just as well because 'it is pretty exhausting looking after shooting parties — up at 6am to make sure the toast is on the table and not into bed till 2am with the backgammon board always at the ready'. The house can accommodate up to eight Guns plus their wives (always a good move to promote matrimonial harmony), and this is a big attraction as at most commercial shoots Guns have to find accommodation at the local hotel or inn. One guest, however, restricts his party to six Guns so that no one is ever out of the shooting and they can shoot double guns. But 'all our guests need to book early as everyone wants to come back'.

Lord Normanton does not accept many shooting invitations: 'There is too much work to be done and I would be out three days a week.' And he is 'not a big bags fanatic. The Americans want 300 to 500 birds but over that is really too much'. He is more interested in quality. Shooting since he was twelve, he uses a pair of Woodwards and his favourite quarry, as with many great shoot owners, is driven grouse. He works very hard at making his guests comfortable and providing good sport through constant experimentation with new drives, which the regulars seem to like. With the aid of walkie-talkies he and John Staley are able to fine-tune the entire proceedings. Staley is assisted by three keepers and a trainee, and one of the more unusual services they provide is cleaning all the guests' guns. They put down just a couple of hundred partridges 'for fun as everyone likes to see them about'.

Roebuck stalking has been let to two Germans for nine years and the salmon fishing is let per Rod from February to August. Christchurch Angling Club takes the tail-end of salmon fishing and river coarse fishing, and the Ringwood club takes the lakes coarse fishing. As Lord Normanton said, 'One has to capitalise on everything nowadays just to keep the roof on.' Other commercial ventures include taking paying guests in summer, accommodating business conferences, letting the house for wedding receptions and even filming — for example, Burberry have been to photograph their collection of coats and the TV series *Mansfield Park* by Jane Austen was made there over six weeks. The house is not, however, open to the public, but the garden is sometimes opened for charity.

Conservation is obviously very important at Somerley with its wide variety of valuable habitat and there are two Sites of Special Scientific Interest (SSSIs) — the Avon Valley (Bickton–Blashford section) along some 3 miles (5km) of the flood plain, and the New Forest (Rockford and Ibsley Commons). The former is most important for its winter population of wildfowl and breeding wetland birds, and the latter as part of the largest tract of unsown vegetation in lowland Britain — the New Forest, with its variety of habitats.

It is certainly a beautiful area in which to shoot, and on the commercial day I visited the guests of a merchant bank were certainly having fun. Some of the shooting may have been less than expert with the birds, especially the deceptively fast gliders, often too much for the Guns. But conversation was very pleasant, mid-morning soup (laced with sherry or vodka) and a good lunch back at the house were both enjoyed and the day ended in all-round satisfaction, especially for one lady who quietly thanked John Staley for 'putting a smile on my husband's face'.

GURSTON DOWN

Few people outside the shooting world will have heard of Gurston Down, at Broad Chalke to the west of Salisbury, but within the gunroom everyone knows this as the finest example of a shoot created out of virtually nothing in modern times. The 850-acre (345 ha) estate has been farmed by the same Wiltshire family for over a hundred years, but it is entirely due to the enthusiasm of the present owner, David Hitchings (born 1928), who took over in 1954, that so much has been accomplished in so short a time. Gurston cannot compete with the likes of Holkham and Blenheim in terms of historical greatness, but David has certainly worked at creation of atmosphere as well as liberal provision of some of the very highest birds in Britain.

Much of the bleak downland was for long deemed of little use to agriculture because of terrain and aspect, and in the 1880s David's great grandfather was a pioneer of watercress growing in the water meadows there. The main valley was primarily used for sheep and poultry and the chickens set the scene for a rather amusing shoot story. One day it was decided to round up all the chickens but three had taken to living in a small copse and could not be persuaded to leave the trees. When the shooting season came round the chickens were still there and David's father had invited a rather pompous guest. David told him that there was a white pheasant about and he might shoot it as it was thought unlucky. So, subsequently, when the drive began and the chickens fled the trees like the finest pheasants, the pompous man watched for and bagged what he believed to be the unwanted pheasant. Imagine his surprise when he found a white leghorn pullet at his feet.

Another important source of income in the days before myxomatosis was rabbits. David told me some 14,000 a year were shot in the valley in the 1930s 'and at sixpence a time this was more productive than growing corn'. At the end of the last century few people had realised just what fine sport the high downs could provide if properly planted. Being scarce there, cover holds game easily, for birds prefer lurking under cover to the wide open spaces where predators watch. And as the land around is open for miles, with no networks of hedges or ditches, there is very little ground vermin, and it is easily trapped. The only necessities for maintaining the pheasants are a good supply of drinking water — for which dew ponds were dug in the early days — and the provision of food where cultivation has been abandoned. Some shoots used to make do with a few rough crops of mixed barley and oats, but today at Gurston David plants maize and kale. Also today cereals are made to grow almost anywhere and there are 600 acres (240 ha) of them at Gursdton, with 120 acres (49 ha) of rough grazing and 130 acres (53 ha) of small plantations.

Knapp and Gurston Farms have always been shot together, but little is known of the period 1900–20 except that partridges and hares were plentiful and pheasants unknown! Between 1921 and 1936 the shooting was let to a Captain de Mobray who, with a few friends, walked around after partridges almost every Saturday, the partridges benefitting from the large areas of grassland existing during the Depression. The first pheasants were seen towards the end of this period.

From 1937 to 1946 there was only a little shooting for David's father and friends. Pheasants were on the increase but partridges declined with the wartime ploughing-up of downland. Between 1947 and 1952 they shot only about twice a year, with an average bag of just 20 pheasants, 10 partridges and 30 hares. David took over then but no rearing was done pre–1965, before which time the hares had already begun their long decline, as had the partridges, except for odd years. Yet shoots were planned in great detail and even the beaters had instruction sheets. The only well known people who came were Sir Anthony and Lady Eden. David and his keeper Eric Penny drove some bushes for them on just two occasions.

The 1966–7 season was the start of a new era, with pheasant rearing on a small scale, and the wonderful thing is that David has logged all the important developments plus details of his private thoughts in the gamebooks ever since. Unfortunately there is insufficient space to print them all here.

The Duke of Westminster shooting grouse on his Abbeystead estate
The late Luton Hoo owner Nicholas Phillips grouse shooting at Abbeystead

Unlike the old-established great shoot owners, who have had time to learn through experience, David had to call in the Game Conservancy for valuable advice on a planting programme and planning of drives. In the beginning he 'followed the other sheep who believed the only way forward was with a syndicate'. But that lasted only one season as he 'couldn't stand the prospect of facing the next twenty years with the same group of Guns'. Today there is no syndicate and virtually all the seventeen days let are sold singly to individuals who bring their own teams, either charging them accordingly or inviting guests when they do not have their own shoots. This makes running the enterprise very much easier, and replacement of Guns taken ill very simple.

By 1970–1 David was able to note: 'It is now possible to invite anyone without fear that they would be bored. Lord Radnor said that "most shoots have one or two high drives, but with yours they are all high".' Local TV had already been to film his methods, and the sporting press, including *Shooting Times* and *The Field,* had complimented him with coverage; they were to return over later years. He was also already on that circuit of shoots which all those with the time and money just had to try, if only to say they had fired at 'the highest pheasants in England'. Yet David is fully aware that height is not everything. On the contrary, a stream of birds at extreme range is not only dispiriting and even boring for many, but can also lead to a large number of wounded birds. No, half his skill is in adjusting each and every shoot to suit the skill and temperament of the guests. The better you are the harder they come, but everyone welcomes at least a little variety and this David duly provides. He even adjusts the drives to provide encouragement for the average Shot where necessary. There's nothing like a couple of easier drives to foster confidence early on, but the cocky should watch out, for very soon they may be punching holes in the sky. However, David always ends with something to restore confidence.

The shoot has also long been known for its exceptionally high partridges, and in 1971–2 redlegs were introduced: 'For the English partridge the world is his oyster and a released bird might be twenty miles away in six weeks. The French partridge is entirely different — a mini pheasant.' The 'Frenchie' is valued for being much easier to rear, though many shoots have frowned upon it for its incessant running. But David hit upon the idea of rearing mixed coveys of French and English so that when the greys spring they take some of the French with them, thus providing the popular English birds and avoiding a heavy flush of French at the end of each drive. So he now rears them together from day-olds in the proportion 20 per cent grey, 80 per cent French. He claims that mixing them later is useless. In October 1972 David went to North Farm, Washington, Sussex, to study their techniques because they had pioneered much of the new success in rearing and showing partridges. He had been disappointed with his two partridge days that season and wasn't too proud to go back to school.

Watched by his American wife Whitney, Consolidated Goldfields Chairman Rudolph Agnew swings to take a Somerley pheasant which has just been missed down the line. Left is one of the riverside duck hides

(inset) Somerley – the Guns in merry mood after lunch, when even the dog dresses up!

The following year started badly when the blade of a scrub cutter David was using came off and entered his leg just below the knee. Eric Penny, at last full time, had to complete the rearing on his own. Nonetheless, on 29 October David was pleased to note: 'A day I shall remember for a long time to come. A blue sky, a strong breeze and hundreds of partridges flying high and fast. Wonderful, accurate shooting. The perfect day. A dream come true.'

Even the cock day is not regarded by him merely as a 'filler'. His gamebook for 1 February 1982 notes:

This is one of the few shoots which makes a very great occasion of the cock day — so many are quite content with fifty birds. It is not surprising that everyone connected with the shoot looks forward to the day. Sloe gin before we start and the same sort of lunch as the Guns enjoy throughout the season goes a long way to making this a special day. If you add to this a bag of over 200 birds and a chance for all the regular beaters and pickers-up to stand in the bottom of the valley as Guns and try their luck with the high birds, then you can easily see why they look forward to it so much.

The following further extracts from the Gurston gamebooks illustrate just how much David Hitchings strives to perfect his shoot. As he emphasised on the first occasion we met; 'It is all very well getting a shoot to the top but keeping a shoot at the top is a different ball game as the initial enthusiasm wanes.'

They say that a huntsman can never tell how good the scent will be until the day has started. I am having a similar problem in forecasting how well the pheasants will fly. The conditions today were bright with a light breeze and yet the birds did not fly anything like as well as last week. I feel that a bright sun must go to the top of the list of reasons for poor flying, with too strong a wind a close second. (31 October 1983)

The first snow of the winter was forecast for today but fortunately it was only a light sprinkling and by 11 o'clock the sun was shining. It is such a shame we look at the sun and say 'Oh no, not again.' Flying pheasants into the sun off Dogberry and Rowberry produces pheasants with an enormous variation in height. I believe that some birds when dazzled climb to avoid hitting something whereas others drop to try and get out of the sun. (12 December 1983)

. . . I am so thankful for the valleys. No wind and a steady rain all day would be a disaster on an ordinary shoot. One thing I have never understood about wet days is where do all the birds go . . . birds do not run forward so readily on a wet day but it still doesn't quite add up. Everyone today was more than happy considering the circumstances . . . for the first time the pheasants really started to fly; I honestly think that this late start is mainly caused by a very mild six weeks with, consequently, an enormous amount of leaf still on. Lunch today: steak and kidney casserole and sherry trifle. (12 November 1984)

In 1984 David produced a splendid card to mark the coming of age (1966–83) of the shoot, which gave full details and analysis of the bags over the total of 210 pheasant and 47 partridge days. Pheasants released: 64,570; shot 38,489; 59.61 per cent recovery. Partridges released: 21,945; shot 9,410; 42.88 per cent recovery. Of the 257 shoots only 3 were postponed because of snow and 4 curtailed through rain, fog or snow. The

David Hitchings gets much pleasure in helping out with the donkey work on his Gurston Down shoot

largest day bag of 369 pheasants and 28 partridges, in 1983, was just one bird more than the entire bag for 1966. The bag for 1983 was 4,498 pheasants (8,000 released) and 1,164 partridges (2,500 released). The figures include the joint partridge shoot with neighbour Colonel Godfrey Jeans. These figures have been exceeded only slightly since then as there is no wish to make excessive bags.

If he had his time over again David would attempt to make the plantings a little more natural. Nonetheless, from a conservation point of view, those done before the Knapp Down SSSI was notified in 1971 have been of great benefit to a whole range of flora and fauna. As he says 'the dawn chorus now is tremendous compared with when the valley was just a windy hollow inhospitable to pheasants'. Fortunately though, much of the valuable sheep downland with its steep-sided spurs and valleys and its variety of aspects — west, south-west and south slopes predominating — remains unchanged. This supports a wide range of plant communities including dwarf sedge, sheep's fescue, glaucous sedge, frog orchid, autumn ladies' tresses and bastard toadflax. The planting programme is virtually finished now, with a swing back to chalk-loving species, which is just as well as 'it is a labour of love to get trees to grow on just 3in of soil on top of pure chalk'.

Maize is regarded as essential for good partridge driving and David's system of planting strips of maize between trees has been widely copied. With pheasants, 'thorn is our basic thinking, but we see the whole as variety. The pheasant must have something for every occasion, for all his needs within his patch — somewhere to roost in safety and a wide variety of foods. Thus we have species such as conifers with horizontal branches for roosting and many berry-bearing shrubs for food'.

Of special value on the shoot are the connecting strips of cover around the heads of the valleys — 'like gold dust'. These enable the shoot to keep a finger on the pulse in adjusting the supply of birds throughout the day. If, after lunch, the bag is down, they can sweep more birds together for the Guns — in stages — to get the bag up where marksmanship has been poor. On the other hand they can hold it down if a party of crack Shots did well all morning.

On this type of shoot the main problem is to get the pheasants to fly across the valleys. Thus the birds are reared on one side so that when they are driven they naturally want to fly back home. Pheasants are great sun-worshippers, so if the release pens are sited on the colder north-facing slopes the birds will automatically work their way across to the warmer sides. They stay out late, too, and at dusk David often sees large numbers of them flying back across the valleys to roost of their own accord. 'It is very important to let the pheasant get back to his favourite tree with his tummy full.'

David now uses a pair of Hussey 12-bores on about thirty days a season. He has about four of his own guest days at Gurston and consequently gets invited back to shoot at a wide range of wonderful places all over the country. But he does not care to shoot with his guests at home as he 'can't get any enthusiasm for shooting something he has spent six months rearing. It's like kissing your sister'. He prefers to direct operations and get in there with the beaters.

He started shooting when he was twelve. A ferret was lost in a bury on the farm and had to be found. A friend said that if David got the ferret back he would let him have a shot with his 16-bore; so David waited for ages near the hole determined to retrieve that ferret, and he did. He then went to the farm lad's mother, who loaned him the gun and *one* cartridge; then up to the head of the valley where he persuaded his five-year-old sister to walk up through the scrub on the old turf towards him. Sure enough, as expected, up lumbered an old jack hare. Almost trembling with excitement, David fired his first-ever shot and was relieved to see the hare tumbling dead down the slope. And from that small beginning he has developed into one of the greatest exponents of pheasant shooting in the 1980s. His advice is in such demand he even goes to Europe to talk to sportsmen. Not surprisingly, he is working on a book on how to produce high pheasants, Sir Ralph Payne-Gallwey having written the classic on how to shoot them.

In 1985 a let day cost about £4,600 plus VAT, the buyers being mostly British and a few Germans. The shoot does make a reasonable profit; it has to because the land is actually farmed by David's widowed sister-in-law and two nephews. But David has succeeded where most others have failed. He has preserved a wonderfully relaxed atmosphere in a wholly commercial environment. When his shoot is at full capacity he does sometimes buy days on other shoots of the very highest quality so that visiting sportsmen can extend their stay in the country. His own favourite shoot is Wrackleford in Dorset.

Lunch is always a great treat at Gurston, where straightforward, hot, traditional English meals of the highest quality are served by Mrs Gwen Hitchings in a purpose-built lunch hut superbly sited high up in the valley. There is also a second hut for the keeper and beaters. This comfort is absolutely essential on hills where the relentless wind really heightens the chill factor. But it is also a beautiful place and, not surprisingly, just behind the lunch huts is the lonely grave of a local poet who chose to be buried there in the 1920s. What a magnificent place to rest!

WRACKLEFORD

As soon as I saw my shooting card I knew that my day at Wrackleford would be full of good sport and hospitality. My host, Christopher Pope, born 1937, Chairman and Joint Managing Director of the Dorset-based wine-shippers and brewers Eldridge Pope & Co, showed almost unique consideration in listing the Guns in alphabetical order. Usually a shoot proprietor puts nobility first, local bigwigs second, best friends third and 'fillers' last. In addition, at the beginning of the day, each of us was given a typed card listing all the drives, peg numbers and Guns' names. Such fine attention to detail showed that here was a man who not only cared passionately for his sport but was also most concerned about his guests' enjoyment.

I had been told about Wrackleford's exceptional sport by several very prominent people in the shooting world. Yet it is only in recent years that the patience and planning of the Pope family has brought this shoot as close to perfection as is ever likely in this country.

This photograph of World War I German prisoners planting a shooting covert on the downs at Wrackleford was found many years later behind a mirror in Wrackleford House

Unlike Gurston in Wiltshire, these Dorset downs were planted up for shooting long ago — by Christopher Pope's great-grandfather between 1890 and 1925. As is traditional, the coverts were given names commemorating notable events and people. One was called 'Great War' and another 'Prisoners of War' after the Germans who were 'borrowed' from the nearby camp to plant the trees. This has created a bit of friendly fun among visiting German Guns who now buy days.

Alfred Pope planted the coverts in his seventies, at a time when most men would not be thinking much about the future, though he did live on into his mid-nineties and saw some of the results of his efforts. He was, however, mainly a hunting man. Alfred's son, Major Rolph Pope, was hampered by the Depression and two world wars, so the original coverts were never really used to their full advantage. Christopher said, 'Grandfather died in 1951 and was of the type who thought it honourable to pay maximum taxes, so the estate was dragged down by our devastating taxation system and indeed there are still liabilities from his death over 36 years ago. He had also inherited late and thus did not have the same incentive to plan for the future.' Before World War II it is unlikely that a bag of a hundred was exceeded and these would have been nearly all wild birds.

As at Gurston, the success of this shoot's production of high birds is due to the coverts being well situated in conjunction with the valleys. Birds not only have to cross the latter but have also to go even higher to get over the trees on the other side. But unlike Gurston, Wrackleford's hills and coverts have acquired mellowed wild variety which comes only through age. Variety in sport, too, has always been a feature of Wrackleford, not just in the way that pheasants and partridges can be driven or walked up, but also in variety of quarry. Ground game has always been prolific, especially before World War II, pigeon abound in the cornfields and woods, and duck in plenty visit the Frome and its tributary, Sydling Water.

Langford Meadow, the SSSI on Sydling Water, is the result of a disused network of feeders and drains. In the seventeenth century the area around Salisbury became the centre for a new system of water meadows which were deliberately flooded to give an early 'bite' of grass for stock; buttercups thrived under this regime as they were distasteful grazing, but many plants were flooded out. Over three hundred years the system gradually lost popularity as it no longer became economic to graze stock on water meadows or sun-dried hay, but partly owing to the Pope family's love of the wild sport and beauty this meadow provided, this area remained wet while agricultural practice changed the surrounding land. As a result the SSSI now boasts many uncommon plants plus eighteen species of grass and eleven sedges. Grimstone Down is also of considerable nature conservation interest for its herb-rich chalk grassland and insects — a paradise much enjoyed by the young Pope boys when rabbits were prolific, and thus preserved. The bogland attracts a wide variety of mammals and birds including teal and wigeon, and there is a duck flighting pond nearby, though mallard are the mainstay.

There were few elms at Wrackleford so their loss was of minor importance. Of greater significance, as at Holkham, are the evergreen oaks which have featured in early and recent plantings, with their provision of shelter and food. Altogether this shoot provides an excellent example of the way provision of habitat for game is of great benefit to wildlife and landscape generally. No other shoot adjoins, and the beauty and variety of the Popes' land is in striking contrast to the barren hills of their neighbours; new plantings here on this exposed soil could not be made primarily for timber profit. There is a big and welcome population of badgers and Christopher Pope is 'very keen to see birds of prey around'. The land is rich with buzzards, hawks and owls. I saw a buzzard on my first visit and on a shoot day a barn owl came quartering over me during a drive.

But there is no soft option for vermin and all egg thieves are dealt with immediately. Keeper Roger Grocott has an assistant whose duties include river work — weed cutting, bank maintenance, stocking etc. The estate has 4 miles (6km) of river fishing, including the smaller streams. There are five beats (four let) with a single angler per beat, and the beats are fished in rotation so that the river is not 'flogged' all the time. The two keepers produce all the shoot's requirements of pheasant and partridge eggs, and then work on a part-exchange basis with another estate for day-olds, thus ensuring a healthy mix of blood. The rearing unit is spotlessly clean and business-like, a conversion of redundant farm buildings. The transfer to wood is made at six weeks.

Winter feeding is continued to encourage the wild stock, and special efforts are being made to re-establish the grey partridge in the wild.

Some 16 days are shot each season (including one for beginners and one for beaters) with an average bag of 185 pheasants and 30 partridges (record 330 pheasants and 265 partridges — separately), but the emphasis is very much on quality rather than quantity. Some 2,500 head has been the average season's bag in recent years.

The atmosphere remains that of a private family shoot but in the 1985–6 season some days were let at about £3,000 per day and the main buyers have included Belgian, German and British Guns. And it was indeed one of the Belgians, Nicky Emsens, who originally encouraged the planning and development of quality. They shoot over some 1,000 acres (405 ha) of the 1,500-acre (610 ha) estate, which is farmed by two tenants, largely the family company controlled by brother Thomas, who provides the game crops. One unusual feature is that the beaters have their own 250-acre (100 ha) syndicate shoot on the estate. Christopher Pope heads what is very much a family shoot — his wife, two of his daughters, son and most relatives all shoot. He is also a keen flyfisher and deerstalker and the family allows the Cattistock Foxhounds and the Ytene Minkhounds to hunt Wrackleford regularly.

On the day of my shoot a hard frost and the chance of snow gave way to heavy, unrelenting rain by lunchtime, discouraging the birds. Conditions were bleak for the Guns too and, not surprisingly, Thomas Pope said 'In the old days we would have all gone home.' I'm glad we didn't! Very welcome relief from the weather was provided by the superb old lunch cabin high on the downs. Earlier this century a sporting writer said of this:

> Right up on the downs is a charming little shooting-box, shut in by firs to shelter it from the wind but giving a view from its wide-opened windows right over the rich valley of the Frome, up past the wooded heights of Bradford Peveril, away to the heath-land where Hardy's monument looks defiance towards the sea. It is a stiff climb to this resting-place but never did its well-filled cupboard fail to reward the thirsty sportsman, though once the keys left behind suggested one of the minor tragedies of life until a strong arm broke down the opposition of mere wood.

And better even than the relief was the fare. Already sustained by a mulled Pope special earlier in the morning, our lunch of stew, jacket potatoes, bread and cheese, cake and Stilton, chocolates and cigars went soothingly down with dry sherry, wine, pints of best bitter and homemade sloe and plum gin, all served at the appropriate moments — and all by the side of a roaring log fire. Such are the times to remember.

One of the drives was Stratton Down. Tom Pope said Stratton means 'settlement on a Roman road' and indeed the Roman road still marches across the estate. Incidentally, Stratton was the last parish to be enclosed in England. With 4-wheel drive Subarus outshining the Land Rovers on some sticky patches, we sped on to Lawyer's Piece, great-grandfather Pope having been a lawyer. One Gun remarked: 'I suppose the largest wood on the estate is found here!' Birds flew particularly well on that drive, a few coming over out of range even as they appeared on the horizon; for Guns further down the valley they were very exciting indeed. Yet even down there one peg was in the bottom of a dip, and afterwards the Gun who had taken that position remarked, 'this was adding insult to injury'. The drives' success is in providing good birds spread both horizontally and vertically and well separated in time. We had one flush later, but that was in the middle of a steady flow and the whole day was a great mixture of fast, swerving partridges and wily pheasants which always gave their utmost. Finally we went back to Wrackleford House to thaw out with tea and whisky, and cake to restore energy. Shortly the keeper was in the porch with braces of pheasants for the Guns.

As I drove home through the Dorset countryside one abiding memory was of fellow Gun, Fido May — an enthusiastic Shot who is often out three days a week — standing in his magnificent ankle-length, Edwardian-style raincoat in torrential rain, *whistling*. There's happiness for you!

Wrackleford owner Christopher Pope (centre) with his son Oliver and keeper Roger Grocott outside the old shooting box high on the downs

MIXED BAG

Stratfield Saye is today a highly regarded Hampshire shoot, much of its success being due to the enthusiasm of the present, 8th, Duke of Wellington — Arthur Valerian Wellesley, born 1915 — who has been a good supporter of fieldsports and President of the Game Conservancy.

Built in 1630, Stratfield Saye house remains substantially unaltered and the estate relatively rural in character, but it is increasingly on the fringe of great urban development, with Reading and Basingstoke close by. Not unnaturally it has played a considerable part in bringing town and country folk closer together. The Country Landowners' Association Game Fair, the biggest country fair in Britain, has been held there, and the Wellington Country Fair is now well established. The area, though, is very different from what it was when the 1st Duke of Wellington bought the estate from Lord Rivers in 1817. Created Duke in 1814 for his military leadership, especially at the Battle of Waterloo when he commanded 63,000 troops against Napoleon's 70,000 men, he paid just £263,000 for Stratfield Saye from a trust fund bestowed on him by a grateful nation.

The present Duke found his 10,000 acres (4,045 ha) of farmland in poor heart when he inherited in 1972, but since then he has improved much. The Wellington Country Park was opened in 1974. A modest man, he said that by no stretch of the imagination could one compare Stratfield Saye with shoots such as Holkham, Blenheim and Highclere. But he added:

I, as a keen shooting man and conservationist, have done my best during my term as owner, to improve the estate in both areas. I think I have not been unsuccessful, and I like to think that I shall leave this legacy behind me, but I can't pretend that we shall ever have a great shoot.

Stratfield's gamebooks go back to the second half of the nineteenth century but according to the Duke there was

. . . a considerable hiatus between the wars when my uncle was in charge and, although a very keen shooting man, he concentrated his efforts, as far as Stratfield Saye was concerned, mainly on the rabbit shoots, and I would imagine during his years it must have been one of the best shoots of this kind in England. For his more serious shooting he went elsewhere, and took a number of expensive guns in syndicate shoots.

Records for this period are very sparse. It is only after the war when my father succeeded, and I subsequently took over the shooting, that there has been a major improvement.

Parts of the estate have been let to syndicates over the years and shooting did continue with largely military Guns during World War II, though of a rough nature. The fine covert shooting which used to have more than an air of snobbishness about it throughout the Hampshire of the thirties, generally gave way in post-war years to high, fast-flying pheasants from strategically placed crops on hillsides. Development of efficient rearing systems kept pheasant stocks high in the face of comparatively low wild-bird production under modern agriculture.

And the way in which birds were treated certainly went through a revolution. For example, a Stratfield Saye keeper's remedy for gapes in young pheasants earlier this century was:

> Three ounces each of these powders — bittaloes, hickory, ground ginger, rhubarb, alum, black pepper, cayarnne [sic] pepper, nitre plus two shillingsworth of Friar's Balsam and half a pint of turpentine. Mix the powders well together in a pail. Pour two gallons of boiling water and stir well. When cool enough to bottle add the spirits. Sprinkle over soft food once a day about half a pint to 1,000 birds. This may be used when birds are young but not so strong.

In Wiltshire, the Earl of Shelburne's **Bowood** shoot is well thought of. When the present Earl's father inherited in 1945, this estate too was in almost total decay. On 7,000 acres (2,830 ha) just one small farm was let, there were 800 acres (325 ha) of timber, 300 cottages needed repair and the main house had dry rot. The latter was easily cured by demolishing part of the building, but it was necessary to sell off outlying farms to raise capital.

Galloping inflation was the next problem and everything had to be made to pay, including the shooting. Bowood is not blessed with a natural shoot; it lies just north-west of the Wiltshire Downs and hunting is the local sport. The present Earl has run the shoot since 1963 and in the early seventies a new policy became vital. Commercialism was inevitable, so the estate established the sale of pheasant eggs and poults and day shooting to foreign and British Guns. By the time of the Game Fair there in 1979 the gamebooks just about balanced.

Covert Coat from **35s.**,
Breeches and Gaiters, from **30s.**

Fishing Suits from **42s.**

CHAPTER 10

HOME COUNTIES AND MIDLANDS

HALL BARN

Lord Burnham's Hall Barn Estate, near Beaconsfield in Buckinghamshire, is typical of those shoots whose nearness to the capital brought early ascendency in the history of social shooting, but which sadly eventually contributed to its decline in the face of urban and road development.

In 1985 the late Lord Burnham (the 5th Baron, William Lawson, born 1920) wrote:

> There is no doubt that Hall Barn was in its day a great shoot, but it has not been such since the early 1930s. Most of the land had to be sold before the 1939–45 war to pay estate duty, though by coincidence I obtained the shooting tenancy on the death of the late Lord Portman in 1967. This, with my own land, has had the effect of bringing back together the land of the original Hall Barn shoot.

Unfortunately, in 1986–7 Portman Estates quadrupled their shooting rents so Lord Burnham, who died in 1993, 'retired' to his own 1,500 acres. With the constraints of modern farming, he and his friends were 'very pleased' to shoot 150 pheasants on one of their best days. Today his brother Hugh runs the shoot in the same relaxed way, in some contrast to the syndicate which now shoots the old big drives and recently put down over 20,000 birds.

Hall Barn's total of 3,937 pheasants on 18 December 1913 is recorded as the largest pheasant bag ever made in this country, although there are reports that this figure has been exceeded by at least one greedy shoot in modern times. The Guns on that record day were King George V, the Prince of Wales, Lord Charles Fitzmaurice, Lord Ilchester, Lord Dalhousie, Lord Herbert Vane-Tempest and the Honourable H. Stonor, the last two being exceptionally fine Shots. The bag also included 3 partridges, 4 rabbits and 1 various. It was by way of a birthday celebration for Lord Burnham — his eightieth was ten days later. An enormous marquee was provided for lunch and the five courses took 1½ hours to consume, with twenty further guests joining the celebrated Guns. The result of all this was a rumour reporting the King as saying, 'I think Burnham rather overdid it today.' But the shoot was not a slaughter and respectably high birds were bagged. On the Parson's Underwood stand the tally was over 1,000. On the previous day the same party had shot 1,705 pheasants in Egypt and Dorney Woods about a mile away.

For the 1913–14 season 11,316 pheasants were shot, 25,000 eggs yielded 17,600 chicks and 13,700 poults went into the woods. This 45 per cent return was a big improvement on the 33 per cent in headkeeper John Hyde's last year in 1911–12. In those days many birds were sent regularly to the *Daily Telegraph* of which Lord Burnham was proprietor and given to the staff. For example, after the royal shoot on 12 December 1912, when 2,400 pheasants were killed, 2,198 were sent to Fleet Street for Christmas.

Partridge bags were surprisingly good at that time, approaching 300 on some days. It is said that Lord Burnham liked to take young Etonians out in September as he could rely on them to shoot a hen pheasant by mistake and he maintained that this was the only time they were worth eating. He gave up the idea on the day Julian Grenfell hit him in the leg. Shooting continued at a lower level during World War I, but there was a partial revival under the 2nd Lord Burnham in post-war years. There was still an occasional bag of 1,000 pheasants.

Fifty acres (20 ha) of the park were expropriated for the construction of the M40 motorway and general disturbance has been considerable. On the other hand, this has helped preserve privacy of that part of the estate south of the M40.

Hall Barn's day really belonged to the era of Edward VII, who looked back on it with great affection towards the end of his life when days of walking-up partridges were over and he really needed comfort and easy sport. He first went there as Prince of Wales in 1892 and from then on, except in two years when he was ill, he shot there every year up to his death. Indeed, it was at Hall Barn on 24 January 1910 that he enjoyed one of his last few outings, having had what he described as one of the best days he had ever known, shooting 2,400 pheasants with the Prince of Wales, Prince Albert of Schleswig-Holstein, Count Gleichen, Lord Ripon, the Honourable Harry Stonor and Sir Charles Cust.

Edward usually spent two days at Hall Barn, mostly arriving from Windsor with the Prince of Wales. The latter was a slow starter at Hall Barn, though as George V he became an excellent Shot. Lord Burnham recalled how the Prince, at the end of one day, sat in the study and declared, 'I can't hit a feather! But I have been at sea for a good many years, and one doesn't see many pheasants there.' Shooting began at 10.30am and went on until lunch at 1.30, resuming at 2.30 and finishing at 4.30pm. It was a special day for the district as well as the estate. Jack Westropp, a runner with the Old Berkshire Hounds, used to appear — decked out in a tall hat which Lord Burnham had given him, and which he kept to wear on extra-ceremonial occasions — to carry the King's cartridges. Lord Burnham always looked after the King very well, his favourite oysters usually being provided.

Edward showed his gratitude by sending his host a bust of himself and a beautiful silver pheasant, the latter 'as a recollection of the best day's shooting I ever had'. He advised his host to put the bird on the dinner table, and this has been done every Christmas since then. And on the Christmas before his death he sent Lord Burnham a handsome gold snuffbox. The King addressed the package with his own hand and the manuscript has been carefully preserved.

LUTON HOO

This well-known shoot in Bedfordshire has entered the commercial arena yet is in the ascendancy and enjoys sport as good as any in the past. The estate has been family owned since 1903, when it was purchased by diamond millionaire Julius Wernher, and, since the death of Nicholas Phillips in 1991, is being very successfully managed until such time that his son Edward, now aged 13, can take over. Edward is already very keen on shooting and enjoys taking part at Luton Hoo whenever possible.

The house was built by the 3rd Earl of Bute in 1760 and he commissioned Robert Adam to expand and modernise it in 1767. More important from the shooting point of view was the commissioning of Capability Brown in 1764 to landscape the park, which effectively conditioned the spatial development of Luton town. Brown's design added 900 acres (365 ha) to the park of farmland and woodland immediately south of Luton and the town has subsequently expanded in every direction except south; despite the sale of 200 acres (80 ha) of estate land on the edge of Luton in the 1930s, the town's shape is still lopsided. This is now one of few privately owned extensive parklands adjacent to a town. Not surprisingly, therefore, poaching is a problem against which constant vigilance has to be maintained.

Sir Julius made much of his money through mining interests in South Africa but today is chiefly remembered for founding the fantastic art collection which is still housed at Luton Hoo. This ranges from magnificent tapestries and paintings to enamels, German silver-gilt and ivories. His wife (later Lady Ludlow) collected fine English porcelain, his son Sir Harold added English furniture and his daughter-in-law (daughter of the Grand Duke Michael of Russia) inherited the important collection of Fabergé gold, jewelled and enamelled objects.

Lady Wernher provided the social ambition while Sir Julius was rather retiring and had advanced social ideas. Fortunately the age of invention kept pace with ambition, for had it not been for the motor car Edward VII would not have thought of travelling the twenty-eight miles from Buckingham Palace to Luton Hoo to lunch with his friend Sir Julius and return to the palace the same evening. Since then the estate has received many famous sportsmen and celebrities including the Royal Family.

The shoot has always revolved around pheasants, but at the beginning of the century partridges were also important on the 4,500 acres (1,820 ha) of loam on chalk, with 85 per cent cultivation to grass and the land tilled on a 4-year course of cropping. In 1911 headkeeper Ross wrote:

> Hedges with additional quicks planted, with annual planting of some young plantations in narrow belts, or in clumps with a southerly exposure, with a view also, if possible, for driving over. Where free from public footpaths, small enclosures of about a yard square are made of wire-netting, left open for six inches at the bottom, to allow the birds to pass through freely.

We find as many nests as possible early in the season; when the herbage gets long, much harm may be done by poking about, making birds forsake. I find the weather is very often unsuitable for doing much among nests in the early morning, and that it is better to give attention to vermin traps, etc, when heavy dew or morning frost show footprints too plainly, and visit the nests later. All eggs in dangerous places are lifted, and incubated to chipping point, when they are changed again with the sham or clear eggs which were given to the partridge instead.

I cannot say that rearing partridges has been very successful here so far. In this hunting country some of our neighbours rear a few partridges in wired enclosures of about 20 acres with a 4-inch mesh netting. It is true this helps to give a good stock, but the birds are found to give poor sport, and the expense is out of all proportion to the result. I do not believe in Hungarian birds for change of blood. I think they spoil the stamina of our English birds and make the stock less capable of withstanding wet summers. To keep our stock healthy we change eggs from one part of the estate to another, and also with eggs from a distance.

Foxes are strictly preserved here, which means a heavy annual loss of both partridge and pheasant nests. Where there is a fair number of rabbits the foxes do not trouble the nests quite so much. To guard against foxes we wire-in the young covers with 6-foot netting, sprinkle human urine, paraffin oil, and tar near the nests, and leave sprung traps, old and broken traps etc set, or iron hoops lying close by. Some of these remedies have been successful at times.

Hedgehogs are our worst vermin, eating eggs and even attacking sitting birds from behind, though I do not think they meddle with the young birds much. Rooks, cats and rats are the next worst enemies. The brown owl sometimes plays havoc among pheasants just taking to roost; and in this district there is a Dutch or small owl [the little owl introduced to England in the 1880s], nearly as bad as any hawk, flying about in the daytime and doing much harm among the young partridges. The kestrels are quite as bad as sparrow hawks with young birds.

Pheasants are mischievous if too plentiful on partridge ground, laying in and taking possession of partridges' nests, defacing nests, and opening them out for rooks etc to find. Turkeys are sometimes troublesome in the same way. Hares and rabbits give much annoyance unless kept well within limits. French partridges I consider good for nothing, neither for change of blood nor for sport.

We feed our partridges in snow and continued frost; also on ground where green crops or pasture-lands are scarce. Our birds sometimes suffer from gapes, scouring, and red ticks on the head. I believe basic slag to be bad for partridges, except when washed into the soil early in autumn.

Our beats are compactly situated and 1,200 acres each. We consider a brace of partridges for every 10 acres a fair stock to leave. Our stock has been decreasing of late years, chiefly owing to bad seasons, but partly from changes in crops, very few roots being grown now, and the corn–fields getting ploughed up so early, leaving little feeding ground for the winter. In a good year we have killed 1 bird to 2½ acres all over the ground; in an average season 1 bird to 4½ acres, and in the last three years only 1 bird to 12 acres.

At that time a great deal of land in Bedfordshire and Huntingdonshire was laid down to sainfoin and the mowing of it was one of the most serious causes of partridge destruction. The new reaping machines seemed to transfix the frightened birds to the spot.

Today on the 4,000 acres (1,620 ha) at the Hoo there are about 500 acres (202 ha) of broadleaf woodland, approximately one third of the land is farmed in hand and some of the sporting rights are let to the tenants on the peripheral land. Within the core area, where the great majority of the shoot lies, there are about 1,300 acres (526 ha) of arable land with approximately 350 acres (142 ha) of grassland/parkland. There are 2,800 acres (1,333 ha) of cereals. No hedges have been planted or removed in recent times but some 5 acres (2 ha) of broadleaved trees are being planted each year. Ten acres (4 ha) of cover crops have been planted for game, with more to be added soon.

Some shooting days are let, and the shoot expected to break even financially over the 1995–6 season.

Two keepers catch up the hens in February and some 10,000 pheasant chicks are hatched in incubators. Converted farm buildings house the chicks from day-old to eight weeks, when they go to release pens. Foxes are now always removed. Whereas the emphasis was previously on grey partridges, French partridges have been put down from 1994 and have been doing well. There has also been recent experimentation with new pheasant blood lines and the introduction of new drives.

ECHO ANSWERS.—*Short-sighted swell (to gamekeeper, who has been told off to see that he "makes a bag").* "Another hit, Wiggins! By the way—rum thing – always seem to hear a shot somewhere *behind* me, just after I fire!" *Wiggins (stolidly).* "Yes, sir, 'zactly so, sir. Wunnerfle place for echoes this 'ere, sir!"

BLENHEIM

Although its pheasants were not always among the very best, Blenheim in Oxfordshire has long been in the 'super league' by virtue of its associations with the rich and famous. The Dukes of Marlborough have varied greatly in character and interests, and consequently the shooting parties and the intensity of their sport have varied too.

Blenheim is in the record books, but surprisingly for rabbits. On 7 October 1898 they bagged the most rabbits ever shot in one day in this country — 6,943, along with 26 hares and 13 partridges. The Guns were the Duke of Marlborough, Prince Victor Dhuleep Singh, Prince Frederick Dhuleep Singh, Sir Robert Gresley and Mr Stephen Wombwell. The night preceding the shoot was fine with a dull sky and a slight wind; ideal for shutting out the rabbits from their warrens. Shooting started at 9.10am and stopped at 5.40pm, thirty-five minutes being allowed for lunch. There were seven drives, and if daylight had lasted another 500 rabbits could have been killed. High Gun was Prince Victor who killed 1,651 head for 2,500 cartridges. In all, 10,180 cartridges were fired. It is said that no one was tired in the evening and no one had a sore shoulder. Indeed the next day the same Guns killed 1,700 pheasants, besides a large number of hares and rabbits, and on the day after that, 614 partridges.

Although trapped rabbits were always preferred to shot ones for eating, rabbit shooting was a big sport among gentlemen in the nineteenth century and most took place in parks or park-like lands where bracken abounded. It was best to fence-in the rabbit shoot. Many of the large recorded bags were false in that not all the rabbits were shot. Some were killed with sticks and by the beaters, and others were cornered in such a way that slaughter was more applicable than sport. But overall, a good shoot was classed as one where the average Gun shot 200 rabbits in a day. Not surprisingly therefore, a lot of doubt was cast on the Blenheim record as it meant that 5 Guns averaged nearly 3 rabbits a minute for over 8 hours!

The story of Blenheim begins with John Churchill who, with the accession of Queen Anne in 1702, was created 1st Duke of Marlborough and Captain-General of the Forces. For his tremendous victories over France, Parliament granted him the royal manor of Woodstock with 15,000 acres (6,070 ha) and £100,000 to raise a mansion. There was also a Post Office pension of £5,000 for him and his successors. As with many other English parks, Blenheim extends over undulating country, a good portion of which is today wooded and covered with fine timber. As these coverts have plenty of 'bottom' in the form of rhododendron, laurel, snowberry and other warmth-producing shrubs, they are suitable homes for pheasants and offer the sanctuary necessary where a large head of game is to be maintained. And with dips or small valleys between the woods the problem of showing game well is made much simpler, for with the Guns in a hollow it is comparatively easy to drive the birds over them.

With politicians in the family, Blenheim was a particularly good centre for the Victorian/Edwardian socialite who wished to join the smart set's circuit and move up in life. When the Prince of Wales first went to shoot at Blenheim in 1896 the party included Arthur Balfour, later Prime Minister. But he was bored by the whole thing and wrote:

> There is here a big party in a big house in a big park beside a big lake . . . the Princess of Wales, the royal couple's two daughters and a son-in-law, two sets of Curzons, the Londonderrys, Grenfells, Gosfords, H. Chaplin etc etc. We came down by special train — rather cross most of us — were received with illuminations, guards of honour, cheering and other follies, went through agonies about our luggage, but finally settled down placidly enough.
>
> Today the men shot and the women dawdled. As I detest both occupations equally, I stayed in my room until one o'clock and then went exploring on my bike, joining everybody at luncheon. Then, after the inevitable photograph, I again betook myself to my faithful machine. So far you perceive the duties of society are weighing lightly upon me.

Before World War I things were done in great style, with twenty keepers in green velvet coats with brass buttons and black billycock hats, while much of the adventurous social programme was organised by the 9th Duke's wife, Consuelo Vanderbilt. The Duke ('Sonny') was a staunch Tory and Winston Churchill was then a radical Liberal, but the two cousins were good friends. Winston was a regular visitor, though he was not among the Guns on that record rabbit day, as is sometimes reported. But his father, Lord Randolph, the 8th Duke's younger brother, did once have the misfortune to shoot a pet dachshund belonging to a lady of quality. He tried to make amends by having the animal stuffed to present to the lady at Christmas, but this only made her more upset.

Lord Carnarvon was another regular guest of 'Sonny'. He particularly liked Blenheim and Lord Lambton's Biddick above all other shoots because 'each of the hosts knows his estate well and places his Guns and makes arrangements, as I have always done at Highclere, to bring out hot soup and warming, cheering drinks. These are handed round with a biscuit and a bit of cheese some time during the morning'. But Carnarvon also said:

> 'Sonny' was a pompous little man and I remember one Boxing Day, just as we were finishing breakfast and looking forward to a day's shooting, the butler came in and said, somewhat nervously, 'Your Grace, I have a message from your head keeper to say that he is ill and will not be able to come out shooting today. He wishes to assure Your Grace that he has delegated all his responsibilities to the keeper on the beat and he hopes you will have a good day.' Sonny listened in chilly silence which communicated itself to all the guests. He replied: 'My compliments to my head keeper; will you please inform him that the lower orders are *never* ill.'

Lord Carnarvon recalled how Consuelo had a passion for King Charles spaniels, housing about fifty of them in various bedrooms about the palace. 'They turned the place into a shambles and their smell pervaded the whole of the first floor.'

With the 10th Duke (John), usually known as 'Bert', shooting always took precedence over agriculture, and he wouldn't have sheep in the park because they would eat his cover. Like the present Duke, Bert was a very fine Shot with perfect,

The Duke of Marlborough plucks a pheasant from the Blenheim mist

unhurried style, though he was renowned for putting himself in all the best positions. One day shooting with film star David Niven he bagged a carrier pigeon. Niven said 'See if there are any messages for me, will you Bert?'

Unlike the 9th Duke, who had given most of his time to gameshooting proper, Bert was as enthusiastic over duck and snipe shooting as over the more orthodox sport offered by pheasant and partridge. And Blenheim had much to offer him as the lake attracts a large number of wildfowl during winter, to swell the resident population. In Bert's day there were several lake shoots each season, duck being put off the water by keepers in boats and giving good shots for strategically placed Guns. Quite a few snipe were then to be found at marshy spots near the lake and good mixed bags could be had. One day in December 1883 the Duke of Roxburghe, Lord Walsingham and the Honourable Edward Marjoribanks killed 106 snipe at Bleinheim.

When the present Duke (the 11th, John Spencer-Churchill, born 1926) took over in 1972 he had already been effective owner, on paper at least, of most of the estate since the early 1960s — the family having transferred assets before death to help reduce the inheritance taxation which would have taken four-fifths of the Spencer-Churchills' fortune and ended their reign at Blenheim. Today 'Blenheim is very much a business with a turnover well over £2 million'. In 1984 there were 361,500 visitors between March and October when there are 120 employees, and even in winter there are 90 on the payroll.

When the Duke assumed responsibility for the estate in the 1960s he assisted in modernising the shooting 'from the old system of broody hens'. Not surprisingly, with his family's history and nine years in the Life Guards (he joined from Eton in 1944 and 'thoroughly enjoyed it'), he runs Blenheim very much on military lines.

He began shooting when he was 11 in the late thirties with a 28-bore on pigeon and rabbits. 'We used to shoot grouse in Scotland and I became interested through my father,' and today his favourite quarry is grouse, 'really the only wild bird in quantity. On the other hand I also enjoy a hedgerow afternoon with a keeper or friend after a hare or pigeon. With pheasants I always think that January offers the best for then the cocks are so cunning and it is a real battle of wits'. He accepts few shooting invitations, but enjoys shooting for the outdoor life, being with friends and the exercise. He uses a set of three Woodwards made for his grandfather around 1907 and he used to shoot partridges in Spain quite a lot.

Actually the Duke likes foxhunting more than shooting and spends many Saturdays with the Heythrop, along with the Duchess. He says that if a good hunt could be guaranteed he would always choose foxhunting — 'it is far less predictable than shooting'. The Heythrop meet at Blenheim sometimes. For a shoot to be great, the Duke puts quality of birds first and foremost. 'Terrain is important too, and ambiance is a factor. Helmsley in Yorkshire is a fine shoot, but cold. The best shoot I have been to is Duncan Davidson's Lilburn Tower, near Alnwick, Northumberland.' The best Shots he has seen are the late Duke of Roxburghe and the present Lord Lambton.

Gundogs are an important part of the Duke's day — 'a lot of fun especially in grouse shooting. Pheasant shooting is not too good for dogs nowadays, with too many birds lying around. It is good to start a young dog in the heather where they really have to hunt for birds. My favourites are yellow labradors'.

The Duke has six keepers and always discusses a shoot with them the day before, 'and on the actual day we alter the plan according to the weather'. Some eleven or twelve days are let, at a cost of £13 per bird in 1985, mostly to overseas Guns. Poults and eggs are also sold.

Some 4,000 (1,620 ha) of the estate's 11,500 acres (4,654 ha) are shot over and a third of the land is farmed in-hand. There are 1,500 acres (610 ha) of commercial woodland (60 per cent hardwood) plus amenity woodland, cereals, dairy units, grassland and parkland. The elms were devastated by disease in the 1970s and much of the beechwood lost in the 1976 drought.

The rearing programme is traditional, with all birds derived from caught-up stock and the average bag is now 500 pheasants per day and 10,000 for the season. Some twenty-five days are shot throughout the full season, during which time the staff are often fully stretched with house parties for up to sixteen guests for a long weekend, Thursday to Sunday. The men usually breakfast in the dining room, whereas the ladies, less interested in the sport, recline with trays in their bedrooms. Shooting starts at 9.15am, lunch is back at the palace at 1.15 and tea is in the Duchess's drawing room at about 4.30. Dinner is at 8.15 pm.

When I went to Blenheim to take photographs at the end of November the cold weather of three weeks was giving way to mild conditions from the south-west and the result was the pea-souper fog common to the area. Conditions were poor for

Pernod boss Claude Foussier with his French loader waiting for a drive to start at Blenheim

photography, but we soldiered on hoping the gloom would lift. The Guns were wealthy Greeks and Frenchmen including Michael and John Chandris and Dino Goulandris of shipping fame, and Pernod boss Claude Foussier; and had it not been a commercial day the Duke would have cancelled through bad weather.

We started with duck over the Guns on the bridge where Dino Goulandris remarked 'the ducks can't see us and we can't see the ducks.' Everything was that much harder for Claude Foussier as he had lost one eye in a shooting accident in Spain — quite a blow for a man who had been in the claypigeon shooting finals in the 1960 Olympics. He has been shooting in Britain for over forty years and his little French loader had then been with him for twenty-seven years. The Duke blows a hunting horn to start and end drives and works very hard throughout the day to ensure that everything runs efficiently. He is meticulous about where the Guns stand and where the flagmen should be to get the birds up. As usual, I found travelling around with the loaders rewarding, but many of their comments about various Guns are not printable. We were in a Land-Rover and the Guns in a convoy of Range Rovers, and as we sped through the grounds we passed a number of visitors, even in that awful weather. Although the house closes in the autumn the park remains open.

Despite the still, damp conditions, birds flew quite well; any shooting day wants a bit of wind to make the birds lift. The Duke stood either as an end or back Gun and took many testing tall birds which are the norm in such positions. And all the while shooting progressed, his labrador padded around collecting shot birds. The headkeeper and Duke certainly knew their business and the day offered more than enough good marks.

With a beautiful parkland setting, this is a great shoot. There have been no special problems with poaching on the estate and the Duke gave the impression of having rather a soft spot for the old-fashioned one-for-the-pot man. 'But today, instead of a bike, the poacher works out of a car and then he must be dealt with.' He believes that public access to the countryside is about right:

> People should not get too up-tight about it as long as the public keeps to the footpaths. On the whole I find people behave well and we must do everything we can to encourage the townsfolk to appreciate the beauties of the countryside and the role of fieldsports. Shooting is something for which there will be a large demand and will continue to increase. There are now plenty of facilities for people from all walks of life to enjoy the sport.

There are four Sites of Special Scientific Interest on the estate so now it is as well the Duke is very interested in conservation. Blenheim Park itself is an SSSI as it contains one of the finest areas of ancient oak-dominated pasture woodland in the country, being descended from a twelfth-century deer park and Anglo-Saxon chase. The lakes, which were excavated and landscaped in the early eighteenth century, are some of the largest areas of open water in Oxfordshire and are of regional importance for breeding and wintering birds. Some of the stag-headed oak pollards may be lineal descendants of those recorded in Domesday Book and the invertebrate fauna includes three beetles listed in the British Red Data Book. The other SSSIs are remarkable for their plant and tree communities.

Never before has a Duke of Marlborough had to take account of so many diverse interests and whoever inherits will have to take his duties as seriously as the present incumbent if a place for shooting is to remain.

MIXED BAG

In recent years the Duke of Bedford's son, the Marquess of Tavistock, has really commercialised **Woburn** Estate yet first-class gameshooting remains. The Russell family was granted the site in the 1540s by Edward VI, who created the 1st Earl in 1550. Henry VIII and Anne Boleyn stayed at nearby Ampthill Castle to course and shoot deer with dogs and crossbows, the King enjoying the sport so much he authorised the steward to collect 201 red deer from elsewhere to increase the stock. In 1625 a royal warrant of Charles I ordered the Ampthill steward to keep the game more carefully.

The 4th Earl bought up as much land as he could in Bedfordshire and Buckinghamshire adjoining Woburn; the 5th Earl was created Duke in 1694. It was the 4th Duke who 'converted a rabbit warren of over 100 acres' within the park wall into an area of sporting, scenic woodland known as the Evergreens, which still provides the nucleus of the shooting. Gamekeepers have been employed at Woburn since the Civil War and the accounts for 1694 refer to money 'expended in the prosecution of deer stealers and poachers'. In 1806 the eleven keepers were each given two guineas at the beginning of March in appreciation of their labours. Pheasants were reared under broody hens in coops on the traditional open-field system which involved constant day and night watching and cooking of elaborate food mixes. Eggs were collected from wild nests and there are records of 'payouts for finding nests to sundry persons'. The habitat was managed for partridges too.

Ground game shooting was very popular in the nineteenth century, but gave way to pheasant, partridge and duck during the last hundred years. At the turn of this century shooting days were numerous with mixed bags of pheasants, partridges, hares, rabbits, woodcock and snipe yielding some 2,500 head per annum.

The 11th Duke's wife, the famous 'Flying Duchess', so called for her love of flying her own aeroplane, in which she mysteriously disappeared, shared the Duke's love of collecting and observing the fauna and flora and was a keener Shot than the Duke. She often shot alone or with park-keeper Lawton.

Today the royal warrant of 1625 is still obeyed in the preservation of all forms of game and the apprehension and prosecution of poachers.

Lord Rothschild's **Tring**, Hertfordshire, shoot provided an interesting example of advanced thinking at the beginning of this century: his whole system was one of artificial rearing, the headkeeper was also head woodman so that the interests of shooting and timber would not clash, and the aim was to shoot hard early so that there would be less conflict in a good hunting country. Each group of three keepers reared 2,000 pheasants so that there was adequate manpower for round-the-clock watching.

Nottinghamshire has always been a good shooting county but some of the former glory was lost with the breaking up of several of the larger estates in the district known as 'The Dukeries'. Fortunately, the Duke of Portland's **Welbeck** has remained largely unscathed. In Edward VII's reign this estate had some 12,000 acres (4,855 ha) of partridge ground, mostly cultivated. There were separate keepers for pheasants and the best beat was just over 1,000 acres (405 ha). But being in an industrial district, plenty of men were needed for guarding against poaching. Among Welbeck's best days were 739 brace of partridges on the Blue Barn beat in 1906, the year's total for the beat being 1,669 partridges. Bags rose from just 5 partridges for the whole estate in 1879 to 6,183 in 1906 and over 6,500 in both 1929 and 1934. Thereafter the trend was downwards.

At the turn of the century Lord Craven's **Coombe Abbey,** near Coventry, had been turned into a very fair partridge ground despite being on heavy, cold clay. In just five years, good management and application of new rearing methods took average bags from 25 to 30 brace walked up, to 100 brace driven. The successful experiment acted as a great spur for other shoots on clay ground in the Midlands, Essex and other counties.

CHAPTER 11

SOUTH-EAST ENGLAND

There are very few really outstanding shoots today in Kent and Sussex. In recent decades some have become established on a grand scale, but in Kent particularly these have been associated with the worst side of commercialism and even deliberate record seeking. One may even have established a new partridge record, but the damage done in stirring up anti-feeling is considerable.

Leeds Castle was once a great shoot but is now an ordinary farmers' syndicate. Lord Romsey's father, Lord Brabourne, has an excellent shoot at **Mersham Hatch**, but understandably wishes to keep a low profile as the region is subject to anti-sport eruptions emanating from the capital. Probably the most interesting shoot is that run by John Shipton at **Chevening**, once the home of Prince Charles and now the official residence of the Foreign Secretary. Here, extraordinary circumstances bring continued sporting success in the face of great disturbance.

Chevening was first mentioned in the King's Rolls in 1199–1203, but other records indicate a church and probable village before that. Eventually the Manor was sold to General James Stanhope in 1717 and he was created 1st Earl in 1718.

When the 7th and last Earl Stanhope died in 1967, aged eighty-seven, he had already made a trust agreement which, through an Act of Parliament, decreed that Chevening should be used by the nation. Firstly, it should be offered to a member of the Royal Family — Prince Charles was nominated, and used it from May 1974 to June 1980, though he seldom spent the night there. Failing royalty, it should be occupied by a leading minister of the Crown: thus Douglas Hurd is now in residence. Failing that it may be used by the High Commissioner of Canada or the USA, or lastly the National Trust.

Chevening's shooting history followed the typical pattern. The 4th Earl established most of the woods in the first half of the nineteenth century and this paved the way for the era of big shooting parties in the late Victorian/Edwardian period, the gamebooks going back to 1874. John Shipton's father leased the shoot and formed a syndicate in 1965, but things were very different from when the shoot was in its heyday in the late thirties. The woods had been neglected and gone well beyond maturity so that a huge re-planting programme became necessary, but John Shipton says this at least keeps him and his keeper on their toes in providing alternative drives. The major re-planting programme is under the control of the trustees, who have borne in mind the need for a good shooting income in the long term.

Despite being just nineteen miles from Hyde Park Corner, Chevening enjoys exceptional isolation — hence it is ideal for the Foreign Secretary in entertaining important visitors; this means that the estate is very well policed, thus reducing problems with poaching. Unique spurs running off the North Downs help provide testing birds on a grand scale. Some 2,000 (810 ha) of the estate's 3,500 acres (1,416 ha) are shot over, about 1,200 acres (485 ha) being woodland. Some 16 days are shot each season, including the keepers' and tenants' days, and bags have averaged 2,850 in recent years. Day bags are in the ideal range of 100-300 pheasants, and about a a dozen woodcock are shot each season. No whole days are let but some single guns are, as guests of members of the syndicate, the cost in 1985 being about £350 per gun. The two keepers catch up some 600 hens and exchange a few eggs (some sold occasionally), but there is no need to buy day-olds. For the weekly shoots they get together a typical team of twenty to twenty-five beaters, many of whom come from an urban environment and look forward to their Saturdays in the countryside.

John Shipton, of J. K. Shipton & Company, an independent members' agency at Lloyds, follows in his father's footsteps at Chevening and holds a four-year lease. He took up the sport at fifteen and now thoroughly enjoys 'a day in the country, the company and enjoyment of the seasons' after working hard in the City. He also relishes the challenge of running the shoot and has the satisfaction of having sons in the line. Sadly, they are never likely to enjoy the 'supreme' partridge days such as those at the Bourne shoot in the late fifties, which John remembers with great nostalgia. But they won't be doing badly if they escape from commerce to shoot some fifteen or twenty days a season as John does now. He regards Six Mile Bottom (pages 141–4) as the most outstanding shoot he has been to.

Despite all the upheaval, John remains optimistic. He, too, is very concerned about the large, commercial shoots, but Chevening is fortunate in enjoying increasing co-operation with the trustees. Some of the best drives have been changed, but innovation at least helps to maintain interest, and 'with persistence and co-operation this can remain a first-class shoot, particularly bearing in mind its location and despite its relative isolation from neighbouring keepered shoots'.

In Sussex, a recently greatly improved shoot is **Balcombe** run by Richard Greenwood, where the woods are managed largely for pheasant shooting, yet they consistently win prizes for forestry. **North Farm** at Washington, owned by the Gorring family, is where the Game Conservancy did much of their Partridge Survival Project work. This was the first shoot in the UK to develop redleg partridge shooting properly. **Cowdray** has always had a good shoot and so too has **Whiligh**, where the land has been in the Courthorpe family since the Norman Conquest, if not earlier.

More famous was **Wadhurst Park** where over 1,652 hand-reared duck were killed on a single day in 1909 when the guests included the Prince of Wales (later George V). He was entertained by the Muriettas, but it was the thirty-year occupation of Julius Drewe which got things going. At the end of the twenties Mr Grant Maclean took over, the days of duck released from bags had been outlawed and the shoot became truly sporting. The greatest asset on the 1,820-acre (730 ha) estate was the ¾ mile (1.2 km) long, 33-acre (13 ha) artificial Great Lake, and it took considerable work on the 550 acres (222.5 ha) of woodland with steep hillsides and deep valleys to get the pheasant bag up. With little arable, it was never partridge country. In 1938 they shot 1,100 out of 1,300 duck put to water. At the time Mr Maclean said, 'It is sometimes amusing to see people who shoot really well at partridges and pheasants making ambitious shots at duck which are quite out of reach.' After two or three duck days each season he would turn his attention to pheasants, but even on pheasant days the number of duck bagged was considerable because of the many duck pits in the pheasant coverts.

The problem of showing only a modest proportion of pheasants reared in large, hilly coverts was also evident at the **Worth Park** shoot of Mrs Montefiore at the turn of the century. But, as in Wales and the West of England, these deep Sussex woods showed fine sport in beautiful surroundings, none of which were laid out specially for game. With plenty of woodcock around to inject excitement, and frequently uneven footing, a Gun has always to be particularly safety conscious in such country.

Adjacent to 'Glorious Goodwood', is **West Dean**, one-time home of the famous Anglo-American shooting host Willie James, who entertained King Edward VII. In fact the James's only son, born in 1907, was duly christened Edward after his royal godfather.

Part of the estate was specifically planted up for shooting by Willie James or his predecessor. Big bags were subsequently obtained and West Dean became fashionable. Edward VII stayed regularly for partridge shooting in October and pheasant shooting in November, in each case for about three days at a time. He contributed to day bags of 333 partridges in 1909 and 1,430 pheasants a month later. All the Guns were crack Shots and included the Honourable Harry Stonor. The nineteen keepers reared heavily, but even so they used to catch up and despatch a quantity of pheasants the day before Edward VII was due to shoot. The corpses were hidden in the undergrowth behind the King's stand, the idea being that if the King fired, say, a hundred cartridges, the pickers-up could gather and lay out 99 birds at His Majesty's feet. Other guests included the Czar of Russia, George V as Prince of Wales, King Alfonso of Spain and Prince Francis of Teck, who turned up at many other shoots. In November 1901, the Grand Duke Michael of Russia contributed to bags of 525, 878 and 674 pheasants on three consecutive days, though King Alfonso shared more the following year.

When Willie James died before World War I, Sir James Horlick leased the shooting, and standards continued very high indeed, with rearing on a grand scale, some eggs being picked up, others produced in an aviary and still more bought in. A keeper often worked in the rearing field from 6.30am to 10pm for 16s a week if single, or 22s if married.

The eccentric Edward James was not a shooting man but a patron of the arts and famous collector of Impressionist paintings. Brilliantly far-sighted, among the many who benefited from his munificence and encouragement were the late Poet Laureate Sir John Betjeman — whose poems were first published by the James Press — and Salvador Dali. He was briefly married to the dancer Tilly Losch, who was also unsuccessfully married to Lord Carnarvon, owner of the great Highclere shoot. Edward was also devoted to his collection of exotic golden and silver pheasants, many living wild.

From 1949 to 1969 the shooting on the greater part of the estate was leased to Freddie Standfield, who ran a syndicate whose largest bag was about 200, but the quality remained very high.

CHAPTER 12

WALES AND THE WEST

On the one hand this region suffers from high rainfall which does not suit gamebirds, but on the other it has the terrain to present birds in the best possible way. There were once some truly great shoots in Wales, in every sense, but most are now shoestring affairs. The quality is certainly there, and great variety, but quantity is lacking and it seems very little is being done to develop potential. This is especially surprising when one considers how close Wales is to centres of population in England.

Most preserved shoots lie in the north and south along the Welsh borders; the main central massif is largely undeveloped, the very large area of grazing land partly accounting for this. The majority of partridge and pheasant shoots are in the drier grain-growing counties of Dyfed, Clwyd and Powys.

Rough and DIY shoots are very common in Wales and it is often very difficult to get sufficient land together to form a sizeable game shoot. Also lack of vermin control is a handicap. Partridge shooting is insignificant in Wales and over-grazing of sheep and afforestation have cut grouse bags right back on the rapidly disappearing grouse moors. On the other hand, there is good woodcock and snipe shooting, an increase in blackgame in some areas, and plenty of duck. Anglesey and Pembrokeshire, both forming important stepping stones on migration routes, have always provided a particularly fine variety. And there is no doubt that the high-flying pheasants of the Welsh valleys deserve their reputation. Many people would prefer to shoot six of these fast, wild birds in spectacular scenery than sixty in a comparatively dull Home Counties' park.

Devon and Cornwall are mostly counties of very small fields with many large fences and hedgerows so that partridge shooting has generally taken a back seat — flushed coveys simply disappear over the fence out of view and driving is most difficult. A whole new system with teams of 'drivers-in' as well as beaters had to be devised. The former 'collect' coveys from stubbles and grass and urge them into fields of roots where the beaters proper work a short drive to the Guns. While the drive is on, the 'drivers-in' are working another area; but they must not be too far ahead, especially when the roots are wet, for the birds will leave such fields rapidly. There are good birds in Devon, however, especially where the hills open up more in the manner of Dorset.

L LANGEDWYN AND RUABON

For many years, these two famous shoots belonged to one of Britain's great sporting gentlemen, the late Col Sir Watkin Williams-Wynn, 1904–88. Probably best known as a foxhunter, having been Master of the pack bearing his name from 1946, he was also a keen game shooter from the age of fourteen, regularly fishing for salmon and trout, and stalking deer. He is succeeded by his son David, another keen fieldsportsman.

Llangedwyn is 5,000 acres (2,025 ha) and Ruabon 7,000 (2,830) but the estate, in the family for some 250 years, was larger before death duties claimed a slice on Sir Watkin's taking over in 1949. The heyday of the shoots, near Oswestry, was 1900–39. Both world wars had a particularly disastrous effect on the scale of operations and things were never the same after 1945. Shortly before his death, Sir Watkin told me:

> I have never had the finance to run the shooting alone since I returned from the war. I have always had a number of personal friends to share it and contribute to the costs and I keep some of the guns for myself. There are four beats at Llangedwyn and two days driving on the moor. In 1975 I let one beat at Llangedwyn and in 1985 I let another. In 1955 three of the four keepers retired with 150 years service between them! I still have the home beat which will provide two separate days of first-class shooting. I do not feel equal to starting another large enterprise at my age.

In 1985 the approximate cost of a let day was £2,000 and the takers were Austrians and Italians.

BROTHERLY CANDOUR.—*Jack (to lady, come out to lunch).* "Are you coming with the guns this afternoon, Miss Maud?" *Miss Maud.* "I would, but I don't think I should like to see a lot of poor birds shot!" *Jack.* "Oh, if you go with Fred, your feelings will be entirely spared!"

Some of the land is farmed in-hand and all the sporting rights are retained. There are 650 acres (265 ha) of mixed woodland, some 200 acres (80 ha) having been replanted since the war. Ruabon Hill is a Site of Special Scientific Interest (SSSI). The hanging coverts, hills and dingles are both good for game and good for wildlife generally.

Grouse, of course, vary greatly with the season, but 40 brace is a very typical bag and 20 days of 100–200 pheasants in a season bring a fairly steady 2,000–2,500 head. There are 10 grouse days and 3 duck days bringing seasonal totals of some 700 and 100 respectively. Pheasant hens are caught up and some 4,000 birds put down. Cocks are changed with neighbours and some 500 eggs occasionally bought. Sometimes eggs and poults are sold. There are no partridges.

Llangedwyn and Ruabon Hill are not hunted but at Wynnstay, on low ground, foxes are always spared for the Hunt. Crows, stoats and mink are other serious pests, and the carrion crow is probably worst of all.

Sir Watkin's enjoyment was in 'outwitting the quarry, observing nature and working my dogs.' He really enjoyed working his springer spaniels — 'I have the fifth generation since the war.' His favourite quarry was grouse and, apart from a 16-bore when he was a boy, he 'never used anything else other than a pair of Charles Lancaster 28-inch 12-bores left to me by someone killed at the Battle of Mons in 1914'.

The following statistics give some idea of bags obtained in earlier days. When Mr Wynne Corrie took over the tenancy of the 7,000 acres of Ruabon in 1898 the bag was just 787, but over the next 10 years was never less than 2,189 and in 1911 reached 6,682 — 42,901 birds in 11 years. The best day was 781 brace.

WESTON PARK

Although Weston Park, seat of the Earls of Bradford for over 300 years, is now owned by a charitable foundation, the 7th Earl has retained a lease of the shooting rights within the Park and the family still owns some 12,500 acres (5,000 ha) at Weston-under-Lizard, on the border between Shropshire and Staffordshire. Ownership may have changed, but this remains one of the classic English shoots.

After gaining a degree in agriculture at Cambridge and a spell of farming in Australia, where the family owned land, Lord Bradford returned to England where his passion for good food and wine lured him into catering. He earned a reputation as a gourmet chef and his Henrietta Street restaurant, Porters, continues to produce superb English cuisine. In 1985 his book *The Eccentric Cookbook* was published. This includes a wild range of recipes from the Roman, Apicius, on how to cook snails, flamingos and ostriches to broadcaster Terry Wogan's 'Murphy's Revenge'.

At Weston Lord Bradford has created what he describes as 'an oasis in a gastronomic desert', and regularly holds gourmet dinners in the stately dining room. Residential shooting parties have long been able to enjoy the sumptuous delights of this magnificent hospitality.

Born in 1947 the Earl took over on the death of his father in 1981 and is continuing the revitalisation of the estate including considerable re-planting of neglected coverts. At the turn of the century the park itself provided excellent days on about 1,000 acres (405 ha), the best stands often being at Newport Plantation. There was also generally reasonable partridge shooting over the estate.

He himself took up shooting at the age of seven under the influence of his father, a very keen Shot: 'He made it look easy. He and Francis Stafford are the two best Shots I have seen.' His favourite quarry are pigeons and rabbits and he shoots a total of thirty or forty days a season with two 20-bores, one Atkin and one Lang. For him the quality of sport is important, but so too is the size of the bag: 'I hate wasting a day for very little.' Unlike some owners who are obsessed with providing very high birds, he has the right attitude in wanting to provide variety, with snapshooting and unusual drives as well. In common with many shoot owners, he would like to see the pheasant shooting season changed to 1 November – 15 February or so, but most unusually he would like to see woodcock protected.

Up to 12 days are let at Weston, including rough. In 1986 the cost was £15 per bird including VAT, which Lord Bradford believes should be taken off such sport. The shooting shows a small profit. Day bags range from 75 to 450 on average and there is just 1 keeper with a young assistant, with only about 15 beaters. Some 15 or 16 days are shot each season. No game crops are planted, there are 1,500 acres (610 ha) of woodland and none of the tenant farmers has sporting rights. This is a beautiful estate with a wide variety of wildlife.

As everywhere, foreign Guns are regarded with suspicion over safety and the wide range of species they want to shoot. On one occasion a party of Germans accidentally shot three beaters and one loader. Lord Bradford told me: 'The next day the leader of the shoot came up to me and complained — "Alzo, ve did not have zuch good shootink today, zere ver not enough beaters." How I resisted saying: If you had not shot so many yesterday . . !'

MILTON'S (EXMOOR)

Until 1988 this shoot near Dulverton in Somerset was a very interesting example of a purely commercial operation in an area which does not naturally hold much game. Alan Milton's enthusiasm and determination developed great sport for the expert in beautiful surroundings and the shoot's reputation was well deserved. But in later years financial constraints brought inevitable sacrifice of quality.

Most of the 2,000 acres (810 ha) shot over belong to Christopher Thomas-Everard whose family has owned the land since 1086. He does not shoot and the family interest waned when two sons and one son-in-law were killed in World War I. The earliest shooting records are from 1883, but when Alan Milton took over in 1974 there had been no shooting since 1937; it was thus a tribute to his organisation, and testimony to the shooting grapevine, that so many big names attended Milton's Exmoor Shoots Ltd in so short a time. These included Captain Mark Phillips, Prince Bernhardt of the Netherlands, Prince Michael of Kent, Prince Lichtenstein, the Duke of Westminster, the Duke of Roxburghe, the Grand Duke of Luxembourg, England cricketer Ian Botham ('a competent Shot') and showjumper David Broome.

Born in north Devon in 1932, Alan Milton followed in his father's farming footsteps until the age of twenty-seven when he became a forage merchant. He started to buy and sell Land-Rovers, and eventually sold the forage business to his brother and continued the motor side, becoming a main Subaru dealer. Alan shot down-the-line clay pigeons for England in 1961 and became captain of the England team in 1977. He won many titles.

Under Alan Milton this shoot was run as a major business rather than as a commercial venture simply to bolster other income. Only 6 of 60–70 days per season were not let to wealthy clients including property developers, bankers, oilmen, landowners and companies who came from America, the Continent and all over Britain and who paid, in 1985, £4,000–£5,000 for a day of 400–600 birds (record 685 pheasants) — a remarkable statistic as there are no wild birds, the land rising to 1,300ft (400m) above sea level being too wet and cold for successful breeding.

There were seven keepers (now three) including the head. All the partridges and pheasants were bought as $6\frac{1}{2}$-week-old poults. The partridges were all redlegs and chukar crosses (now all redlegs) — the natural choice for this type of shooting as these species are much more controllable than greys and will flush separately and higher. With them the shoot got a much higher return on birds released, and anything which contributed to virtually guaranteed bags was a must. On a private fun shoot, where the size of the bag is much less important, the sporting qualities of the quarry come first. The partridge day record at Milton's is 673 and the 3 years to 1985 produced an average seasonal bag of 15,743 head including pheasants (2 days a week) and partridges (3 days a week).

Six tenant farmers run cattle and sheep on the land and there are some 900 acres (365 ha) of mixed woods. Game crops planted have been kale, mustard and buckwheat. Daily winter feeding of wheat to pheasants is also invaluable to songbirds in the Exmoor area where snow and hard frost are common. There is also an enlightened attitude to other fieldsports and there is no attempt to eliminate foxes entirely. They are controlled as necessary, but there are always some for the hunt — the Exmoor Foxhounds, the Dulverton East Foxhounds and the Dulverton West Foxhounds. There is no stalking as the deer are hunted by the Devon and Somerset Staghounds and the Tiverton Staghounds.

On the commercial partridge day I attended in mid-October 1985 Guns assembled at the pretty little Royal Oak at Winsford, where some were staying. In keen attendance was a man from Roxton's Sporting Agency who let all the Milton days. Appropriately, the pub had a pair of thatched pheasants on the roof as if highlighting the importance of shooting and fishing in supplementing the revenue of local hoteliers and innkeepers.

We were joined by the loaders and keepers and everyone took off in a fleet of cross-country vehicles. There were four drives in the morning and two in the afternoon, all in fairly deep valleys of mostly grazing land. With such large numbers of birds put down on largely barren land, flushes were inevitable; but there were also singletons and pairs to give fairly steady shooting. It is strange to see scores of birds running about on a hilltop, wary and reluctant to fly until the beaters are up to them, instead of rocketing, 'unseen' partridges with Guns concealed behind tall hedges. There was no real attempt to conceal the Guns and there was only one way the birds could go, but once launched they glided to deceptive speed and this was quite enough when combined with the extraordinary height. The most entertaining drives, however, were those where there was a little more cover in trees, less notice of the birds' approach and a little breeze to enhance their speed.

Such commercial shoots are ideal for keen sportsmen who do not have a first-class shoot of their own but who want to reciprocate invitations. A wide variety of shooting skills is inevitable, but this generally lends amusement to the day. Lunch of roast, cherry pie and clotted cream, with ample wine and other drinks, was simply and warmly presented in the cosy atmosphere of the keeper's cottage. It was good and plentiful.

Not surprisingly, Alan Milton is a very good game Shot — 'Driven pheasant provide the finest of any shooting'. Rather fittingly for this north Devon man, one of his game guns is a sidelock by E. Gale & Son of Barnstaple. He certainly put it to good use on the shoot's famous high pheasants and partridges.

And Alan found time for humour, too. In 1983, when a very popular party of Americans was there for three days pheasant shooting, there was one drive where the Guns stood partially on a cricket pitch near the River Exe and a public road. Alan arranged for a mobile public address system to be driven very slowly past the Guns in the middle of the drive playing the 'Stars and Stripes' and 'The Yellow Rose of Texas'. That's what makes people come back.

In 1988 Alan Milton sold his shooting interests to Classic Sporting, owned by well-known house builder Charles Church, who already had rights on Devon's West Molland Shoot, once described by famous Shot Prince Alfonso de Hohenloe as having 'the finest pheasant drive in the world'; Somerset's Chargot Shoot, with its famed high pheasants, and Wiltshire's Minal Shoot, as well as the two shoots on his own estates at Roundwood and Steventon. Charles Church planned to develop Milton's and all his other shoots to produce birds of the highest quality, some of which he would shoot himself. Sadly, he died soon after when flying his Spitfire, but his widow, Susanna, continues to carry out his aims and ideals and still shoots with the same regular team of friends. Under shoot manager Steve Potter and headkeeper Bob Hunter the scale of shooting has been drastically reduced. Far fewer days are let and only the best drives that made the reputation of Milton's have been retained. As a result it is still highly regarded for its consistently very high birds.

A Holkham pheasant rises rapidly to cross the line
The Earl of Leicester picking-up at the end of a drive

MIXED BAG

Commercialism is quite prominent in Wales and the Marches now, and bags can more or less be made to measure according to depth of pocket. Also they often come in conjunction with complete sporting holidays — a very important factor bearing in mind how far many Guns have to travel. Prominent among those well known for laying on excellent sport is John Ransford who organises shoots over three estates including the 5,000 acre (2,025 ha) **Vaynor Park**, home of Colonel John Corbett-Winder, Lord Lieutenant of Powys. It is all stuff of arched backs and vertical guns and the customers keep coming back.

Llanarmon in north Wales is a legend as far as high birds are concerned. Before World War II George Cornwallis West had one of the best pheasant shoots in the country there. It was always said that you could wave your hat at the birds with as much effect as you could fire a gun at them, though whether that constitutes good pheasant shooting or not is another matter. Sir Malcolm MacAlpine then took over and it was said that those returning to London after shooting there bore an older and wiser look, like men who had returned from some great Antarctic adventure.

The belief that pheasants could not flourish above a certain altitude took a knock when the **Glanusk** estate in Breconshire reared them successfully at over 1,000ft (305m) above sea level during the closing years of the nineteenth century. They were high-class birds and produced in sufficient quantities to give over 1,000 on some days. There, as anywhere, the sunny side of the hill was important, but little could be done to prevent the birds' tendency to stray downwards rather than up.

Another big name among high-flying Edwardian Sports was **Stanage Park** in Radnorshire, where Mr C. C. Rogers laid on some truly stratospheric quarry. But perhaps no more so than on the nearly adjacent and very similar estate of **Powis**. There it was said that 'Pheasants did not fulfil the condition of their existence, which is to end — and before they are old and tough — on the dinner table. Here also, the birds, often invisibly impossible to kill, ran greater risk of dying of lead poisoning from eating the shot than from any external application of the same'. But systematically, Lord Powis, a great exponent in those three requisites so necessary to dealing with pheasants — the arts of bringing them up, over, and down — reduced many formerly unwieldy tracts of woodland into a scientific shoot before Victoria left the throne. His success was in creating new rides, having some stands inside the woods and pushing birds quietly, with heading stops, away from home, then flushing them to fly back to base. His innovation paved the way for a great shoot.

But perhaps the most famous of all the Welsh shoots from the days of the big blow-ups was **Rhiwlas**, just north of Llangedwyn and west of Oswestry. There Mr R. J. Lloyd-Pryce made the science of rabbit farming his special study and 5,086 were killed by 9 Guns on one day in 1885; the Marquis of Ripon bagged 920 of them. Mr Pryce let his moors to Lockett Agnew from 1909 and with a more modern approach the latter made a great success of the grouse. The pheasant shooting there, too, was legendary, though many of the stories are as tall as the pheasants. For example, it was said that in order to bring them within shot of the sky-scraping birds Guns were put up on scaffolds, which rocked to and fro in the wind like ships anchored in a swell.

Lord Coke (now the Earl of Leicester) with retired Holkham headkeeper James Preston

Typical small grouse-shooting party in Breconshire, circa *1900*

Sir Alexander Hood's **Fairfield** estate in Somerset was an early leader too. Despite the soil varying from rich, red loam near the Quantocks to heavy clay near the Bristol Channel, it was always a good partridge manor and foxes were carefully preserved for the West Somerset Foxhounds. Many drives were necessary in the small fields and, most importantly, there was good co-operation from the tenant farmers who all turned out for the shoot with their cider and home-brewed nut-brown ale, in the great West Country tradition which continues today.

Few Devon shoots have great ancestry, though the Earl of Devon's **Powderham** estate on the south coast continues a glorious history. Perhaps the star today is **Castle Hill** near South Molton where a powerful syndicate, including wealthy Greek John Chandris, rent from Lady Fortescue to enjoy superbly testing birds.

Woodcock, too, feature prominently in both Wales and the West. On a November day in 1894, ninety-five were shot at Captain Barclay's **Manor Bier** shoot at Tenby, Pembrokeshire — a remarkable bag. But on 21 December 1920 the Melton Constable (page 102) record was beaten when 106 'cock were shot at **Lanarth**, Cornwall, along with 6 pheasants, 9 snipe, 3 woodpigeons and 1 rabbit. The Lanarth coverts are well-placed, being at the eastern side of the Lizard peninsula and on the direct line of migration; but from 1900 special care has been taken to improve the woodcock habitat. A new record of 133 was shot there on 30 January 1982.

CHAPTER 13

NORTHERN ENGLAND

*The Duke of Westminster's keepers in jovial mood at his World's End shoot
earlier this century*

The precise geographical definition of the North is uncertain, and in any case bears little relation to gamebird shooting for there is tremendous variation in climate accentuated by variation in altitude. But in that portion of the country from Derbyshire northwards we do have a marked difference in terrain — the incidence of moorland and hills increases and that definitely has a marked bearing on gamebird biology and behaviour. Pheasants find the going tough on very high ground, and in much of the North the winter feed bills add considerably to costs. Partridges more often struggle against lack of suitable habitat and even the traditional moorland home of the grouse is increasingly threatened with factors such as afforestation, acid rain and over-grazing by farm stock.

Once many of these colder counties were protected by their remoteness from the capital, but now ramblers are increasingly numerous and there is a worrying disturbance of nesting birds, both game and protected species. Also the spread of commercial sport means that virtually every valley is valued for its potential, and consequently rents have rocketed.

Of all the counties in England, Yorkshire might well claim to be the current leader in shooting. Its tremendous variety of habitat, climate and terrain provides not only good bags of partridges but also some of the best pheasants in Britain and almost certainly the most superior grouse. Indeed, it was probably here that driven grouse were first shown.

CHATSWORTH

The principal home of the Cavendish family since 1549, the 'Palace of the Peak' in Derbyshire has long been a centre of sporting excellence and gatherings, both private and public. But even in the short period between two Game Fairs at Chatsworth — 1966 and 1987 — there have been many changes linked to the burden of taxation.

In 1877 the family owned almost 200,000 acres (80,940 ha). This had shrunk to 120,000 acres (48,530 ha) in 1950 and to 62,000 (25,090) in 1967. And when the 10th Duke died early at fifty-five, the present Duke, Andrew, was faced with daunting death duties of £4.72 million which took seventeen years to pay off. The house was unoccupied from the death of the 9th Duke in 1938 (except during the war when it housed a girls' school) until the very end of the fifties when much repair and renovation was necessary. The successful rehabilitation was largely due to the energy of the Duchess who, prior to her marriage in 1941, was the Honourable Deborah Freeman-Mitford, youngest daughter of the 2nd Baron Redesdale. Today Her Grace remains an excellent and enthusiastic Shot but the Duke (born 1920) gave it up at the age of thirty,

In earlier days the Duchess of Devonshire set off on her pony to the Bolton Abbey butts while the rest of the party rode in a Land-Rover. Today her enthusiasm for shooting is undiminished

having taken it up when he was twelve but later stopping 'because I can't hit anything'. Under the influence of his father, the Duke found grouse shooting 'very exciting' but 'reared pheasant shooting does not appeal to me at all. Unfortunately I have never had the opportunity to shoot partridges'.

Capability Brown had considerable influence on early sport when he replaced the 1st Duke's formal gardens with many copses to make the view more natural. This enhanced the game holding and showing potential of an estate which, like so much of Derbyshire, produces a great variety of quarry. But in the old days, apart from Hardwick and Haddon Hall, Chatsworth was almost alone in Derbyshire in attending to good game management which in most areas was very necessary to compensate for heavy land and high rainfall. Partridges would always be scarce but pheasants would respond well if given shelter through planting programmes, and protection from a high predator population. And poaching is a special problem in Derbyshire where industrial towns encroach on the coverts.

Not surprisingly, Chatsworth led in the splendid world of the Victorian/Edwardian shooting party. Everyone who was anyone, from the King down, attended the battues. When the King and Queen stayed in 1907 the party was too big for all the men to shoot, so the Duke did not select the Guns until very late at night and delayed announcement until the morning. Even Lord Rosebery who came down to breakfast dressed for the field was left off the list, and he promptly left for London in a huff.

The glittering parties and odd incidents, such as when King Edward flukily shot a very high pheasant while still in his bath chair, gave the press an opportunity to be facetious. For example, in 1913 the *Yorkshire Post* reported that the King had

> . . . another crowded day of sport at Chatsworth . . . At first it seemed as if birds must be scarce, for they ventured across the road in single spies or in twos or threes at the utmost [but later] the birds rose in clumps of a dozen or twenty at a time, thus exhibiting what seems almost an instinct of self-preservation, for in the circumstances some are bound to get away. With the King, however, a pheasant, if it did but know it, usually runs much less risk by merely skirting the tree tops, for if there is choice he aims preferably at the high fliers.

The 8th Duke, 'Harty Tarty', was not such a good Shot. Once he shot a wounded cock pheasant, but he also killed the retriever which was after it. The dog's owner and the Chatsworth chef were also hit, but the Duke was only concerned because the chef's injury might have put dinner in jeopardy!

The present Duke told how in his grandfather's time there was no shooting until Christmas:

> It was really a family occasion with the big shooting over the Christmas period, especially Boxing Day, and pretty intensively for about two weeks thereafter. This was from the mid-twenties to 1938. The shooting is very much a social thing and there has never been a syndicate here.
>
> I was given a 20-bore by one of my godfathers and a pair of 12s for my birthday later on. We always used to go for Woodwards. But I was always a bad Shot. And another problem I always found taxing was that if you want people to stay from November to January you have to ask them a long time ahead.

The young Duke of Devonshire picking-up on his Bolton Abbey grouse moor in Yorkshire. Now he no longer shoots

The Duchess of Devonshire with keepers who received Country Landowners Association long-service awards at Chatsworth, where the Game Fair was held in 1966, 1975 and 1987

Today the impetus for the shoot stems from Her Grace and son Peregrine, Chatsworth heir and Marquess of Hartington. The Duke thought the late Lord Arran was possibly the best Shot he had ever seen, but 'we always used to joke at the number of clothes he peeled off as things became hotter. Sir Martyn Beckett, the late Lord Harlech and the late Sir Hugh Fraser were good too.' As for the best shoot in the country — 'Lord Lambton's at Biddick, Durham, but Garrowby and Helmsley are marvellous shoots'.

One of the great problems of the Peak District has been accommodating very many more visitors in recent years, but Chatsworth has done its best to alleviate the impact. The Duke believes 'it is very important that the public should be allowed as much access as possible. This has always been done on the estate and there is virtually no friction between those walking on the estate and those shooting over it'. He is also very interested in conservation of habitat and landscape and has 'the highest regard for the Peak National Park, with whom the estate collaborates. We have all sorts of esoteric bodies here, including insect hunters from universities and fungi gatherers'. He considers Chatsworth special for shooting because 'a lot of the woods were planted to show pheasants and the countryside is so lovely. One disadvantage is that there is a lot of sycamore and pheasants don't show well out of sycamore.'

Today many of the twenty-five days shooting are let, generally to English Guns, and some eggs are sold. There have been six keepers for the last thirty years or so. Hens are caught and penned in February at the ratio of seven to a cock. Chicks are reared indoors until 3½ weeks old, then penned on grass for a further 2½ weeks before being released into the woods.

Today's average pheasant bag is 300. The recent seasonal total has averaged 8,000 and the record is 8,500. About a third of the estate's present 12,000 acres (4,855 ha), part of which is tenanted, is shot over. There are 1,000 acres (405 ha) of broadleaved woods and 2,000 (810) of coniferous forest.

Grouse are few at Chatsworth now, the family's main moor being the renowned Bolton Abbey in Yorkshire. It is well worth the two-hour drive from the magnificent Cavendish seat.

EATON AND ABBEYSTEAD

The present centre of the Duke of Westminster's shooting interests is the Abbeystead estate near Lancaster. Shooting ceased at Eaton, near Chester, in 1983 principally because the potential at Abbeystead was so much greater; but it is hoped to resume shooting at Eaton in a few years' time.

In the meantime an almost unique plan — the Landscape Conservation Plan published in 1983 — has been drawn up to overcome conflict between major land uses at Eaton. This highlighted the destruction of habitat through agricultural practices, pollution and other factors, resulting in loss of wildlife and of game. The 10,800 acre (4,790 ha) estate astride the River Dee had been partially planted for game but lack of attention reduced its potential and also the estate is much smaller than it was before World War I. There is no doubt that effective conservation costs money and planting for game does too, but each interest has so much to offer the other and it will be a great shame indeed if shooting does not return to Eaton's coverts, which have shown great sport since the eleventh century.

Eaton has been in the same family since 1068 when William the Conqueror granted the lands to his nephew, Hugh. He is said to have been Duke William of Normandy's closest companion at the conquest of England and a huntsman — *veneur* in Norman French — whose bulk earned him the nickname 'Gros Veneur'. As well as being given Eaton, he was accorded the rank of Earl of Chester with the responsibility of keeping Welsh cattle rustlers out of Cheshire. He was so successful he became known as Hugh Lupus or Hugh the Wolf, and is said to be the model for the bronze, heavy-set Norman warrior on horseback in the middle of the goldfish pond on the lawn at Eaton, representing the origin of the Grosvenor name itself.

The 1st Duke of Westminster (created 1874) was also called Hugh Lupus. Master of the Cheshire Hounds 1856–66, he was also considered one of the best Shots in the country and in his lifetime (1825–99) followed fashion by turning Eaton into a first-class gameshoot on the Prince of Wales' great circuit. But there was certainly nothing ordinary about him! Pheasant bags increased four-fold in the 1880s to 4,000, and by 1900 approached 6,000 per season. Yet while most hosts invited friends 'for some shooting', an Eaton invitation never bore these words. Wiser guests always packed their guns, but often they were not even told until well after breakfast that they would be shooting that day, even though the Duke had prepared meticulously, to the extent of having names put on the pegs. For him, the pleasure of company overrode the shooting. One very surprised guest was Lord Hamilton, who was led to believe that he would merely poke about the hedgerows with the Duke for a bird or two. Imagine his surprise when seven Guns did not set forth until 11am but shot 1,000 pheasants in two hours! And the keepers had instructions to start driving at 11am whether the Guns had appeared or not. Lunch marked the end of the day as the Duke never shot after it; he was only interested in very active periods of shooting. Yet he was shooting snipe just a few weeks before his death.

The 1st Duke also forbade keepers' tips, saying that guests should not pay for the privilege of shooting his game. Fair pay for the staff was his business alone. Many proprietors today though would find it difficult to keep staff if all such perks were abandoned, for there is no doubt that keepering is an underrated profession. But the 2nd Duke's headkeeper, Garland, was at least able to speak his mind — he had been with the family for over forty years. The ground was never easy to get birds well up over and when Prince Francis of Teck suggested to him how he might get birds higher the old retainer replied: 'Well, Your 'Ighness, if I was to do it you wouldn't 'it 'em.'

There were 300 men and women on the 1st Duke's payroll and 80 men in the forest and game departments. He built 48 farmhouses, 360 cottages, 8 schools, 7 village halls and 3 churches to make their lives better. The 2nd Duke, Hugh (1879–1953), known as 'Bendor', was also a Master of the Cheshire and an excellent Shot. But he put weight on easily and needed to exercise hard. There was a private racecourse at Eaton where the Duke always left his cigar on a post by the mounting block. It became the tradition that the cigar was claimed by the beatkeeper. There were twenty keepers until World War II. The head wore a green velvet cutaway coat with brass buttons, matching waistcoat, white breeches, box-cloth leggings and a bowler hat trimmed with gold braid; the underkeepers wore dark, three-piece tweed suits with bowlers and box-cloth leggings. The eighty beaters, who were estate workers, wore scarlet felt, wide-brimmed hats and white smocks held in at the waist by a wide brown belt with a large, brass buckle.

A horse-drawn float carried the leather cartridge boxes embossed with their owners' names or crests, along with all the other paraphernalia such as shooting sticks. The loaders had a horse-drawn bus and each had a lad to carry a further two cartridge bags, each containing 200, plus extra clothing and sticks. Despite the great weight the poor lads were never allowed to put anything on the ground. Besides being impatient — beaters were always well ahead with the next drive while shooting was in progress — Bendor tended to give himself the best positions. But no doubt on some days he would have been the only Gun competent on the very high birds anyway.

Before World War II ladies were not allowed to be present in the morning but in the afternoon they went out with the men on the private narrow-gauge railway, often with

Bendor wearing the driver's cap. Bags often reached 2,000 a day before 1939. The typed-out game cards with the Grosvenor crest were placed before each Gun at dinner in the evening and for a big two-day shoot there would be a fashionable London band to entertain some 150 dancing guests.

Unlike the present Duke, who has a particularly enlightened attitude towards fieldsports, Bendor shunned publicity to such an extent that poachers were only prosecuted if they had physically assaulted a keeper. An effective alternative, similar to systems at other estates, was to record the names and addresses of the offenders, confiscate their equipment and tell them they must pay £1 to whichever hospital was nearest home, the receipts for the 'donations' to be sent to the headkeeper within a month.

Winston Churchill was among Bendor's many famous guests. Once he went to the Duke's leased 'World's End' moor at Llangollen, 20 miles (32km) away, which had been taken on to reduce the risk of disease at hard-shot Eaton. The house party was still at Eaton, but because of the distance the ladies didn't go out in the afternoon, though lunch for the Guns and 180 loaders, keepers, beaters and dogmen was sent all that way. Churchill had just returned from America, where he had been knocked down by a car on Fifth Avenue and was unfit to walk. Vehicles couldn't manoeuvre at World's End so Winston was provided with a donkey — it was easier to get on and off than a pony. And later, when Churchill was too tired to dismount, he shot from the saddle but the accustomed animal remained steady.

Bendor's kindness towards staff was shown one day when he was shooting woodcock alone with three keepers, one of whom was struck by a ricochet. The Duke hastily apologised and offered the man whisky or champagne in compensation. The keeper chose whisky but that very evening the Duke's secretary was at the man's cottage with a case of whisky *and* a case of champagne for good measure.

Game often graced Bendor's table. In particular he liked snipe and always had some on hand to take back to London. Once he set himself a target of a hundred in a week and stopped when he reached it. He also liked plovers' eggs and always had them for his Aintree house party. He does not appear to have eaten squirrel, but when Eaton was overrun with the pests he ordered his keepers to kill as many as possible as he wanted 800 skins to make the Duchess a fur coat. He also collected woodcock pin-feathers to cover a fire screen.

All this rich history at Eaton ended when Gerald Grosvenor bought Abbeystead from the Sefton trustees in 1980 and transferred his eight keepers there. The young man (born 1951), said to be the richest in Britain, had thus added some 21,500 acres (8,700 ha) with greatly underdeveloped shooting potential to an empire which includes 300 acres (120 ha) of London's most expensive and select areas in Mayfair, Grosvenor Square, Park Lane and Belgravia. And with typical enthusiasm, just two years after the purchase, he entered and won the country's unofficial race to put the season's first grouse on the table. Using his own helicopter, he supplied Abbeystead grouse to the Grosvenor Hotel in Chester before they were even cold.

But Abbeystead had already been famous, for it was on the Littledale and Abbeystead beats that the Earl of Sefton and seven other Guns made the record bag of 2,929 grouse on 12 August 1915. The bag for the season was 17,078 on some 17,000

Eaton beaters on parade early this century

acres (6,880 ha); about 17,500 acres (7,080 ha) are shot over at Abbeystead today.

When the Grosvenor estate purchased Abbeystead the bag rose to 770 brace from 441 the year before. By 1985 this had risen to 3,612. The Duke achieved this largely through the application of 'good old-fashioned moor management', only really possible when you have the money to provide the manpower. Yet agriculture is not ignored and they run about one ewe to every three acres. And a thorough heather-burning programme has kept down disease. Other pests such as stoats and weasels are also strictly controlled. Among the measures which the Duke introduced to the neglected Abbeystead moorland to get the grouse stock up, and at the same time improve grazing, was the ploughing up of over 1,000 acres (405 ha) to let the land dry out and the heather regenerate. Drainage ditches have also been dug, access roads reinstated or created and bracken sprayed from the air.

As mentioned, conservation is very much to the fore in the Duke's mind, some £25,000 having been spent on the plan for Eaton alone. At Abbeystead, where there is traditional hill farming, sheep, beef and stock rearing and limited forestry, there are two SSSIs which are important for their botany and birds. The Duke commented: 'Clearly, with the control of the environment and vermin there are many types of flora and fauna that have benefited enormously. The balance of management of woodlands and the management of uplands because of shooting interests have had untold benefits to the countryside.' It is certainly encouraging to report that in 1985 there were merlins, harriers and at least one pair of peregrines at Abbeystead.

The Duke, who told me 'Every good grouse keeper should look like a grouse', really seems to have fired his staff with enthusiasm, which is a welcome change from those many estates where the owners have become generally blasé towards the greatness available to them. It may be something due to youthful energy, but whatever the cause, when I was there in teeming rain the Duke was the only Gun who really wanted to carry on.

Gerald Grosvenor, who is now President of The Game Conservancy, shot his first gamebird, a woodcock, 'at the age of seven at my then home in Northern Ireland, walking bracken banks with my father'. The Duchess, Natalia, uses a gun only occasionally. His Grace likes walking-up best of all, 'for the love of the countryside, the exercise and working the dogs'. During the season he shoots most weekends and occasionally on weekdays. He has a number of fine English guns but his favourites are 26in Holland & Holland Royals with no choke and weighing 6½lb. Number 7 shot is always used. He has been a deerstalker for many years but he does not hunt, as his wife does. Both are keen fishermen.

Changing guns on Abbeystead Moor

If the year is 'big enough to achieve it', the Duke lets 10–15 grouse days, the number of days shot averaging 30 for the season (twice a week) plus 10 on pheasants. There are now eight keepers (four on grouse and four on pheasants) and they are always appointed by the Duke. Their main problem is the constant battle against the Lancashire climate — the 80–90in (203–228cm) of rain experienced in 1985 was just what a number of diseases thrive on. Despite the great wealth of the Grosvenor estate, the Duke told me 'the shooting costs are watched very carefully at all times and the keepers are acutely aware of this, but if improvements are to be made they generally are'.

Insofar as His Grace takes most of the shooting for himself there is no attempt to make a profit but, as he can't be there all the time, some days must be let to keep the stock at the required level. A local agent is used and in 1985 the cost was £38 per brace on a 10-year average for the month. No pheasant days have been let. All days are let to individuals who organise their own teams, principally British. Surplus eggs and poults are also sold.

The Duke always places his guests, but on let days the Guns draw for pegs. When I stood with the Duke on a very wet day, the first drive got underway at 10am. Labradors — he keeps two — are the favourites of this very keen dog man, and as we made the first pick-up he remarked: 'Dogs like this count for 10–12 per cent of the bag.' On the second drive about 2,000 acres (810 ha) were brought in by two lines of beaters, one getting underway ahead of the other. But the weather was not our friend, the grouse packing exceptionally early in the season, and when one manoeuvre went slightly adrift His Grace cursed: 'There will be grouse all over Lancashire now, swirling in every direction.' The grouse were really needed for subsequent drives, but luckily there were still plenty to go round.

Also among the Guns were brother-in-law the Duke of Roxburghe; the Honourable Peter Morrison, MP for Chester; St John's Ambulance President Mrs Gina Phillips (the Duke's mother-in-law) and very well known crack Shot Hugh Van Cutsem. They all seemed to thrive on the Duke of Westminster's keenness and if what he is trying to do towards integrated country management in the North is copied elsewhere, there really is a bright future for shooting and conservation as bedfellows. He believes 'It is right there should be public access to the countryside providing that it is in sympathy with those who live, work and play within it. Recently we have seen the enormous erosion problems within the Peak Park. I feel shooting has a healthy future providing it is well managed. There is no doubt that there are now many more people involved in fieldsports and this is a welcome development.' As regards antis, he believes that 'If we disagree with something it is quite correct that we should say so, but I do not agree with the methods of violence and intimidation which are becoming so much a part of the anti movement today'.

STUDLEY ROYAL AND DALLOWGILL

Yorkshire's Studley Royal estate rose to the height of shooting fame largely through one man — the 2nd Marquess of Ripon, who is often regarded as the greatest Shot of all time. Certainly his worldwide lifetime bag was prodigious and at home he wiped the eye of the likes of Walsingham and Harry Stonor on many occasions, although some of his reported achievements are hard to believe.

At Studley, he entertained the royalty and nobility of Europe in the typical big Shot way, and when he died in 1923 he had recorded 556,813 head of game, from rhinoceros to snipe. Fortunately he also left a unique record of his exploits in the form of fifty-three leather-bound volumes for the seasons 1871 to 1923 plus fourteen cloth-bound pocket books and about thirty game cards, all of which were auctioned by Sotheby's in 1986. But before they went under the hammer I had read every page and gained a fascinating insight into the life of this legendary figure.

The following are a very few of these private notes from this man who is said to have been obsessed with shooting (though unlike Walsingham he could afford it) and not only to have had seven pheasants dead in the air at one time, but also to have killed twenty-eight pheasants in a minute at Sandringham. Today it would be considered very bad form to compare performances at a gentleman's shoot so Ripon's meticulous record may make him appear egotistic; yet he was not a conceited, arrogant bore. He was married to Gladys Lonsdale, one of the most vivacious ladies of the period, and he was a good friend of George V, a man who did not tolerate fools.

1872

2 Jan	Holkham; Scarbro' Clump: Killed 106 at the Clump: 12 Guns shot well.
9 Jan	100 pigeons. Mostly from trap at 30 yards. Killed 43 out of 48.
4–19 May	21 woodpigeon, 1 hare, 24 rabbits, 2,134 various. The rooks, with exception of 400, killed with a rifle — small Purdey C.F., Rigby Express C.F., Breech Loader Purdey No. 2.
10 Sept	1 snipe, 1 heron, 1 sea fowl. Gull shot flying with small Rigby rifle.
16 Sept	Cormorant shot with Rigby rifle.
15–17 Oct	Chillingham: HRH Prince of Wales killed a wild bull with one shot. Covert shooting poor.
23 Oct	16 partridges, 1 pheasant, 1 hare, 1 various. Alone for two hours walking: 4 times killed 2 birds at one shot.

1873

2 Jan	Holkham: Did not get many chances owing to good shooting in first two lines.

1874

19 Oct	Warter: plenty of birds.
26 Oct	Elveden: On our way from the station met Maharajah and shot a small wood — 50 pheasants.
27 Oct	Elveden: Shot well. Killed 38 shots running at one corner.
17 Nov	Sandringham: 12 Guns! 212 birds. Not many. Top score by 2.
25 Nov	Blenheim: Rain! Rain! [To him 2 snipe, 1 wild duck and 3 various in an afternoon's walk.]

26 Nov   Blenheim: Snow which spoilt the day — 4 inches — cold — beastly — irritating.

27 Nov   Blenheim: Spoilt again by snow. Fox killed by Marjoribanks' dog! 7 Guns! 2 Reeves cross bred with common pheasant killed.

1877

4 Dec   Luton: Over-gunned [and] low birds.

1881

10 Jan   At Bradgate with the Prince of Wales. 3,000 head (1,600 rabbits and 1,250 pheasants. A peaceful crowd of people — 3,000 at least.

11 Jan   Bradgate: Spoilt a great deal by the masses of people who crushed in everywhere driving the game away in all directions.

12 Jan   Bradgate: Spoilt by between 15,000 and 20,000 people. No ground game. [No wonder with all those people trying to see the Prince of Wales.]

1882

21 Nov   Huttons Court: 950 head. Poor Clare died on the 11th so we had to put off shooting last week.

1883

4 Dec   Crichel: Birds badly managed and not put over the Guns. Calvert was thrown from the box of a fly last night and received a compound fracture of the leg.

11 Dec   Melton Constable: Not much stuff.

1884

10 Dec   Chatsworth: I killed most of the pheasants.

1885

13 Aug   Askrigg (grouse): Caley and Hastings did not shoot the last drive for fear of losing the train. Weak and feeble.

1891

1 Oct   Studley: Had a drive of one turnip field with 3 men to get a pheasant for the house.

1894

6 Dec   Spa Gill: The nitro powder did not hit as hard as I expected and the black did *much* the best at the real high birds.

1895

28 Nov   Highclere: Killed 300 pheasants myself at High Rise. Started at 8.30 [heavily underlined].

1913

13 Aug   Dallowgill: [150 grouse to him but 234 to George V and 164 to Lord Derby, with the others lower.] Tom Corner beat.

25 Nov   Lambton: Again with the King, and four others in bagging 2,331 pheasants etc. His share 611 pheasants, 1 pigeon, 8 hares.

1923

22 Sept   [The last entry in the books] Dallowgill: Tom Corner. Lord Ripon 166, Mr Morris 26, Mr Wade 21. At the end of the last drive Lord Ripon killed 51 grouse, and at 3.15pm, while the last birds were being brought in, he fell down dead. He missed the snipe with his first two shots and killed it with the third shot: from his second gun.

So the man who devoted his life to shooting actually died at the end of a shooting day. A lonely memorial still marks the spot and is the scene of at least one interesting sequel. Lord Porchester told me that when he was shooting there once he shot fifty-one grouse. His northern loader turned to him and remarked: 'Do you realise that this is a piece of history. Come and look at this.' So he showed Lord Porchester the plaque commemorating the fact that Lord Ripon had shot fifty-one grouse and one snipe from that butt before expiring. Lord Porchester replied to the loader: 'Thank goodness that snipe's brother didn't come along.'

Ripon appears to have kept much of his competitiveness private, though once at Gopsall he did claim 124 birds for 127 cartridges although he had fired over 150. And at High Force his rivalry with Lord Wemyss led to the black powder from the latter's gun setting fire to the butt. 'The fire took a fortnight to extinguish, and the entire local workforce had to be employed in carrying buckets of water from the valley below to stop it spreading.'

At the beginning of this century *Country Life* magazine described Studley's 24,000 acres as a 'veritable paradise for the sportsman'. Many of the birds were genuinely wild

The Marquis of Ripon, said to be the greatest Shot of all time,
died while shooting grouse on his Dallowgill Moor

and even crack Shot Lord de Grey said that he never saw such high pheasants as those at Ripon's seat. It was, they said, 'an estate which seems made by nature and art to be the haunt of pheasants and the shooting ground of favoured man'. Nonetheless, rearing became very important there because when it ceased temporarily in 1898 the bag for one week in November fell to 1,481 from 5,784 in the corresponding week of the previous season.

The entire Studley Royal estate was sold in 1965 and split into four parts. Shooting continues over most of it, even on the central part, including Studley Royal Park, Fountains Abbey and Fountains Hall, which was purchased by the West Riding County Council and is now owned by the National Trust. The Trust does not hold the shooting rights.

Probably the most interesting section of the estate today is Dallowgill, bought by Mr Godfrey Bostock in 1965. Born in 1915, he was educated in Switzerland and then entered the family business, from which he retired in 1961. He then joined a merchant bank and pursued his farming interests, but his great love is shooting and a visitor is immediately impressed with the obvious enjoyment he derives from making his friends happy on the famous moor.

Driving began at Dallowgill in 1861 or 1862 and Lord Ripon first shot grouse there when he was just seventeen. For the last quarter of the nineteenth century seasonal bags averaged 3,000–5,000 birds and the moor was very well-managed with systematic burning etc. When I attended a shoot on a bright mid-October day it was fascinating to see the same little shooting box where Lord Ripon had sheltered in the last century and to see the butts at Tom Corner still proving their worth. The shoot is exceptionally well run and is a fine example of a whole cluster of famous Yorkshire grouse moors where excellent sport continues.

The Guns gather in the yard of the Drovers Inn, which is next to the Moor House, which Mr Bostock built in 1970 to accommodate the shooting parties.

As Mr Bostock drove me around in his Land-Rover he pointed out two small fenced off areas which showed how heather recovers when sheep grazing is limited. Concerning bracken control, some fern had been pulled by hand and other areas sprayed by helicopter. Dallowgill's new owner was proud of the new moor management which would not have been possible without the hard work and enthusiasm of the keepers.

In common with most good shoots, the Guns were very keen to work their dogs and share in the picking up. On the way back to the assembly point after one drive I paused to talk to one picker-up. A Gun called over: 'Did you get the one here?' The picker-up commented, 'That's the third person this grouse now belongs to.' It was all very relaxed. Lunch at the Drover's was also very good indeed. But the merry-making halted abruptly when Mr Bostock threatened to cut one drive in the afternoon. Godfrey Bostock stressed 'It is very important that everybody enjoys themselves — keepers, beaters, loaders and Guns.' And I must say how interested everyone was in the entire proceedings: nothing was done begrudgingly. Mr Bostock makes a point of getting involved in local affairs such as the harvest festival even though he lives in Stafford most of the time.

The present (8th) Duke of Leinster on Dallowgill Moor

Studley Royal shooting party 1901: (left to right) Mr F. St Quentin, Mr H. V. Higgins, Lord de Grey, Lord Ripon, Mr O. H. Wade (behind) and General Thynne, commander of the troops at York

The afternoon was magnificent, and hot. As we waited for the beaters to approach over the brow there was silence, save for the dogs panting, and even they held their breath momentarily to identify sounds unheard by human ears — perhaps a distant jet or the rustle of birds in the heather. And as the sun fell away its golden shafts of light revealed myriads of insects. The last birds were picked up and it was back to the Moor House for tea, scones and cake prior to farewells.

Before leaving I looked at the gamebooks, begun by Lord Ripon. There are just three and Godfrey Bostock has had them beautifully re-bound. The first entry was for 15 August 1871 when the Marquis of Ripon, Lord de Grey, Mr H. Cowper, Mr C. Vyner, Mr Cayley and A. N. Other shot 1,505 grouse at Tom Corner in 11 drives. That season ended on 15 November and brought a total of 4,713 birds for 7 days. By way of contrast, on 13 August 1984 the Earl Cawdor, the Earl of Lichfield, Lord Nelson of Stafford, Mr R. E. Ansell, Jeremy Graham, Mr R. F. Kershaw, David Stern, David Wigan and Godfrey Bostock shot 355 grouse. The season, which started a day late as the 12th was a Sunday, produced 4,982 grouse, 24 snipe, 35 wildfowl, 1,164 pheasants, 20 partridges and 265 various. Two days were let to a Dutch party including Prince Bernhard.

These books also reveal a little more about Lord Ripon's last day in 1923, referring to a 'seizure' and that he 'fell down and died in 10 minutes after he had shot Caley Fort last drive'. The entry concludes: 'He was 71 years of age last January 29th and was well-known as a famous Shot.'

HELMSLEY

Some of the proprietors of the great shoots in this book regard Helmsley in Yorkshire as the best pheasant shoot in Britain. It has been calculated that on average one bird is shot there for every eight cartridges fired, yet difficulty of shot is not everything and in some ways the shoot's most atmospheric days may have passed.

It was the 3rd Earl of Feversham who really got the shoot going, and before his untimely death in 1963 he ran it as a private syndicate assisted by one of Britain's most remarkable headkeepers, Adam Gordon, who had been employed originally by the 3rd Earl's grandfather as falconer and dog trainer. The 3rd Earl's brother, architect Sir Martyn Beckett, who has been to many of the great shoots in his lifetime, told me:

> Born in Perthshire in 1886, Gordon first came to Yorkshire in 1911 as an under-keeper from Windsor Castle and as one of many answering an advertisement from Lord Helmsley for a man who knew about falcons and could train gundogs. He met Lord Helmsley at Nawton Tower and was taken by him for a short walk through the woods to see what he knew. They had only been walking for a few minutes when Gordon asked Lord Helmsley to make his dog sit and to walk back with him ten yards. Gordon pointed out a woodcock a few feet from the path, sitting on its nest and so well camouflaged as to be almost invisible.

Gordon was given the job on the spot.

Sir Martyn continued:

Gordon was first a peregrine and dog trainer and eventually became headkeeper to the [Earl's] Duncombe Park estate — until 1935 about 70,000 acres (28,330 ha) until he retired in 1960. After retirement he was kept busy stuffing birds and animals privately and for museums, as well as designing and painting the background habitat for each species. He continued to do this almost to the year he died, in 1982, aged ninety-six.

During World War I he joined the Yorkshire Hussars, but then became an infantryman. Being a crack rifle Shot, he was made sniper and often was left alone in 'no man's land' to pick off unwary Germans. His bravery was renowned; he was wounded twice and was awarded the MM and DCM and bar.

On return from the war he was made headkeeper under the young Earl and in between the wars had ten keepers under him and several shoots to supervise. A number of these underkeepers have since gone on to become headkeepers themselves of renowned shoots. All of them acknowledge the debt they owe to Gordon's knowledge and tuition. There is no doubt that he was one of the outstanding keepers of his day. His knowledge of nature, of birdlife, of fauna and flora — especially wild flowers — was extraordinary, and people came from all over the country to learn from his first-hand experience and see his collection of birds of prey and bats, which he stuffed himself and kept in his parlour. He even discovered a parasite which used brown trout and grayling as host and was named after him — *Salmincola gordoni*.

On top of all this he was one of the best Shots I have seen and a beautiful fisherman, of course making his own flies and minnow baits. I got to know him well in the thirties when I started shooting with a 20-bore. One day when out walking partridge with a small party of Guns and beaters, I felt ill and handed my 20-bore to Gordon (though it was far too short in the stock for him) at lunchtime. He managed to shoot 24 head with 26 cartridges, including one partridge at 75 yards.

Gordon was also an expert on deer, having served the Duke of Portland at Welbeck. His bat collection was presented to Yorkshire Museum in 1976. He was the first to record the barbastelle in Yorkshire and rediscovered the lesser horseshoe which was then thought to be extinct. He found them both in the dungeons of Helmsley Castle.

One of Gordon's favourite shooting stories involved Jim Robson when he was a young keeper at Duncombe. Having collected pheasant eggs, he was carrying them tucked into his shirt to keep them safe and warm prior to placing them under a hen, when he met a new curate to the parish. The curate was amazed and remarked on what a very difficult job it must be to carry the eggs so carefully until they hatched, and Jim encouraged him to think this. Unfortunately the curate was entertained by the Earl that evening and during dinner commented on this 'exacting job' the keepers had hatching eggs through the warmth of their bodies. Next morning Robson was up before the Earl and severely reprimanded for telling untruths, especially to a churchman.

In 1962 Lord Feversham gave a special dinner to mark Gordon's retirement. In his speech he recalled the latter had been shot twice, 'once by a German sniper and once by an English boy. The latter was me. I peppered him instead of a hare. He had to be taken home and I wanted the ground to open up and swallow me'. He also described Gordon as a 'real gentleman':

His closeness to nature probably assisted his knowledge of people. And believe me there have been some 'hard nuts' among them; especially among shooting tenants. A few of

Helmsley's legendary headkeeper Adam Gordon with a hooded crow – just one of the many birds and mammals which he mounted himself

them, it was soon discovered, were much more at home in the city than in the coverts, more conversant with cigars and champagne than partridges and cartridges. But Gordon always provided them with the memory of an enjoyable day and made them happy in the belief that they had done well. What they did not appreciate was Gordon's gift of tolerance and tact, and when they had gone, his enormous sigh of relief!

Gordon had virtually created the Beckdale and Riccaldale beats, and these, along with Ashdale, were originally let to a local syndicate of which Sir Martyn was a member:

> It started soon after the war and by today's standards was a fairly modest affair with 3,000–4,000 pheasants reared. But the quality was always superb, and in the thirties, when my father took the shoot from Lord Feversham, the birds were nearly all wild. The plan was then to walk up one side of the dale [Riccaldale] in the morning with three Guns on a rickety path in the wood and three or four Guns in the valley spread out 80–100 yards apart taking high pheasants, crossing over, having lunch in a farmhouse and then walking down the other side in the same fashion, nearly always finishing in the dark — 120 wild pheasants was an excellent day.
>
> In 1955–6 Lord Feversham saw the potential of the combined three valleys running roughly parallel north to south, and about this time he asked me and Gordon to 'walk the course' with him and plan out its future. The contours and slopes have, of course, remained the same, but in thirty years the woodland has changed. Riccaldale, once all deciduous oak, birch, ash and alder, is now principally coniferous. Ashdale, as the name implies, has an amount of ash and no river in the valley. It is also much smaller than the other two; it is, in fact, only half a day's shooting and is therefore combined with parts of either of the other two. Duncombe Park has been developed much later as a shoot. Some would say in quality it is the best of the lot.
>
> Initially Gordon planned the Helmsley shoot and for the first ten years was in charge. After he retired he was succeeded by his protégé Dick Norris, who went as headkeeper to Chatsworth; Joe Cowton, whose father had been keeper at Duncombe; and then John Masterman. Bags of 500-plus in a day are achieved until the end of the season, giving some idea of the number of birds reared. Celebrities come to shoot from every walk of life and country and the best Shots are tested to the utmost. Yet, it might be nostalgia, but I look back on those days of the thirties with 120 wild birds in Riccaldale as the acme of the sport of pheasant shooting.

Kit Egerton managed the shoot after Gordon's retirement and it was let to Felix Fenston in conjunction with Prince (Statch) Radziwill. Mr Fenston died in the early seventies, whereupon Prince Radziwill was joined by Lord Ashcombe, who took it on his own after the death of the Prince in the mid-seventies. Kit Egerton told me:

> In the early sixties we were rearing about 8,000 pheasants a year, all under broodies on an open field. What a job it was to get the broody hens gathered up, then shutting up each evening. The coops were moved to the wood when the chicks were about a month old at 0400 hours. No release pens in those days. However, gradually the shoot was modernised with electric brooders and rearing and release pens.
>
> The contour between the top lip of the dales and the bottom is about 200 feet. The birds are driven from one side to the other in a sort of herringbone pattern which gives great quality, and each drive tends to help fill the next but one.

The present Lord Feversham still lets the shooting to Lord Ashcombe.

WARTER PRIORY

Once the ancestral home of the Warter family, Yorkshire's Warter Priory is known for once holding the record for the number of pheasants shot in a day. On the Golden Valley beat on 5 December 1909, 9 Guns — the Duke of Roxburghe, Lord Dalhousie, Lord Lovat, Lord Savile, Lord Londesborough, Lord Cecil Manners, Lord Chelsea, the Honourable C. Wilson and the Honourable G. Wilson — killed 3,824 pheasants, 15 partridges, 526 hares, 92 rabbits and 3 various — 4,460 head. The following day the same Guns shot the Highcliff beat but, owing to a very high wind, stopped at luncheon when the total was 3,045 pheasants, 11 partridges, 182 hares, 42 rabbits and 2 various — 3,282 head. Had it been possible to continue shooting all day the bag would easily have topped 4,000 pheasants. All the big Guns were guests of Lord Nunburnholme and they enjoyed quality as well as quantity, though some later complained of headache and fatigue after shooting such high birds all day with up to four guns each!

Big days continued into the 1920s when there were still sixteen keepers. Much of their work was concerned with rabbit catching. Indeed, the sale of rabbits at 1s 6d a couple had to pay much of their 30s a week wages and rabbits were caught at the rate of some 50–100 per day. The keepers were also expected to help the farmers in reporting broken fences and watching for straying stock. No one was allowed to smoke on a shoot and anyone speaking on a partridge day was severely admonished. The twenty or so beaters were each paid 6s a day and given 1½ pints of beer. Some countrymen supplemented their low incomes by catching cock linnets and bullfinches and selling them as songbirds for 2s 6d each.

In 1929 the excellent Shot, the Honourable George Vestey purchased Warter from the trustees of the late Lord Nunburnholme. It was then 14,000 acres (5,665 ha) of excellent game ground, far removed from any industrial area. The undulating, high wold land with large arable farms intersected by long, winding, deep dales had been systematically planted in the past, making excellent pheasant drives. In most years the arable land was very satisfactory partridge and hare country; but there were also many acres of dale which were not planted and of no agricultural value — steep, rough banks and prairie grass and whin — ideal shelter for game and good walking-up country.

In the late thirties the keepering staff was still large — five on partridge beats, eight on main pheasant beats, two rabbit catchers, a cartman and a head. Some 12,000 pheasant eggs were set each year. Hens were only spared being shot in certain main coverts which had been shot twice. Seasonal bags then averaged 8,235 pheasants, 1,857 partridges, 1,669 hares and 3,988 rabbits (a further 44,696 rabbits trapped). Unlike the Nunburnholmes, Mr Vestey made no attempt at records and did not pick a team of crack Guns. Shooting parties were what they should be, mostly local friends and neighbours and near relations.

Just after World War II, Mr Vestey had some 9,000 acres (3,640 ha) in-hand, farmed very traditionally. The hedges were untrimmed, many of them 20ft (6m) high and 10ft

(3m) thick — ideal nesting cover which provided for a marvellous wild shoot.

The Marquis of Normanby's family trusts bought the estate in 1969, but as Lord Normanby had a shoot at Mulgrave Castle it was decided to let the Warter shoot. Sadly a new farm director set out to modernise everything on the home farms, including the grubbing up or cutting right down of some 30 miles (48km) of hedgerow, and that was the end of the wild shoot.

Rich shipping magnate Stavros Niarchos took the shoot in 1970 and Kit Egerton was appointed shoot manager. He told me:

> We had to start from scratch as no birds had been reared there since 1939. Tom England was in semi-retirement and there were seven underkeepers. We had a pilot scheme for the first year, rearing some 4,000 birds and this was increased to 20,000 in the following years.
>
> Warter had the most superb potential for pheasant shooting. There were three main valleys on the north side: Highcliff, very high and steep sided, providing four main drives; Golden Valley which divided twice, making it possible to have about ten different drives; Silver Valley, not so deep as the others but the birds loved it. South of the road were a number of coverts overlooking smaller valleys which showed terrific birds.
>
> The woodlands had been neglected for years and had no ground cover. The whole estate was overrun with rabbits; between the wars some had been imported to strengthen the breed! The result of the woodlands being bare was that it was easy to run the birds on to where you wanted them to flush, but some were very cold and we had to plant cover crops to hold them in the high places. But because the farms grew a good deal of kale there were field drives which often produced some marvellous birds.
>
> Mr Niarchos used to shoot in batches of three days at two-week intervals until Christmas. After that there were some tremendous 'mopping-up' days. The Guns used to complain that it was very expensive in cartridges and tips! Mr Niarchos was very good to work for. He told me what he required, I gave him an estimate of the costs and was then told to get on with it. If I needed any more money I just had to give the reason and it was forthcoming. His behaviour was impeccable regarding tenants, keepers and beaters. But the lease was terminated after four years.
>
> Mr Niarchos had a nice sense of humour too. On one occasion we did a field of kale, third drive. I put the sticks out the day before and the field was stuffed full of pheasants. When we came to drive only one bird flew out. I went in fear and trepidation to 'the Boss', as he was then called, to apologise. He grinned from ear to ear and said 'Don't worry — but don't do it too often.' A post mortem revealed that the stop we had sent out had made far too much noise and all the birds walked out before we got there.
>
> Normally we aimed to shoot 500–600 birds a day, three times over, and bear in mind these were all very high pheasants. Niarchos paid for the whole thing himself. His guests often included his brother-in-law George Livanos, Prince Bernhard of the Netherlands, Prince Hohenloe from Spain, Joe Nickerson from Norfolk, Lord Lambton (a most graceful Shot) and many other distinguished European and English gentlemen.
>
> After Mr Niarchos' lease was terminated the shoot was allowed to slide into oblivion; a great shame. All but three of the keepers were sacked and those who remained were demoted to rabbit catchers.

Lord Normanby told me that 'Since that time no pheasants have been reared but in the interests of good estate and farms management a reasonable degree of vermin control has been maintained. The occasional wild pheasant and partridge shoot takes place with small bags but excellent quality'.

HAREWOOD

The Queen's cousin, George Henry Hubert Lascelles (born 1923), 7th Earl of Harewood and Chairman of the English National Opera, has always been interested in shooting. He started when he was twelve: 'My father shot well, so did most of my relations, and I always wanted to do it.' His remarkable knowledge of music was developed much later, as a prisoner of war in Colditz. The first grandchild of George V, another bearded Gun, he enjoys shooting for 'being in the countryside, being a long spell in the open air and attempting to do something difficult which, when achieved with the ordinary skill I have, gives genuine satisfaction'. His wife and eldest son (Viscount Lascelles, to whom the estate has recently been passed over) also shoot.

Harewood has been in the Lascelles family since 1737 and the grounds are yet another Capability Brown enterprise. In the opinion of recently retired head gardener Geoffrey Hall, who spent fifty years at Harewood after working at Warter Priory, Brown ruined the whole effect by over-planting with beech and yew. But overall this probably helped the shooting.

When the estate was 20,000 acres (8,095 ha) there were smaller groups shooting different areas, but now all the shooting rights are retained by the Earl. With the untimely death of his father in 1947, the present Earl was faced with an estate duty bill of nearly £1 million; sadly, as well as some house contents, 13,000 acres (5,260 ha) of the West Riding had to go. Today there are just 4,300 acres (1,745 ha) including Trust Settlement land, and of the 4,000 acres (1,623 ha) shot over, some 1,700 acres (688 ha) of park and woodlands form the main shoot. In 1962 a terrible gale made serious inroads into the main woods, over a tenth of which (some 20,000 trees) was blown down and 123 acres were re-planted over four years. Lord Harewood's aim is a final crop of hardwoods (mainly beech and sycamore) with larch and Scots pine as nurse trees. Three hundred acres are farmed on a management agreement.

Lord Harewood does not consider public access a serious problem, 'but the park is crossed by several footpaths and bridleways, including the Ebor Way and Leeds Country Way. It is all becoming more of a problem as each year goes by — dogs, "no map", "lost", gates left open etc.'

In 1959 there was an unusual poaching incident when a group of Chinese — six or so — were seen walking in line through the best root field near the main road. The keeper was near to apopolexy. 'We welly solly. We make big mistake. We shoot everywhere in China — welly solly, we pay damages. We not come again.' 'Not bloody likely,' said the headkeeper.

It was by accident really that Brown's landscaping coincided with the contours of the land to produce several of the best driven pheasant stands in England — Burden Head, Stubhouse Ride, Nan Pie — and today there are three keepers to look after the coverts. Harewood has moved on to buying-in poults and game is no longer reared on the estate. This has immense benefit in releasing keepers' time from the rearing field to other duties of vermin control, security and general estate work. Some grey partridges are released, red-legged partridges being regarded as a poor substitute. Apart from foxes, the worst pests are cats dumped by their city owners on the eve of their annual holidays.

There are 22–24 'big days' (200–300 pheasants) each season and 4–6 small ones with partridges etc. In recent years the seasonal bag has averaged 5,000 pheasants (50–60 per cent of birds put down), the best year being 5,500. There is probably as much shooting at Harewood now as there has ever been, but the accent remains on quality. Lord Harewood told me: 'If a drive begins to produce low birds for any reason it is abandoned or re-thought.'

Some 5 days are let to an outside group. In 1985 this was based on £12–£14 per pheasant shot. The estate has now moved away from charging per bird shot and instead costs are related to the day itself. For example, a Park day before Christmas, with 200–250 head recently cost £5,000, while an 'outside' day across new drives on tenant farmers' land and with a bag of about 100 cost £2,000. There is no surcharge or compensation should the expected bag be exceeded or not achieved.

Lord Harewood is yet another owner who likes grouse shooting best of all, but he has to rely on friends for invitations. He also does some roughshooting with his wife and a few friends. He shoots between twenty and thirty days a year and uses long-barrelled Purdeys which belonged to his father.

As regards the future, he is cheerfully optimistic: 'Once the basis of shooting in the country is recognised as being widespread, it will be harder to attack. It is a country sport and its future will, I am sure, be based on co-operatives rather than the exclusive style of Edwardian times'.

THE SINEWS OF SPORT.—*The Marquis (to head keeper).* " Now, Grandison, His Royal Highness will be tired of waiting ; why don't you send in the beaters ? " *Head keeper (sotto voce).* " Beg pardon, my lord, the London train's late this morning with the pheasants—we must have half an hour to get 'em into the coverts ! "

Conservation is very much to the fore at Harewood. Indeed, there is a Bird Garden which concentrates on breeding rare and exotic species and showing them to the public. Lord Harewood believes that anyone controlling areas of countryside has a duty of trusteeship which is more important than ownership. 'I believe, too, very strongly in participation of all kinds, but I think that what has happened to the Pennine Way must sound a warning note to even the most access-minded person.'

MIXED BAG

The **Gunnerside** estate in Yorkshire has a most distinguished history, though the changes in farming practices since the last war have resulted in a considerable reduction in the heather habitat. The heyday of shooting here was the mid-thirties, and it is only through exceptional moor management that good stocks are maintained.

For many years it was owned by Lord Peel. Born in 1947, he started shooting when he was thirteen and, not surprisingly, likes grouse best for 'enormous variation and natural extension of my involvement in management'. Variation in presentation is something in which Gunnerside prides itself. Any number of grouse days from none to thirty are shot at Gunnerside, according to the season, and there are some six pheasant days. Lord Peel believes that the grouse season could be brought forward a week in exceptional seasons to allow a sufficient number of birds to be shot.

The American Mr R. W. Miller bought the estate in February 1995 and intends to enjoy the shooting himself rather than let it out. Of 32,000 acres (15,950 ha) over which shooting rights are held, some 15,000 (6,070) are now shot over. There are four SSSIs on the estate and there is no doubt that the shooting interest has benefited a wide range of animals and plants in maintaining, and now extending, the semi- natural heather habitat. Estate staff assist the five keepers (previously eight) in maintaining the fine sport on this estate.

By 1872 a decade of regular driving had brought the Yorkshire moors to their best. In that year five of them shot over 1,000 brace in a day, while at **Wemmergill** and **High Force** the season's total reached 17,074 and 15,484 respectively, the latter figure being the product of 19 days driving. Such figures were hard to surpass thereafter.

Blubberhouse is possibly Yorkshire's most famous moor, having been in the limelight since Lord Walsingham killed a record number of 1,070 grouse there to his own gun on 30 August 1888. The first drive started at 5.12am and the walk home ended at 7.30pm. He fired 1,550 cartridges (including 40 signal shots) over 20 drives. The 2,000 acre (810 ha) moor is shaped like an hour-glass and Walsingham stood at the narrowest part where the birds were concentrated, two lines of beaters driving the birds backwards and forwards. Passers-by said grouse lay by the road too tired to move. Walsingham's half-brother, John de Grey, who succeeded him, later said: 'The stone passages of the farmhouse where we were staying were stacked with grouse three and four feet deep. For a fortnight the place was swarming with the lice they left behind.' It was said that Walsingham shot the record because the King refused his invitation and friends said his moor was 'too little'.

R. H. Rimington-Wilson's **Broomhead** Moor was another showpiece shoot, where 9

Guns bagged 2,843 grouse on 27 August 1913. Though just 4,000 acres (1,623 ha), the moor also produced 2,648 grouse on 30 August 1893, but in 1858 the record day was only 82! Often only two days were shot and the great success was virtual elimination of disease through fine moor management and stock control. Unlike Walsingham's twenty short drives system at Blubberhouse, six long drives were the daily limit with Wilson. A former Wilson of Broomhead is credited with shooting the first grouse on the wing, in the middle of the seventeenth century.

At the beginning of this century Broomhead was celebrated for producing such fine wild sport so close to 'grimy' Sheffield. Sadly its handiness for Guns is now poor recompense for the mass trespasses which have become a feature of the area in recent years.

These are just some of many fine grouse moors in northern England. Many others are distinguished in their own way — **Allenheads** in Northumberland for its recent consistency, **Bolton Abbey** for its famous guests such as Prime Minister Harold Macmillan (uncle of the present proprietor the Marquess of Hartington, Chatsworth's heir), and so on. Sadly, many now have considerable anti trouble to contend with and maintain a low profile.

Biddick, Chester-le-Street, Durham, is commonly regarded as one of the best pheasant shoots of today and its owner, Lord Lambton (born 1922), one of the most competent Shots. I am reliably informed that they are mostly quality birds coming over the Guns along the river from hanging woods in Lambton Park. The castle is now empty, the safari park closed down after ten years and the estate reduced to 30,000 acres (12,140 ha) after Washington New Town was built.

Antony Lambton still likes to be styled 'Lord Lambton', despite having disclaimed the Earldom of Durham and other peerages in 1970. He resigned as Under-Secretary at the Ministry of Defence and MP for Berwick-upon-Tweed in 1973 over what he described as 'a casual acquaintance with a call girl and one or two of her friends'. Despite a life of self-imposed 'exile' in Italy, 'Lord' Lambton frequently returns to wipe the eye of many top Guns at Biddick. Now many of these Guns come from overseas to pay for the privilege of shooting where George V once sported.

Mr R. H. Rimington-Wilson (1852–1927) achieved excellent grouse bags on Yorkshire's Broomhead Moor

The Duchess of Devonshire, a very experienced game Shot, in action at Bolton Abbey

CHAPTER 14

SCOTLAND

While most people automatically think grouse when considering Scotland, that still sparsely populated country has so much more to offer the gameshooter. There is great variety of quarry resulting from widely varying altitude, terrain, habitat and climate. In Dumfriesshire, for example, it is possible to shoot grouse, blackgame, grey partridge, redlegged partridge, pheasant, woodcock, snipe, mallard, teal, wigeon, tufted duck, woodpigeon, golden plover, coot, moorhen, hare and rabbit.

Fieldsports have become an enormous source of revenue for Scotland, not only because the quarry is testing but also because the land of moor and mountain is an inspiration to be in. Whether you are after fur, fin or feather, Scotland can accommodate you with sport to suit your pocket, and few people are disappointed.

The Scots, however, have been surprisingly slow to capitalise on certain sporting resources. It is only recently that there has been a marked increase of interest in lowground shooting, particularly in the east which has a farming pattern and summer climate very similar to that of the traditional partridge manors of East Anglia. Many people are surprised to learn that good partridge bags have been made in this part of Scotland for over a century, with days of over 400 on more than one beat. On 10 October 1914 six Guns killed 486 at Hutton Castle, Berwick, and on 9 October 1906 Lord Elphinstone with five other Guns killed 513 at Prestonhall, Midlothian. But bags took a general nose-dive earlier this century when many acres previously under the plough were turned over to grass.

The Borders have always been good gameshooting country, being farmed for almost 700 years and now with 85 per cent of the land in agriculture. Here are many of the finest sporting estates whose proprietors also recognise the importance of conservation and public amenity. Sadly, England's 'filling-in' process whereby areas between large estates, usually shot over by owner-occupied farms, undertake their own game conservation, is missing north of the border. Too many still take without giving back. And in even more areas the 'forgotten' fringe between the low arable ground and the heather is a completely untapped resource.

It is also often wrongly assumed that the very many foreign Guns who visit Scotland are push-overs. Most of them have done the 'grand tour' and want value for money. Scottish driven pheasant will be compared with those of big days in eastern Europe, and even the glorious grouse must compete with the very attractive partridge shooting in Spain. It is indeed regrettable that up to April 1995 the Scottish proprietor had the burden of local sporting rates to add to the penalties of inflation.

Scotland's chief worry, however, is the continuing decline of grouse stocks — a problem both little understood and not easy to deal with as grouse cannot be reared and released in the manner of pheasants and partridges. 'Cultivated' birds are unable to adapt well to a natural diet, therefore concentration must be on habitat management. It is noticeable that where the best management prevails, the grouse stocks generally thrive. But that is not all. The whole Scottish uplands are increasingly threatened by blanket afforestation in the heartland and an increasingly adventurous, technologically based agriculture around the fringes. New friends have been found in conservationists who recognise the importance of grouse to wildlife generally, but the pull of pounds sterling is ever there to change the moors' use.

Scottish moors have really declined since 1976 and now the moors of northern England are the main bastion of the red grouse in the British Isles — ironic when most people think of grouse as synonymous with the kilt and haggis. A special research project is underway to examine how best to arrest the decline, and a further irony is that it was a large financial gift fom an Arab sheikh which made this possible. Why sportsmen have been so slow to rescue the grouse is a mystery; the dangers have been exposed since the Lovat Committee's report in 1911 and yet the first modern grouse research unit was not established in Scotland until 1956! Whether the problem is acid rain, over-grazing, weather-related disease, predation or something else, remedial action is going to cost money and that is why the best moors generally continue to be those with rich proprietors or those which have turned grouse into big business. Heather burning and predator control are both labour-intensive, and the overall reduction in keeper numbers is a particular problem where moors are isolated and there is a continual topping-up of vermin from outside. For over a decade the number of foxes killed has been increasing by 7 per cent per annum and on many moors it is not possible to keep them under control. At the same time crows have been increasing by 5 per cent per annum and mink by as much as 18 per cent!

As a general rule, grouse flourish most on the highest ground in southern Scotland and prefer a lower altitude further north. Pheasants will never do well at great height where it is too wet and cold for breeding and there is little for them to eat.

A peculiarly Scottish problem is the extra number of beaters often required to bring the great expanses in. At the beginning of this century parts of Forfarshire were noted for schoolgirl beaters 'striding the heather manfully'. Scotland has always had its share of great characters, such as Horatio Ross, who is credited with killing 82 grouse with 82 cartridges on his 82nd birthday — with a muzzle-loader! Then there are the ever-present poachers, whose tales are legion and who seem to have had a rather easy time because of the great distances keepers need to police. Daylight poaching has been common and it is not so long since grouse were netted in large numbers before the season and sold after 11 August.

FLOORS CASTLE

Guy Innes-Ker, 10th Duke of Roxburghe (born 1954), who was awarded the Sword of Honour at Sandhurst in 1974 and saw active service in Ulster, is one of the keenest young Shots of our time. And as owner of 50,000 acres (20,235 ha) — 30,000 (12,140) shot over — around Kelso in the Borders, it is as well that he is also devoted to wildlife conservation. He is chairman of the Scottish Wildlife Appeal which set out to raise £1.2 million, and in 1986 set up a scheme to extract some of this money from shooting and fishing. Thus the Scottish Wildlife Trust is asking owners to impose a 1 per cent levy on all sporting tenancies, and in urging owners to take part the Duke commented, 'Ultimately, fishing, shooting and stalking depend on the balance of nature being maintained.'

The dukedom was created in 1707 and Floors Castle built in 1721. The Duke now also owns a very good local hotel, a garden centre and a small stud farm.

This great estate has always been blessed with variety. One of the most memorable bags was 560 partridges to the Duke and five other Guns on 22 October 1913, but on the same day they shot 70 pheasants, 81 hares, 1 rabbit, 1 snipe and 3 plover. A further 516 partridges, 69 pheasants and 33 hares were shot on 4 October 1921. Such great partridge days have long gone, as also have the wild pheasants, and the accent is now on rearing. Pheasant days now average 200–300 birds, the best recent bag being 700; the seasonal average is over 5,000 birds for 20 days. When possible there are some 6–8 grouse days, the best in recent years bringing 190 brace but consistently averaging 90–100, the season's total averaging 600 brace. There are now three pheasant keepers within the park and two grouse keepers, one of whom has been there forty-two years. Six thousand day-old pheasants are reared in the park, and the aim is to produce high and challenging birds to test the Guns.

Some twenty days are let to Americans, French and British businessmen and farmers at a cost, in 1985, of around £3,000 plus VAT per day. Overall the shoot makes a loss. Roe stalking and salmon fishing are also let. Some foxes are spared for hunting, but the ever-increasing mink are eliminated whenever possible.

The Duke likes grouse shooting best: 'It offers the greatest challenge and variety of shot, requiring the highest level of skill.' He shoots twenty days each year and uses Purdeys. His ambition is to take part in a first-class Spanish partridge shoot and his favourite shoots are Abbeystead (Lancashire), Lambton Park — Biddick (Durham), Milton's (Somerset), Castle Hill (Devon), Lilburn (Northumberland) and Clarendon Park (Wiltshire).

Guy Roxburghe's attitude to public access to the countryside reiterates the view of many proprietors in this book: 'In principle, this should be encouraged. In practice this leads to inevitable conflict with public, farmers and keepers. In reality the access should be limited to certain areas and with preconditions.'

M<u>OY</u>

Nine miles south-east of Inverness in the Highland region is the ancestral home of the Mackintosh of Mackintosh, whose Moy shoot is now a poor reflection of former glory. The present Mackintosh told me that 'the drastic reduction in grouse stock has led in the last few seasons to us getting only about eighty brace in five days walking up'. And this is the estate which led the way with grouse in Victoria's reign, the moor being entirely suitable for grouse with long, rolling hillsides of moderate height intersected by burns and covered with heather of the highest quality. There are also good shelters from winter's worst storms.

There grouse driving, started in 1869 and regularly taken up from 1879, was brought near to perfection with the employment of a large number of boys among the beaters, the youths being numerous and cheap. Bringing 30 beaters and six 'side-boys' together in Scotland was often difficult, but the Mackintosh always managed it because he was head of a clan and loyalty was great. Just six drives were taken and the beating line extended over three miles!

The butts were sunk in the ground so that the shooter could just comfortably see over their tops, which were raised some 2ft (.6m) at most above the general level of the moor, the 2ft (.6m) shelving gently away on the outside so that there was nothing to alarm approaching birds, and covered with heather. They were not more than 45yd (41m) apart at any drive, and often as little as 15yd (14m), the Mackintosh considering this safer than the more usual longer distances for there was little chance of forgetting the proximity of your neighbour. Good use of whistles and horns was made to indicate when to start and stop shooting.

Numbers rapidly increased with the use of regular driving, though at first it was only resorted to when birds were too wild to sit to dogs and there were no butts. In the famous grouse season of 1872 the whole yield of the moor was only 1,501 brace and the highest individual driven bag 29. In 1900, 10 Guns killed 870 brace in one day and 6,092 in the season. In 1905 the same number of Guns brought down 914 brace in one day and 7,127 for the season. George V became one of the skilled regulars.

With the advent of driving, disease became rare, vermin was ruthlessly destroyed and grit provided for grouse to aid the digestion of heather. The Mackintosh believed that grit was the best preventive of disease and he placed cartloads all across the estate. Other aids to producing a healthy grouse stock were the damming of streams to provide water during high summer, drainage of sour wetlands to increase the area of heather, and sloping the ditches so that young birds could scramble out of them easily. Burning was always carried out methodically in small patches, the only places where the heather remained over a foot high being on the tops of knolls to provide winter shelter when the wind blew the snow away.

KINNAIRD CASTLE

Kinnaird Castle, Brechin, Angus, was the home of one of Britain's most hospitable and sporting gentlemen, the 11th Earl of Southesk, Charles Carnegie (born 1893, died 1992), whose father was one of the most remarkable Shots of all time. Among the latter's achievements were 48 grouse for 48 cartridges (he missed once but killed 2 for 1 shot), 63 partridges for 63 cartridges, 79 pheasants for 79 cartridges, and 228 pheasants for 238 cartridges in 17 minutes. He was in a party which twice shot 51 capercaillie at Kinnaird and among six Guns which shot 3,012 pheasants at Fasque. Between 1893 and 1933 he shot over 100 pigeon on 12 occasions (once 228 in 2 hours) — all at Crimonmogate, Aberdeenshire except once at Kinnaird. And on 7 November 1900 at Fasque, he shot 600 pheasants at one rise.

Days of such bags are mostly gone, of course, but Kinnaird remains a wonderful, picturesque centre of mixed shooting, and should remain so as the present Earl (the son of the Duke of Fife) is as keen and accurate as his grandfather was.

In 1942 the 11th Earl inherited an estate which originated in his family in 1401, though all of it is now in the hands of trustees. He started shooting at ten, when the

One of the most celebrated Shots of his generation, the 10th Earl of Southesk (right) in 1923 with his son, the 11th Earl, and daughter-in-law, the late Princess Maud of Fife

The 11th Earl of Southesk with his first wife, Princess Maud of Fife

keepers rolled turnips down the slopes for running shots, and always enjoyed the thrill of pigeon and duck flighting as much as pheasant shooting. His guns were 12-bore William Powells. He believed that first and foremost an excellent Shot should have 'a good eye and natural swing'.

Throughout his long life, Lord Southesk saw many changes on his estate, now 13,000 acres (5,264 ha) (all shot over), including the decline of partridges and the World War I disappearance of capercaillie through removal of pine forest. There are also now 3,500 acres (1,215 ha) of coniferous forest as well as 500 acres (202 ha) of old broadleaved trees and 9,000 acres (3,640 ha) of cereals and grass. Some 25 acres (10 ha) of trees are planted annually and include mixed hardwoods with Sitka spruce, larch and pine, keeping in mind the requirements of game habitat, shooting and amenity. Before World War I the estate covered 25,000 acres (10,117 ha), but much has been sold off to alleviate the burden of capital transfer tax.

Two SSSIs are partly within the Southesk estate. Rossie Moor is of national importance for the quality of its individual habitats and the extreme rarity of finding them in natural continuity with each other. It comprises a series of lowland oligotrophic to mesotrophic mire communities surrounded by extensive areas of lowland dwarf shrub heath interspersed with pockets of unimproved meadow and birchwood. An unusually large number of vascular plant species are present, including several mosses rare in lowland Scotland. Several species of wildfowl breed in locally important numbers and the invertebrate fauna is of national importance. The Montrose Basin SSSI is found at the only enclosed estuarine basin in the northern half of Scotland. It is of great ornithological importance for overwintering wildfowl and waders.

The 11th Earl reported a decrease in the number of woodcock and a great decline in snipe following blanket afforestation with conifers. Not surprisingly, the number of foxes has increased, and there are also more herons, hedgehogs and moles. The first rabbit was shot in 1833; by 1851 the bag had risen to 475 and by 1862 they were very numerous all over the estate.

Kinnaird's gamebooks go back to 1831, in which year were shot 354 partridges, 130 pheasants, 209 hares, 4 woodcock, 1 snipe and 7 roe deer. The number of Guns varied from 1 to 9 (average 4). They went out on very many days but bags were very small, though 8 Guns shot 58 partridges once. By 1903 pheasant rearing was well underway and the year's bag was 80 partridges, 1,103 pheasants, 230 hares, 16 woodcock, 1 snipe and 475 rabbits. A few years saw grouse in the bag, but the odd patches of heather have now died away. World War I caused felling of trees on moorland and gave some extra grouse shooting before re-planting took place.

There are now just two keepers and a trainee at times, whereas there were eight before 1914. Usually they catch up about 650 hens in February. Some 3,200 eggs are set every Monday for seven weeks. Partridge rearing was abandoned when the number of keepers diminished, though for some years they were successful in rearing 300 or so by turning 10–12 young birds onto each wild barren pair.

In recent years the seasons' bags for the whole estate have averaged 6,000 pheasants, 150 woodcock and 100 duck, the partridge numbers being erratic — just 3 in 1982 and 220 in 1984. On the Home Beat some 26 days are shot with bags varying between about 150 and 300 (7,500 pheasants released). There are also 4 rough days and 4 duck flighting. Altogether with the keepered Carcary Beat this small team of keepers organises 38 days' driving — a remarkable effort.

Four beats, including the Carcary, are let to syndicates, with Aberdeen oilmen becoming predominant. In 1985 they paid about £12 per pheasant and overall the shoot made a small profit and covered the rates. Seven miles of salmon and sea-trout fishing on both banks of the Southesk River are also let. The Earl did not mind having paying guests. On the contrary 'Meeting a variety of businessmen and farmers makes interesting conversation'. However he told me 'Guns are more difficult to find now owing to the expense'.

Anyone who visits Kinnaird today is assured of a great welcome but there are not so many surprises as there used to be. The 11th Earl told me how he 'used to put blank cartridges into the second gun held by the loader and the discharge of a rocket caused much surprise among guests'.

LAMMERMUIRS

American Guns just love visiting the late Lord Biddulph's grouse shoot near Lauder, high among the rolling Lammermuir Hills to the south of Edinburgh, for here is one of Scotland's most consistent moors, and its late proprietor was everybody's idea of what a British lord should be. Robert, the 4th Baron Biddulph (born 1931), had an impish twinkle in his eye and a great sense of humour, but it was his all-round appreciation of the finer points of a shooting day which made his company so welcome.

At the turn of this century grouse shooting in the Lammermuir Hills was not taken very seriously and access was difficult. There were very few places where butts were necessary, long walls running across the moor providing cover for the Guns. Today there is no question of making do, for this is still one of the most professionally run shoots in Britain, being organised as a business. The Biddulphs also have a pheasant shoot at their home 18 miles (30km) away at Makerstoun, Kelso, where they are neighbours of the Duke of Roxburghe.

At the Lammermuirs Lord Robert started with his wife's Maitland family property of 7,000 acres (2,830 ha) in 1961. The shoot had been neglected since the thirties due to the war because the land had been used as tank ranges, so he enlisted a local keeper to help, and together they started to put things right. The sheep farmers to the north were not interested in shooting so he took their land on too. Later he acquired the rights on land to the south and built up a shoot of 20,000 acres (8,090 ha) on properties marching together. Now there are three keepers.

At first there was a syndicate with 8–10 days driving and Guns who paid £250 a year each and came from a wide variety of backgrounds including farming, building and veterinary practice. Then inflation took hold and it was decided to let one week to Americans, the syndicate Guns being guaranteed ten years' shooting in return for helping to build up the moors. Later two weeks were let to Americans, but gradually things became more costly and after twelve years it was decided to go entirely commercial. The original syndicate members were still invited to clean up at the end of the season. There were and still are many overheads. Just part of the programme of improvement was putting in 17 miles (27km) of road and 69 rows of butts. At first the sporting rates were £1,200 per annum. The 1985 assessment was £13,000 on a turnover of £115,000, but with the pheasants included it rose to £17,000 on a turnover of £125,000.

Not surprisingly, Lord Biddulph was very concerned about the disparity in tax and rating systems within the UK: 'The government is certainly not helping me. In England they tend to look after their moors. Here it is an endless struggle against bureaucracy.' At the time sporting rates were levied in Scotland irrespective of whether the shooting was let, so there was less incentive to maintain a shoot well or re-establish one. The rates had to be paid even in bad years, and with the cyclical nature of grouse stocks this was very difficult. Lord Biddulph would have been delighted to see the abolition of sporting rates in April 1995.

Lord Biddulph was also very concerned about restraint on predator control and the way in which the value of grouse shooting is underestimated. He told me how on a recent walk he had seen the remains of some hundred grouse killed by birds of prey. When he arrived in the Lammermuirs 'Vermin had taken the upper hand, it was becoming uneconomic to farm due to lamb losses and there was no wildlife at all'. In the first year, the single-handed keeper accounted for 3,000 crows, 90 foxes and 30,000 rooks and jackdaws. Lord Biddulph thought that authorised persons should be able to use poisons in a prescribed manner to kill carrion crows.

> At first there were no stoats, falcons and harriers on the moors as there was no food for them, but as soon as the crows etc were knocked out the other predators such as falcons, merlins and harriers moved back. The place is alive with all sorts of birds now. Birdwatchers often ask for permission to go on the moor, which is especially good for golden plover, but these 'birdie boys' don't realise that there would be nothing there for them to watch if I didn't keep the vermin down. Someone who just walks about a moor contributes nothing to it. A moor is an incredibly valuable asset and we are beholden to look after that land for its investment and for future generations.

Public access can be a problem here as there is a long-distance footpath — the Southern Upland Way — across the southern portion. As Lord Biddulph commented: 'Suddenly a party of red anoraks appears in the middle of a drive. It's all very well for them to say "sorry", but try explaining that to a party of Americans who have been paying hundreds of pounds a day for their sport.' In Scotland there is nothing to stop anyone walking on the moor, except an injunction if damage is caused.

One American party is led by a gentleman with a very forbidding name — General Patch. He is obviously very well looked after because the Biddulphs attended to every detail and ensured that no shooting took place unless expectations were at least reasonable, unlike some owners who tend to over-shoot to exploit their resources. Lord Robert said: 'I'm not going to go out and shoot nine grouse with nine Guns. That would be wrecking the moors and the business and my customers wouldn't come back.'

Under Lord Biddulph prices ranged from £450 per day per Gun at the start of the season to £100 per day per Gun in October. Apart from the Americans, customers included Britons from all walks of life. Some 50–60 days were let, shooting 6 days a week. But there is the land to do this, and each beat was shot every eighth day. In 1985 a record day bag of 248 brace was shot. 1976 and 1985 were bumper years, with 3,354 and 3,436 brace respectively. After Lord Robert's sad death in 1988 Lady Mary, assisted by her son Nicholas, ran the shoot and continued to achieve record bags.

When I visited the shoot with a party of Lincolnshire farmers there had been a night of continuous, heavy rain on top of an already waterlogged countryside. Guns assembled at a local hotel where they had been staying — Lord Biddulph did not provide accommodation — and we set off with fingers crossed. The falling rain was no deterrent: 'We shoot through thick and thin and have only ever cancelled one afternoon through weather.'

As we togged up by the vehicles out on the moor, Lord Biddulph muttered: 'Damn, diabolical, beastly weather. But we don't mind the rain; the problem is bringing the drives in across the burns. I can see some of these young beaters trying to jump across

Lammermuirs grouse moor, 1985. The late Lord Biddulph (centre) and his keeper (left) decide to cancel the day through severe flooding: the burn is flowing over the bridge on which they are standing

and getting drowned — then what would their mothers say?' Like all good shoot proprietors, Lord Biddulph was concerned that everyone in the field, from Guns to beaters, has a good day. When everyone was suitably attired our host did something which quite a few owners dispense with — addressed the assembled company and explained exactly what was going on and what was likely to happen. Too often in the shooting field (commercial or private) it is assumed that everyone is an expert, often with very dangerous results.

We moved off inspired, but soon met our match in an impassable burn. We jumped out of the lead Land-Rover and stood dismally in the water which was going over the *top* of the bridge. Lord Biddulph cancelled the day; there would be no point in returning later as the day's drives are interdependent. As for the Guns — well, this was the first of two days for them, and, although there was no obligation to refund their money Lord Biddulph told me he would try to find them an extra day or two later in the season.

The late Lord Biddulph started shooting in Hertfordshire when he was nine through the influence of his father and their gamekeeper, and now his two sons are following in his footsteps. He used Purdeys and liked grouse best for their wildness and their countryside, but nevertheless he had a pheasant keeper at his house beside the River Tweed. Of all the moors he visited, Allenheads impressed him most with its fine

A slug of sloe gin compensates for a day's sport lost to the floods

management, good company and sporting birds. But he also thought of Swinton Gunnerside, Arden Hall and Leadhills as being great. Among the best Shots he had the pleasure of shooting with were the Duke of Roxburghe, the Earl of Swinton, the Earl of Leven and Melville, the Earl Peel, the Duke of Westminster and Jeremy Graham. The worst he saw were: 'Italians shooting at everything that moves, including beaters, flankers and themselves!'

Lord Biddulph was on the steering committee of the Grouse Research Project and gave his all to the future of grouse, pioneering and encouraging the use of medicated grit. He said: 'I've seen the best of it now. Fieldsports have become a political issue but I have always said that economies will prevail, and it would be finance, if anything, that eventually did away with shooting.'

Due to death duties, in 1990 the moor was sold to the Duke of Northumberland and is now expertly run by his brother, Lord Ralph Percy, with the same headkeeper and two underkeepers, and a mix of family and let days. Lord Robert, whose memory lives on in a memorial cairn on the moor, would be delighted that his great shoot remains in safe hands.

MIXED BAG

Scotland too has had its days of huge bags, but many of the shoots once deemed great have now sunk into oblivion. The first man to kill 100 brace of grouse in a day was The Campbell at **Monzie**, near Crieff, in the days of muzzle-loaders. In the fabulous year of 1872, 7,000 birds were killed at **Dalnadamph** by driving, and 10,600 at **Glenbuchat** over dogs. Also in that year one Gun had a day of 220 brace at **Grandtully** and 3 Guns shooting separately at **Glenquoich** had a day of 327 brace. But even Moy's record of 914 brace was beaten out of sight in 1911 by a useful family team on the Duke of Buccleuch's moor at **Langholm** who killed an astonishing 1,300 brace.

Some 1,300 hares were once killed by just six Guns on Lord Mansfield's estate in Perthshire, but even in that big bag era this did not imply greatness in the eyes of most true sportsmen. Neither did the bag of 3,012 pheasants to Sir John Gladstone and seven other Guns on 17 November 1911 at **Fasque** in Kincardineshire. Whether it is Scotland or anywhere else in Britain, greatness in shooting is more to do with quality than numbers, and in the end it is really a private thing rather than a path to glory or greater social standing.

ACKNOWLEDGEMENTS

My very special thanks go to all those friends and experts consulted about which shoots to include and to those shoot owners who co- operated so fully in my research. In most cases hospitality was very generous and I must also thank all those families and friends whose privacy I invaded with my pen and camera. Thank you too all those agents, administrators, secretaries, head-keepers, keepers, loaders, beaters and dogmen who fed me with snippets of information, and to all those sporting organisations and journals whose archives I raided and to those scribes whose earlier tomes provided me with much of the historical material. I am sorry that space precludes my mentioning everyone and that I must confine myself to the following: The Duke of Devonshire, the Duke of Marlborough, the Duke of Roxburghe, the Duke of Wellington, the Duke of Westminster; the Countess of Feversham, the Earl of Bradford, the Earl of Harewood, the late (3rd) Earl of Iveagh, the 4th Earl of Iveagh, the Earl of Normanton, the Earl Peel, the late (11th) Earl of Southesk; the Marquess of Hartington, the Marquis of Normanby, the 7th Earl of Leicester, Lord Ashburton, the late Lord Robert Biddulph, Lady Mary Biddulph, Lord Burnham, Lord Lambton, Lord Montagu of Beaulieu, the 7th Earl of Carnarvon, Lord Walsingham; the Mackintosh of Mackintosh, Sir Martyn Beckett, Sir Charles Blois, Sir Denis Mountain, the late Sir W. Williams-Wynne, Sir David Williams-Wynne, the Hon Mrs S. M. Cowen; John Anderton, Geoffrey Armitage, James Booth and his colleagues at Sotheby's, Godfrey Bostock, Brian Bowden, Christopher Brunker and his colleagues at Christie's, Arthur Cadman, David Cant, Gordon Carlisle, David Cock, Charles Coles, Robin Cowen, Christopher Cradock, Noel Cunningham-Reid, Beryl Duncan, Christopher Egerton, William Garfit, the late Harry Grass, Ian Grindy, Roger Grocott, Dr John Harradine, David and Gwen Hitchings, Bill Hughes, Ken Jaggard, F. C. Jolly, Richard Kitson, Ian McCall, W. G. McDermott, Colin McKelvie, C. A. Milton, Peter Moxon, Norman Mursell, the late Nicholas Phillips, Christopher Pope, James Preston, James Ramsden, Albert Saxton, John Shipton, William Sloan, the late Charles South, John Staley, Freddie Standfield, Richard Van Oss; *The Field*, *Country Life*, *Shooting Times*, the National Trust and the Nature Conservancy Council. Finally I thank my family for their general help and consideration.

INDEX